Writing Travel
Series Editor, Jeanne Moskal

Writing Travel
Series Editor, Jeanne Moskal

The series publishes manuscripts related to the new field of travel studies, including works of original travel writing; editions of out-of-print travel books or previously unpublished travel memoirs; English translations of important travel books in other languages; theoretical and historical treatments of ways in which travel and travel writing engage such questions as religion, nationalism/cosmopolitanism, and empire; gender and sexuality; race, ethnicity, and immigration; and the history of the book, print culture, and translation; biographies of significant travelers or groups of travelers (including but not limited to pilgrims, missionaries, anthropologists, tourists, explorers, immigrants); critical studies of the works of significant travelers or groups of travelers; and pedagogy of travel and travel literature and its place in curricula.

Other Books in the Series

Vienna Voices: A Traveler Listens to the City of Dreams, Jill Knight Weinberger
Eating Europe: A Meta-Nonfiction Love Story, Jon Volkmer
Sarah Heckford: A Lady Trader in the Transvaal, ed. by Carole G. Silver

Au Japon

The Memoirs of a Foreign Correspondent in Japan, Korea, and China, 1892–1894

Amédée Baillot de Guerville

Translated, Annotated, and with an Introduction by Daniel C. Kane

Parlor Press
West Lafayette, Indiana
www.parlorpress.com

Parlor Press LLC, West Lafayette, Indiana 47906

© 2009 by Parlor Press
All rights reserved.
Printed in the United States of America

SAN: 254-8879

Library of Congress Cataloging-in-Publication Data

Guerville, A. B. de (Amédée Baillot de), b. 1869.
  [Au Japon. English]
  Au Japon : the memoirs of a foreign correspondent in Japan, Korea, and China, 1892-1894 / Amedee Baillot de Guerville ; translated, annotated, and with an introduction by Daniel C. Kane.
      p. cm. -- (Writing travel)
  Translation of Au Japon, originally published: Paris : Lemerre, 1904.
  Includes bibliographical references and index.
  ISBN 978-1-60235-128-8 (pbk. : alk. paper) -- ISBN 978-1-60235-129-5 (hardcover : alk. paper) -- ISBN 978-1-60235-130-1 (adobe ebook)
 1. Japan--Description and travel. 2. Japan--Social life and customs--1868-1912. 3. Korea--Description and travel. 4. China--Description and travel. 5. Guerville, A. B. de (Amédée Baillot de), b. 1869--Travel--Japan. 6. Guerville, A. B. de (Amédée Baillot de), b. 1869--Travel--Korea. 7. Guerville, A. B. de (Amédée Baillot de), b. 1869--Travel--China. 8. Foreign correspondents--United States--Biography. 9. Travel writers--United States--Biography. 10. French Americans--Biography. I. Kane, Daniel C. II. Title.
  DS809.G87 2009
  952.03'1--dc22
                                        2009032568

Cover design by David Blakesley.
Printed on acid-free paper.

Parlor Press, LLC is an independent publisher of scholarly and trade titles in print and multimedia formats. This book is available in paper, cloth and Adobe eBook formats from Parlor Press on the World Wide Web at http://www.parlorpress.com or through online and brick-and-mortar bookstores. For submission information or to find out about Parlor Press publications, write to Parlor Press, 816 Robinson St., West Lafayette, Indiana, 47906, or e-mail editor@parlorpress.com.

Contents

Introduction: Amédée Baillot de Guerville
  and *Au Japon*   vii
Note on the Translation   lxi
Author's Preface to *Au Japon*   lxiii

1 *To Japan*   3
2 The Ambassador's Wife   7
3 Teikoku   10
4 A Tokyo "Five O'Clock"   15
5 The Yoshiwara   19
6 A Socialite   23
7 Tokyo   28
8 A Few Silhouettes   36
9 Their Women   42
10 Their Children   47
11 At the Imperial Court   51
12 The Real Madame Chrysanthemum   59
13 A Visit with His Excellency, the Governor of O . . .   62
14 The Missionary   67
15 From Tokyo to Tientsin   76
16 Ayama   90
17 Marshal Yamagata   97
18 The Red Cross   104

19 The Spy   *109*

20 The Eggs   *114*

21 Chiu-Ji   *121*

22 Port Arthur   *126*

Appendix A: Prominent Personalities of *Au Japon*   *133*
Appendix B: The Writings of A. B. de Guerville   *144*
Au Japon Notes   *150*
Index   *157*
About the Translator   *159*

Illustrations

Figure 1. Milwaukee Women's College at the time of de Guerville's employment there (1890).   xiii

Figure 2. A. B. de Guerville and his students at Milwaukee Women's College (1890).   xiv

Figure 3. A flyer announcing a public performance by de Guerville's "Cercle Français" in Milwaukee (1890).   xv

Figure 4. A. B. de Guerville Covering the Sino-Japanese War in China (1894).   xxiv

Figure 5. An artist's rendition of the fall of P'yŏngyang that accompanied de Guerville's newspaper account.   xl

Figure 6. De Guerville's headlining account of the fall of Port Arthur in the *San Francisco Chronicle*. 1894.   xliv

Figure 7. A Japanese rickshaw in the 1890s.   11

Figure 8. A street scene in Yokohama in the period of de Guerville's visit.   12

Figure 9. Japanese firefighters in the late 19th century.   32

Figure 10. "Two Japanese Belles," an illustration from Frank Brinkley's guidebook.   45

Figure 11. Japanese children in the 1890s.   48

Figure 12. Mutsuhito, the Emperor Meiji, around 1895.   53

Figure 13. Cherry Blossoms in Tokyo's Uyeno Park (1890s).   54

Figure 14. Japanese women enjoying a traditional bath, late 19th century.   66

Figure 15. An issue of *Toki no koe* (*The War Cry*), the Salvation Army's newspaper in Japan (1897).   74

Figure 16. A view of Seoul at the time of de Guerville's visit.   79

Figure 17. Korea's fainthearted King Kojong.   80

Figure 18. King Kojong's strong-willed wife Queen Min.   81

Figure 19. King Kojong's father, the headstrong and wily Taewŏngun (Tai-Wan-Kun).   82

Figure 20. Main gate of one of the Korean royal palaces in Seoul (1894).   83

Figure 21. A depiction of Li Hongzhang (Li Hung-chang), his son, and grandsons.   87

Figure 22. Japanese in western dress (late 19th century).   92

Figure 23. Marshal Yamagata Aritomo at the time of the Sino-Japanese War.   98

Figure 24. Japanese and Chinese wounded being nursed at the Red Cross Hospital at Hiroshima (1894).   106

Figure 25. Count Oyama Iwao, Minister of War and Commander of the Japanese Second Army.   110

Figure 26. The one-eyed General Yamaji Motoharu, Commander of the First Division.   117

Figure 27. Japanese soldiers during the Sino-Japanese War.   122

Figure 28. A. B. de Guerville and Chiu-ji (1894).   125

Introduction: Amédée Baillot de Guerville and *Au Japon*

> *"Nowadays our countrymen are exploring every quarter of the globe; we find them not only on established routes of travel and in familiar Old-World haunts, but in out-of-the-way nooks and corners where tourists of other countries seldom if ever penetrate. They make pilgrimages to the farthest East; they scour all seas; they throng the sites of buried empires and dig for relics of civilizations which perished in the dawn of time; they study the monuments on which is writ the history of the primeval man and his struggles; there is no obstacle that can arrest, and no peril that can appall them, in their search for new fields of conquest.*[1]

—"The American as a Tourist," *Leslie's Illustrated Weekly*

> *I am of the opinion that the civilized nations ought to organize an academy whose mission it would be to regulate books of travel impressions, and in general all publications that deal with the customs, politics, and laws of nations . . . there should be an index to indicate whether such and such a book is sincere or specious. . . . Why not establish a cordon sanitaire against contumely?*[2]

—Colonel Tcheng Ki-Tong (Chen Jitong), *Les Chinois Peints par Eux-Mêmes* [The Chinese painted by themselves], ghost-written by Adalbert-Henri Foucault de Mondion

I. Amédée Baillot de Guerville (1869—?)

Beginnings

It has been a century since A. B. de Guerville's *Au Japon* first rolled off the Paris presses of Alphonse Lemerre. Written a decade after the last of the book's events takes place, it details the author's travels and experiences in Japan, Korea, and China (but primarily Japan, as the title indicates), first as an Honorary Commissioner for the World's Columbian Exposition and later as a newspaper correspondent covering the Sino-Japanese War (1894–1895). Though the book has long since been relegated to the *purgatorio* of used booksellers, it had its day in the sun. *Au Japon* went through seven printings, indicative of respectable sales.

Even more so than *Au Japon* itself, its author has since retreated into anonymity, his experiences and observations largely forgotten.[3] Who was A. B. de Guerville, this obscure French-American journalist and travel writer? And perhaps more importantly, why should we care about him today? The second, and more easily answered, question shall be addressed later. Tracing the life of de Guerville himself poses more of a challenge. On this question, secondary sources are of practically no use, for there are hardly any to speak of. The biography of de Guerville has never been written, even in the most abbreviated sense. What can be woven together of de Guerville's life today must remain an insufficient patchwork, one stitched together solely from primary sources, often from the pen of the man himself. Yet it reveals a man and a voice worth hearing again, if for the first time.

We know from his own writings and a surviving New York marriage certificate that Amédée Baillot de Guerville was born in Paris in 1869, son of another Amédée Baillot de Guerville and Antoinette Luce. Though the de Guerville name boasted a prominent pedigree going back to its ennoblement in the fifteenth century, by all appearances Amédée's upbringing was on a more modest scale than that of his forebears. His namesake (Amadeus in English, a popular name of the period and a reflection of more middle-class taste in Mozart) suggests this, as do the circumstances of his young life, as we shall see. Though his teaching, writing and editing income must have often been rather modest, A. B. de Guerville never seemed to lack funds, whether for establishing a small French newspaper in Milwaukee or for his extensive travels. Indeed, he later gained entrance into the highly exclusive and expensive Nordach Clinic for consumptives, all of which seem to indicate the possession of at least a modest personal fortune.

A. B. de Guerville, who was always reticent concerning his own background, rarely mentioned his family, though on a few occasions he wrote of his mother and a younger brother with fondness. An obscure notice in an 1853 London *Times* reveals that a man who was likely

Introduction

de Guerville's father (though certainly a relation), Paul Louis Amédée Baillot de Guerville, was in dire straits, in the courts for bankruptcy after stinting several students of the French lessons he had been paid to teach.[4] It's conceivable that the elder de Guerville was one of a contingent of continental exiles following the upheavals of 1848. In any case, though this was still nearly fifteen years before our A. B. de Guerville's birth, it gives us the first indication that A. B. de Guerville had cosmopolitan roots, and based on his later career probably grew up speaking English and French fluently. London is where we first hear the Baillot de Guerville name; it is the last place as well.

We have no specific information regarding A. B. de Guerville's childhood or early adolescence but it would have no doubt been infused with that sense of fatalism that pervaded the lives of so many Frenchmen in the years following the Franco-Prussian War (1870–1871). It was this war that put a dramatic and humiliating end to almost a century of French material grandeur and empire. Though the flame of imperial glory and national honor would be kept kindling with its *mission civilisatrice* in far-off Cochinchina and Panama, and the closer shores of North Africa, names that became intimately familiar to a whole generation of Frenchman of de Guerville's time, French prestige and *amour-propre* never fully recovered from the debacle (as Émile Zola properly termed it) of Sedan and the 1871 declaration of a German Empire in the Palace of Versailles.

To a man of de Guerville's background and temperament—educated, ambitious, adventuresome, young—it was the American frontier that beckoned rather than the tired old lands of Europe with their perennial rivalries. And it was to America that the young Amédée fled when he was barely out of childhood. The exact circumstances that would inspire such a young man to abandon home and hearth remain concealed, but whatever the causes, the act itself certainly reveals a strong-headedness and precocious independence, even for a time when children grew up faster to the world.

Perhaps one may look at de Guerville's flight to America in the same way one regards the flight to Greece and Italy of an earlier generation of youth. The young Louis Napoleon, who went on to rule France as Napoleon III, had nearly gotten himself killed in the Italian Wars, where he had fled seeking the vanished glory of his uncle's day. A later generation of young idealists—if the expression is not redundant—sought meaning in the Spanish Civil War and the struggle against fascism. In short, it was a quest more than a voyage, and it is likely that America held for the young de Guerville all the hope and potential his homeland seemed to lack.

There was another factor. As de Guerville would relate later, from an early age he suffered from that great killer of the age, tuberculosis. The typical nineteenth century remedy for the consumptive (as with de Guerville's compatriot and exact contemporary André Gide), besides generous portions of cod liver oil and open windows, was a change of scenery, specifically to a drier, more arid locale away from the vapors of wetter or lower altitudes that were thought to congest the lungs. In his own irreverent fashion, Mark Twain had recommended a stint in the American West as a palliative for diseased lungs. Robert Louis Stevenson (also a consumptive) found great relief during several months' residence in Napa Valley, California. De Guerville's tuberculosis may also have played a role in his solitary flight from his homeland for the America West in 1887.

The final two decades of the nineteenth century saw a virtual flood of European immigrants to the United States, primarily from Ireland and the states of southern Europe. It was among these boatloads, though probably traveling in a bit more comfort, that de Guerville arrived in the United States in 1887, at the age of eighteen. He numbered among the very first immigrants to witness the Statue of Liberty—a gift from his native France—welcoming the huddled masses into New York Harbor. The statue was placed on its new granite pedestal in 1886, thanks greatly to the fundraising efforts of Joseph Pulitzer's *New York World*.

Of his first years in the United States little at all is known, save that he first sought his fortune in the American West. We know this only because de Guerville reminisced years later, writing about anti-Semitism in France, "I shall never forget that years ago, when a boy of eighteen, struggling for a living in the far West, and suddenly taken ill, a German Jew extended his hand to me, and in those dark days proved the truest, most devoted, most generous of friends."[5]

Though he claims in 1892 to be an American—both in heart and on paper—de Guerville's trail is frustratingly difficult to trace in these early years. Unfortunately, data from the 1890 census (the only one de Guerville would have participated in) was destroyed through fire and neglect. Nor does de Guerville's name appear among the lists of natu-

Introduction

ralized citizens of New York City. In fact, de Guerville seems to have left hardly a trace in the bureaucratic records of the United States.

But from 1889 the outlines of de Guerville's life take on greater clarity. That year found him in Milwaukee, where he was able to secure a position teaching French at the small and nondescript Milwaukee Women's College, one of dozens of small private colleges beginning to train middle class women in the sciences and modern languages. There he taught French during the day while spending many a Milwaukee evening directing the city's French club, *le Cercle Français,* in public performances. He was an able teacher and manager, and local papers lauded both his pedagogical and dramatic skills.

Figure 1. Milwaukee Women's College at the time of de Guerville's employment there (1890). Milwaukee-Downer College. Records, 1852-1964. Milwaukee Manuscript Collection L. Wisconsin Historical Society. Milwaukee Area Research Center. Golda Meir Library. University of Wisconsin--Milwaukee. Used by permission.

A period photograph shows de Guerville sitting for a group portrait with his students at Milwaukee College. He is not an especially handsome man. His face is long, eyes close set, and ears small but notable by their protrusion. His glance is focused and intelligent, and he seems most like a gentle and resigned figure, like someone who had already suffered much despite the gangliness that still betrays his youth.

Figure 2. A. B. de Guerville and his students at Milwaukee Women's College (1890). Milwaukee-Downer College. Records, 1852-1964. Milwaukee Manuscript Collection L. Wisconsin Historical Society. Milwaukee Area Research Center. Golda Meir Library. University of Wisconsin--Milwaukee. Used by permission.

Though barely twenty-one, in Milwaukee de Guerville became a central figure in the city's Francophone community. In 1890 he founded the city's *Courrier Français,* a small French weekly much like the other *Courrier Français* papers in other American cities. He would continue to edit and manage the modest weekly until leaving Milwaukee in 1892. If the small college atmosphere (Milwaukee Women's College enrolled 120 students in 1890) was intimate it was also likely stifling, judging by how quickly de Guerville departed once the opportunity arose. One tends to forget, picturing de Guerville lecturing in French, that he had only just entered his twenties, and was likely younger than many of his students. In this respect, his restlessness may be easily understood.

Introduction

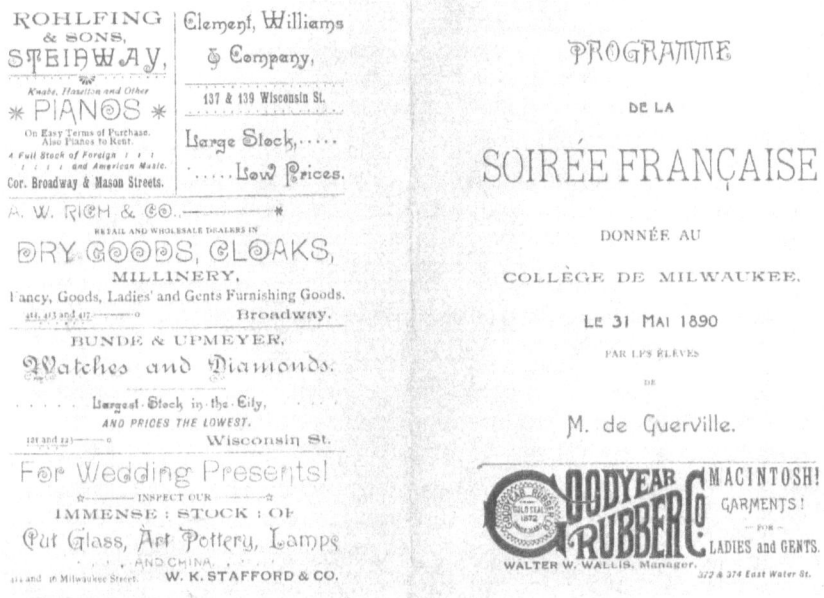

figure 3. A flyer announcing a public performance by de Guerville's "Cercle Français" in Milwaukee (1890). Milwaukee-Downer College. Records, 1852-1964. Milwaukee Manuscript Collection L. Wisconsin Historical Society. Milwaukee Area Research Center. Golda Meir Library. University of Wisconsin--Milwaukee. Used by permission.

By all indications, de Guerville's background and tastes were not such as could be long restrained in Milwaukee. Even in 1890, while living and working in that city, he was moving back and forth between the United States and his native France. In the summer of 1890 he passed through Washington, D.C. en route to Paris, staying in the luxurious Willard Hotel, and "highly recommended to General McCook, visited the Capitol, and before departing . . . shook hands with President Harrison."[6]

Even considering de Guerville's rather worldly air, in 1892 he took what is by any account quite a momentous step—from lecturer in French and editor of a minor paper to Honorary Commissioner for the World's Columbian Exposition, planned as the world's largest fair and then in its formative stages just down the lakefront at Chicago. It was a move that would thrust him into the larger world of politics, travel, and writing that would prove his ultimate calling.

"A Stupendous Thing!"—The World's Columbian Exposition

President Grover Cleveland's exclamatory opening of the World's Columbian Exposition, held at Chicago in the spring and summer of 1893, still qualifies as understatement. The fair, held to commemorate the four-hundredth anniversary of Columbus' landing in the New World (it was held a year later than originally planned), was perhaps the most successful and talked about of all the world's fairs and expositions—which by de Guerville's time were enjoying their golden age. It put Chicago on the map and to many Americans it marked a great turning point in American destinies, the end of the frontier period, and the beginning of a more organized, industrial, mechanized and bureaucratized future that would soon make of the United States a global imperial power. To a young Henry Adams the world shifted on its axis at Chicago.

It was certainly a turning point in the fortunes of de Guerville as well. It launched him from the obscurity of a small town lecturer and newspaper editor to a "globe-trotter," even if he was never to lose his love of the audience. It provided access to persons of fame and influence, both in the United States and abroad, and paved the way for the direction his life would take once the fair's turnstiles had stopped. If one may point to a single hinge of fate in a person's life, then for Amédée Baillot de Guerville it was beyond doubt his designation in 1892 as Honorary Commissioner for the World's Columbian Exposition.

It is not clear today just how de Guerville managed to secure this position, or even with any great precision when. By all evidence, de Guerville had absolutely no background in or familiarity with the Far East. Though *Au Japon* treats in part of de Guerville's activities there as Honorary Commissioner, the author gives us no indication of how he procured that nomination. However, an editor's notation to de Guerville's first article in *Leslie's Weekly* (a publication for which he would come to write widely) claims he was "selected by Mrs. Potter Palmer [chief of the Board of Lady Managers for the Chicago World's Fair] to visit Japan with a view of enlisting the women of that country in the World's Fair Exposition."[7] A small notice later appearing in the *Japan Weekly Mail* seems to confirm this, remarking that de Guerville arrived in Japan carrying "an invitation from Mrs. Potter Palmer and the Ladies Committee to the Empress."[8] The pages of *Au Japon* also clearly indicate that de Guerville's World's Fair business in Japan concerned primarily the women's exhibit.

Yet de Guerville's name goes unmentioned in the otherwise exhaustive official directory to the fair, which details with meticulous precision every officer and official representative of the Chicago World's Fair, whose organization rivaled in size and scope the governments of many small states.[9] One possibility is that Mrs. Palmer, a strong advocate of women's education, paid a visit to Milwaukee Women's College, and perhaps was a spectator at one of the fêtes thrown by *le Cercle Français*. Charmed by de Guerville's manner, perhaps she made him an impromptu offer he could not refuse. Another possibility is that de Guerville, as editor of a small French language publication in Milwaukee, had become acquainted with the press leaders of nearby Chicago and was commissioned privately by city leaders to head to the Far East, as both roving correspondent and quasi-official promoter of the World's Fair, perhaps promoting the women's exhibit in particular.

De Guerville never mentioned that his mission to the Far East concerned primarily, if not solely, the women's exhibit, either in his own writings or, in light of diplomatic correspondence, to political authorities in the Far East. In fact, in Japan there was some confusion concerning just who or what he represented. But in the end that hardly mattered. In the final analysis, the fact that in 1892 the twenty-three year old de Guerville appeared bearing official credentials in the courts and homes of influence (one as important as the other) of the Far East must say something about the young commissioner's charm and facility, personal qualities that would be emphasized again and again in the press in the few years to come.

It is largely the events intimate and peripheral to A. B. de Guerville's mission as Honorary Commissioner that comprise the first half of *Au Japon,* and so there is little point in reviewing them in any detail here. It is worth emphasizing that as the title of the work implies, it was Japan—rather than Korea or China—that left the deepest and most positive impression on the young and impressionable commissioner. One might even say that it was Japan that inspired him to dedicate his life to writing.

New credentials in hand, de Guerville first reached Japan from the direction Rudyard Kipling recommended, from America and the Pacific—from "the barbarians and the deep sea."[10] In fact de Guerville arrived in Yokohama from San Francisco on April 13, 1892, only a week before Kipling made his more celebrated, or at least more remembered, voyage there.

A. B. de Guerville also arrived with the latest technology in hand—a McIntosh Magic Lantern, a device later to play such a prominent role in his public and private lectures from the Vatican to New York City. It seems that during his journey to the Far East de Guerville made the acquaintance of Count Harry Kessler (1868–1938)—Count Harry K- in *Au Japon*—then returning by circuitous route to Germany from New York. Of Kessler, one of the preeminent social critics and cultural figures of his epoch, it has been written, "He attracted magnetically the best and brightest, and, wherever he went, they formed his company."[11] Again, this tells us something about de Guerville's personal qualities. Kessler, who himself became highly intrigued with Japanese aesthetics, would show up at de Guerville's lectures a few years later in New York (and in fact would financially sponsor some).

De Guerville and Kessler had only a few weeks to enjoy one another's company. At the end of April the young Count proceeded via Indochina and India to Germany, while de Guerville lingered in the Far East until the stultifying heat of the Japanese July sent him and his fragile lungs off to summer in Vancouver. He returned to Japan, again on World's Fair business, in October, this time visiting Korea and China to elicit support there.

As is so often the case with new visitors to the Far East, de Guerville's experiences in 1892 comprised an almost overwhelming flood of original sensations that proved personally transforming. Though his initial sojourn in Japan, Korea, and China was rather brief, the events that filled it provided sufficient grist for de Guerville's writings and other activities for years to come. What's more, it made of him an ardent admirer and friend of Japan, willing to support and defend it in word and print.

Nevertheless, it is fair to ask just how successful de Guerville's mission was on behalf of the Chicago Fair. The answer depends greatly on the exact nature of the Honorary Commissioner's charge, specifically in the case of de Guerville. At first it would seem his role was in the same vein as that of previous fair commissioners mentioned in the semi-official *Book of the Fair*, who "visited all the northern countries of Europe . . .and making it a point everywhere to approach the highest authorities, the Prime Ministers or Ministers of Foreign Affairs . . ." in order to obtain assurances of participation.[12] Yet Horace Allen, the chargé of the American legation in Seoul at the time of de Guerville's visit, remarked that despite the appeal of his magic lantern display, he seemed remarkably ignorant on the particulars of the fair itself.[13] The American delegation in Japan was actually under the impression that de Guerville, rather than a representative of the Chicago World's Fair, represented a consortium of Chicago newspapers, while the *Japan Weekly Mail*, the primary English newspaper in Japan, described de Guerville's mission as being "uniquely to spread information."[14]

The *Japan Weekly Mail*'s assessment seems most accurate. From the standpoint of securing foreign participation, de Guerville's success was minimal, as it would have to be. Though the Japanese emperor pronounced the presentation at the palace, "one of the most enjoyable evenings he had ever passed," and de Guerville's magic lantern show with a view of the planned Women's Building briefly inspired Korea's Queen Min to put together a Korean women's contribution for that display (which in the end did not materialize), the fact is both Japan and Korea were already committed, light and picture show or not.[15] Elements of what would be the Japanese delegation to the World's Fair had arrived in Chicago months before de Guerville first arrived in Japan. Indeed, as is revealed in the opening chapter of *Au Japon*, de Guerville's first voyage to Japan was shared with Teshima Seiichi, the Commissioner General of the Imperial Japanese Government to the World's Columbian Exposition, then returning home from Chicago on World's Fair business. The most that can be said is that de Guerville's visit kept the momentum going, which in the case of Korea and its vacillating King Kojong may have proved one crucial factor in that country's participation.

One of de Guerville's greatest successes in Japan had little in fact to do with the fair. Following his laudatory presentation at the imperial residence, the Japanese Red Cross Society requested that de Guerville repeat his magic lantern show for a public, paying audience, to raise funds for that organization. It seems that like his other performances on behalf of Japanese charities, this one met with great success. It was also a service that would not be forgotten by Japanese officials when de Guerville returned two years later as a war correspondent.

As for China, which de Guerville visited soon after his brief sojourn in Korea, the Honorary Commissioner's presentation before Li Hongzhang (Li Hung-chang) and his colorful guests in Tianjin (Tientsin) entertained but did not convince. In *Au Japon* de Guerville briefly discusses his presentation at Tianjin, though he seems concerned in his recollection more with comic effect than concrete results. But de Guerville would describe in more serious tones elsewhere his experience in China before Li Hongzhang. The fact was that in 1892 China was still smarting from the American passage of the Geary Act, which extended curbs on Chinese immigration, as well as by stories of escalating anti-Chinese sentiment in the United States.[16]

As a final note, regarding de Guerville's mission as Honorary Commissioner, not everyone commended the young American's visit. The *Japan Gazette*—one of the three English papers serving the foreign enclave at Yokohama—was disparaging of de Guerville's efforts. It was this same paper that would attack de Guerville even more vituperatively during his tenure in Japan covering the Sino-Japanese War, and was no doubt related to the fact that not all foreign papers in Japan, indeed the majority, looked kindly on those that emphasized Japan's capabilities and potential. Regarding his efforts on behalf of the fair, the *Japan Gazette* openly rejected the notion de Guerville ever called upon the imperial household while belittling his role in general:

> We distinctly remember Mr. de Guerville being on one of the Yokohama Hotel lists, but to our knowledge he never did anything more than other "World's Fair" Commissioners have done, who have drifted this way under the influences of an all round trip, paid for by someone else. He did not even preach a sermon, as some have done as a sort of conscience vent, and we need hardly say that no one has given any illustrated lectures before their Imperial Majesties.[17]

It was not the last time de Guerville's prominent praise of Japan would bring him into conflict with the English press of Japan. In the *Japan Weekly Mail*, however—whose owner Frank Brinkley was also a fervent admirer of Japan—de Guerville found a welcome ally. That paper defended de Guerville's reputation in 1892, as it would again in 1895 when de Guerville's denial of a massacre by Japanese troops at Port Arthur stirred up controversy over matters more serious than palace soirees.

Introduction

War Correspondent

There is no direct evidence one way or the other concerning assertions by the American legation in Japan as well as the *Japan Weekly Mail* that de Guerville represented a "consortium of Chicago newspapers" during his visit to the Far East on behalf of the World's Fair. However, one thing is clear: de Guerville's journeys in Northeast Asia during the spring and summer of 1892 launched his all too brief career as a foreign correspondent and travel writer.

Besides his more provincial writing for his *Courrier Français* in Milwaukee, de Guerville's first known publication is a story concerning his experiences as Honorary Commissioner. "Japan at the World's Fair" appeared in *Leslie's Illustrated Weekly* in September 1892 and was followed soon thereafter, and in the same publication, by "Humor in Japanese Politics" in October 1892. From this time de Guerville would continue to write for *Leslie's*—either the *Weekly* or the more lavishly illustrated *Frank Leslie's Popular Monthly*—through 1897, when he became managing editor of *The Illustrated American*. After his brief stint as an Honorary Commissioner, de Guerville also found a niche for himself as a lecturer, perhaps a calling he had developed a taste for as a university instructor and during his evenings treading the boards for le *Cercle Français,* but certainly strengthened by his experiences lecturing to audiences—royal and otherwise—in Asia.

Using the same magic lantern he had employed with such effectiveness during his presentations in the Far East, de Guerville began to give public lectures in New York City on a variety of topics, from "Interesting and Amusing Experiences of an American World's Fair Commissioner" to "Noted Women of France" and "Josephine, Wife of Napoleon." He was by all accounts a gifted, captivating, and humorous speaker. One newspaper compared him to George Grossmith, a period actor and impersonator famed for his satirical monologues done to piano accompaniment.[18] *Leslie's Weekly* gloated like a proud parent over its random reporter:

> Mr. de Guerville is able to speak of people and things never before made public in a lecture—but they are also extremely amusing and full of wit and sparkle. Ready in delivery, Mr. de Guerville is easily seen to be possessed of the enthusiasm of his subjects; and his clear and penetrating voice, which is both magnetic

and pleasing, and the slight foreign accent which pervades his speech, serve to lend piquancy to his witty descriptions.[19]

From this time as well, travel writing became a staple of de Guerville's pen, with his numerous publications appearing in *Leslie's Weekly* as well as *Munsey's* and *Pearson's Popular Weekly*. Even when he was later deskbound by duties at *The Illustrated American*, he continued to travel in his mind, reminiscing of far-off destinations visited months or even years before as if he had been there only yesterday.

One of his favorite destinations was Spain, where on a May afternoon in 1894 he witnessed the great matador Manuel Garcia "Espartero" gored to death by a bull. Besides his travels in the Far East, de Guerville wrote of his voyages in Italy, Morocco, Turkey, Colombo (Sri Lanka), and Cuba, usually mixing descriptions of scenery and customs with a discussion of current affairs—government reforms in Turkey, the rising tide of rebellion in Cuba, or an independence struggle in Morocco.

The spring of 1894 found de Guerville wandering the courts and capitals of Europe contributing stories to *Leslie's Weekly* on an irregular basis and on eclectic topics. He wrote a nostalgic piece concerning his 1892 visit with Li Hongzhang in Tianjin, along with a series dealing with "Socialism and Anarchism in Europe" (this during the heyday of anarchist *tentatives* in a year that witnessed the assassination of French president Sadi Carnot).

De Guerville seems to have had a remarkable ability for gaining access to political leaders, including a call on Pope Leo XIII (even giving his Holiness a private magic lantern show) and high political figures in Spain (such as the former president of the failed republic) and Italy in the spring of 1894.[20] His linguistic aptitudes and journalism contacts allowed him to publish in both France (*le Figaro*) and Italy (*La Tribuna Illustrata* and *Le Moniteur de Rome*).

In late summer 1894, with the outbreak of hostilities between China and Japan over Korea—the Sino-Japanese War as it is now known, but at the time generally referred to as the China-Japan War—de Guerville was picked up as a "special correspondent" for *Leslie's Weekly*, which dispatched him immediately to the Far East—via New York and San Francisco—with instructions to "proceed as rapidly as possible to the theatre of action and supply us with correspondence and sketches of passing events."[21]

Introduction

The editor of *Leslie's Weekly* took care in one issue to explain the qualifications of his man in the Far East:

> Mr. de Guerville has already represented us on important missions: he had visited China, where he interviewed Li Hung Chang; had represented the World's Fair Commission as a special envoy in enlisting the interest of the Empress of Japan in the great Chicago exhibition [. . .] and had been, moreover, a close student of Oriental affairs. His standing with the two governments was such that, as it seemed to us, he would be accorded the largest privileges allowed by either to correspondents from abroad.[22]

The editor's confidence was not misplaced.

But it was not only *Leslie's Weekly* that de Guerville represented in the Far East. He set out for Japan as special correspondent for the *New York Herald* as well. This was the same paper from which the journalist James Creelman had resigned in 1893, chaffing under the strict editorial policies of its chief editor, James Gordon Bennett Jr., who prohibited him (as any reporter) from putting his byline to his stories. Bennett's *New York Herald*, it should be noted, was in fierce competition with Joseph Pulitzer's *New York World* (to which Creelman transferred in 1894, and for which he also served as a special correspondent for the Sino-Japanese War). Apparently de Guerville offered his freelance services to the editors at the *New York Herald*, who agreed to buy his copy at space rates.[23]

Perhaps to whet the appetite of its readers, even as de Guerville was heading from New York to the Far East, the *New York Herald* published a lengthy exposé by de Guerville detailing his recent experiences in Japan, Korea, and China as Honorary Commissioner. In what must have sincerely vexed Creelman (it certainly did Creelman's wife), Bennett prominently displayed de Guerville's name at the foot of the full-page article.[24]

De Guerville's final sojourn in the Far East, now as a war correspondent, was shorter but more eventful than his first. Here is de Guerville at the top of his game: dispatched to the theater of war as a special correspondent for one of the best-known dailies in the world. Indeed, he seemed, much as *Leslie's Weekly* had recently surmised—on the cusp of great things.[25] A surviving illustration of de Guerville during his coverage of the conflict has him tall and strapping, and dressed in the *de rigueur* outfit of the heroic adventurer of the day: high boots, pantaloons, cape and hat.

Figure 4. A. B. de Guerville Covering the Sino-Japanese War in China (1894). *Munsey's Magazine* (1895).

De Guerville arrived in Yokohama, Japan, on a rainy September morning in 1894. Soon his social and political connections in Japan, cultivated during his initial trip to that country two years previous, had secured him transport on Japanese troop carriers and access to the frontlines in Korea and later Manchuria. His dispatches and subsequent writings on what he witnessed—and perhaps more importantly, *did not* witness—played a central role in the debate that raged in America, Europe, and even Japan itself regarding Japanese behavior during that war and attitudes towards Japan in general at a time when that nation was quickly rising to the status of world power.

De Guerville's writings on the Sino-Japanese War, perceived by many as excessively pro-Japan, also gave rise to controversy and a public clash of personalities between himself and other correspondents and newspapers, most notably James Creelman of the *New York World*.

Magazine Publisher

Despite the praise his accounts of the war in the Far East received, de Guerville's employment with the *New York Herald* did not result in the professional windfall one might have expected and for reasons that will be dealt with later in this introduction. De Guerville spent the next several years following his return to America from the Far East writing, lecturing, and traveling, but he was never to be picked up as a regular correspondent. By late 1895 he was in Europe and North Africa, the year after that stomping from Cuba to Constantinople. His relationship with the *New York Herald* had ended along with the Sino-Japanese War, but he continued to write for *Leslie's Weekly* and other American and European newspapers and periodicals on a sporadic basis. He developed an interest in the "Cuba question," which was increasingly dominating American papers and public opinion, as the United States under William McKinley (and Assistant Secretary of the Navy Theodore Roosevelt) moved ever closer to war and empire. Somewhat sympathetic to Spain, de Guerville's coverage of the Cuban insurrection—including a trip there in the spring of 1896—is characterized by a reflective moderation rather than the belligerence then dominating so much of the period press, especially out of New York City. Had not personal illness intervened, perhaps de Guerville might have gone on to join the host of well-known American reporters covering the war in Cuba in the years ahead.

As a result of his experiences as Honorary Commissioner for the World's Columbian Exposition, in early 1896 de Guerville was also appointed United States General Commissioner for the American program at the International Exposition planned for Innsbruck, Austria, from May to October 1896, an exposition dedicated to physical education, hygiene, sport and associated trades and industries.[26] Meanwhile he continued to maintain a busy schedule of lecturing and writing.

Between his frequent travels and social and professional engagements, de Guerville also found time to marry. In December, 1896, he wed Laura Belle Spraker in New York City. De Guerville was twenty-seven, the bride twenty-four. He had married well. Laura Spraker came from a respected, well-to-do New York family, American to the core. Her great-great grandfather had advised George Washington.

Within a month of his marriage de Guerville and his new bride departed New York for what can only be described as a five month working honeymoon through Europe. In February they were in Spain, where his comments in front of the Madrid Geographical Society stirred up some controversy in both Spain and the United States when he intimated Japan would support America in the case of a Spanish-American conflict, if only in hopes of gaining the Philippines as a result.[27] From Spain the de Guervilles set off on a four-month jaunt through North Africa, Italy (where he had a final dramatic encounter with Creelman), Greece, and Turkey, only returning to New York in the late summer of 1897. In November 1897 de Guerville's wanderings—and his tenure with *Leslie's Weekly*—came to an end when he became President and General Manager of *The Illustrated American,* taking over from Lorillard Spencer, the magazine's founder. One commentator wrote of the new proprietor, "Mr. de Guerville will enlarge the paper and make it even more progressive than it has been."[28] Oddly enough, de Guerville's Sino-Japanese War rival James Creelman had briefly managed the same publication in 1892. De Guerville's tenure was to be brief as well.

By late 1897, with a new marriage and the partial acquisition of *The Illustrated American,* de Guerville seems to have recovered from the disappointments of his Sino-Japanese War experience and reached another professional peak. He had an excellent marriage, was editor of a reputable New York magazine, and was a well-known and respected reporter in the intensely competitive New York City scene. As *Leslie's Weekly* had once remarked, he was well situated to "make a mark upon his time," and he was not yet thirty.

Collapse

Reading the range of de Guerville's work, one receives the distinct impression that he was happiest not behind a desk but independent and on the road. There is always a certain restlessness to de Guerville that he seems unable to elude. Even in his hours of sickness he is constantly on the move, as if it was the search for a cure, not the cure itself, which inspired. His description of himself during these years says much,

"Burning with a desire to see, to know, to sense, to comprehend, I dispensed a limitless energy and vitality."[29]

But at the offices of *The Illustrated American* de Guerville was forced into a more routine, if more harried, existence. By his own characterization, 1897 and 1898 saw him in a swirl of social events and editorial responsibilities—tasks that left him exhausted and often not in bed until nearly morning. His writings during this period seem to effuse a sense of ennui. He revisited old topics or explored uninspiring new ones—"The Plain People of Spain," "Santa Clause around the World," "The Women of Japan," or "Li Hung Chang in Pekin." His last publication for *The Illustrated American,* "Woman's Love in China," was actually only a translation from a decade old work by Colonel Tchen-Ki-Tong, whom he had once met at a magic lantern show in Tianjin. The only topic that seems to have inspired de Guerville was the growing climate of belligerence towards Spain. Here de Guerville refused to pander to the period taste for sensationalism and jingoism, often using the pages of his periodical to criticize what he saw as a reckless drive towards war, notably on the part of the nation's press. It was a lofty stand, but it didn't help sales.

Despite outward appearances of contented success, beneath the surface things were troubled. The hardships of travel were one thing, but de Guerville was less suited to the exertions of the editorial desk and social circuit. In January, 1898, a fire ravaged the offices of *The Illustrated American,* also destroying de Guerville's "private collections"—including an assortment of personal photographs that was described as "probably unsurpassed by any collection in the city"—bringing further stress upon the young manager and editor.[30] When de Guerville acquired *The Illustrated American*, the magazine was already on financially shaky ground, with subscription rates down and competition intense. The fire only compounded the publication's financial difficulties—and indeed it would not survive the century. Based upon subsequent events, there is also reason to believe that de Guerville's marriage was not finding its way to a storybook ending.

With such accumulated stresses, the resurgence of de Guerville's long dormant tuberculosis is not surprising. According to an obscure later publication by de Guerville, in the spring of 1898 he was revisited by the sickness that for so many years during his active, globe-trotting life had remained in check. As a result he gave up the *The Illustrated American* in March, 1898, when it was sold in public auction for

$5,000, and for several months afterward he sought relief from his ailment in North America, from New York's Finger Lakes to Florida, but all to no avail. By summer his six-foot frame, sturdy and vigorous in a photo from 1894, had withered to a mere 114 pounds. His left lung was completely eaten away, with the disease also making short work of the right one; his life, in his own words, "hung by a thread."

In August 1898, living under his doctor's prognosis that he would not survive the year, de Guerville opted to quit America altogether for France, wishing to see his mother and his motherland a final time before dying.[31]

We must take de Guerville's own word on these particulars regarding his health, as such intimate details are not found elsewhere. The condition of his lungs aside, that by 1898 his marriage was ailing we can be certain. In late summer of 1898, when de Guerville quit New York City to seek relief from his tuberculosis, he apparently left his young wife behind. Partially as a result of this, in 1900 Laura Spraker de Guerville made a public suit for divorce on the grounds that her husband had abandoned her saddled with his debts. To these accusations she added elliptically and for good measure that she had "learned enough of his life abroad to justify her in bringing suit for an absolute divorce."[32]

Final Wanderings and Writings

> Like many who are sick, I no doubt repressed my illness a long time before it violently manifested itself. From the age of fifteen my life was very difficult and painful. Numerous exhausting trips to Korea, Cochin China, India, Egypt, Morocco, Cuba and all about the world, in all climates and seasons greatly improved my constitution. But feverish with a desire to see, to know, to sense, to comprehend, I expended immense energy and vitality, increasingly undermining my health as I threw myself into unending adventures.[33]

One wonders if de Guerville read André Gide. They were both Frenchmen, born the same year. Both were consumptive as well. In 1897, when de Guerville was beginning to struggle with the renewed and vigorous assault on his lungs, Gide published his *Les Nourritures Terrestres,* a call of affirmation that emerged from Gide's own battle with the killer disease ("Fevers of bygone days, you consumed my flesh with a mortal consumption . . . O loving beauty of the earth, the flowering of your surface is marvelous! Scenes into which my desire plunges . . . ").[34] Though ostensibly a paean to life on behalf of a young man afflicted, bedridden, and lacking in a life aesthetic, the book came to represent to a whole generation of youth the primacy of lived experience and personal freedom over formal education and the social constrictions of the times. The vocabulary of Gide seems to resonate in de Guerville's short account of his own struggle with "the white death," written in 1904, after he too had reclaimed life.

In August 1898 de Guerville boarded the *Kaiser Wilhelm der Grosse* in Manhattan harbor and bid good-bye to the America that had nurtured and molded him over the previous decade. He would never return. He was going back to a Europe and a France he had never completely left behind. His younger brother had joined the invalid in New York to accompany him on a voyage he might very well not survive. By order of the Kaiser, hanging aboard *Kaiser Wilhelm der Grosse*, as with all passenger liners of the Hamburg Amerika Line, was a painting ostensibly designed by the Kaiser himself: *Die gelbe Gefahr*—"The Yellow Peril." It depicted the Archangel Michael and an allegorical Germany leading the other European powers against an Asiatic (read Japanese) threat rising in the East represented by a golden Buddha.[35]

If anything could get the ailing de Guerville across the ocean in speed and comfort it was the *Kaiser Wilhelm der Grosse*. Launched in 1897, she was the pride of the German commercial fleet, rivaling any ocean liner on the seas. Her massive engines could carry 1,700 passengers across the Atlantic in six days, and to de Guerville in the late summer of 1898 each day was precious. As it was, he was in no condition to enjoy the luxuries the *Kaiser Wilhelm* offered its coddled passengers. He was delirious from a high fever, unable even to feed himself.

But despite doctors' gravest predictions, de Guerville did survive the journey, and the year. He even survived the century. However, what followed were nearly three years of hellish recovery, during which de Guerville often wished himself dead. From Paris de Guerville was dragged and pushed across Europe and the Mediterranean on the advice of various physicians. Normandy, Archachon in Burgundy, Mentor, Nice, Ospedaletti near San Remo, Palermo, Pallanza on Lago de Maggiore, Pégli, Abondance in French Savoy, and the list goes on. He tried every known remedy, including the experimental *igazola*, developed by an Italian physician in Palermo, in which a powder was heated to a gas and inhaled.

It is at Pallanza, however, that de Guerville learned of the remarkable successes being made at a place called Nordach near Baden in the Black Forest by a Dr. Otto Walther. So intense was the demand to get into the limited space of the Nordach Clinic that even for a man who had no trouble obtaining an audience with the Pope, a yearlong wait was required. The personalized treatment of Nordach was also extremely expensive, with the first hundred days having to be paid in advance.[36]

In September, 1900, de Guerville finally gained his coveted entrée to Dr. Walther's clinic, and from that time until May of the following year ascribed to the strict regimen that made Nordach so famous, and perhaps so effective: plenty of rest, high caloric intake, open windows, and most importantly, *no medicines*. This "abode of Spartans" was situated so as to be exposed to every wind. The sanatorium's *Liegehallen* received the cool, often as not freezing, blasts day and night and in all seasons in order to dissipate impure air and facilitate the recovery of the lungs. It had a proven track record. By the early twentieth century the clinic's fame had spread throughout Europe and America, spawning the rise of "little Nordachs" from Wales to Canada.[37]

It certainly seemed to work wonders for de Guerville, who upon his discharge in May, 1901, felt "totally renewed." He even climbed Mt. Righi and Mt. Pilate near Lucerne, both well over two thousand meters. But the greatest testament to de Guerville's newfound health was his pen. He felt well enough to write frankly about his experience with tuberculosis in a small tract entitled *La lutte contre la tuberculose*, which was later published in English and German editions.[38] In 1904 de Guerville was inspired to revisit his experiences in Japan, Korea, and China with the publication of a little volume of reminiscences entitled—'in Japan.' Though its publication in 1904, just as another war threatened to erupt in the Far East, smells suspiciously of profit motives, it should also be seen as sign of de Guerville's return to health. That his mind should turn again to far off Japan is indicative of the place that country continued to hold in his heart and imagination.

Au Japon enjoyed a respectable success, something that seems to have convinced de Guerville to direct his future energies to the writing of travel books. Book writing, rather than the deadline-driven writing demanded by weekly or monthly publications, accommodated de

Guerville's convalescence as well. With tuberculosis in the nineteenth century one doesn't get that close to death and simply recover. Despite de Guerville's optimistic accounts of his own "return" to life, his health certainly remained forever fragile.

That de Guerville chose as his next subject after *Au Japon* the arid lands of North Africa also suggests a still-ailing consumptive. The dry Mediterranean climes of such locales as Algeria and Tunisia were attracting hordes of European consumptives, a reality best illustrated by André Gide's novel *L'Immoralist*. Along with an article on the Sudan for a French travel journal, in 1905 de Guerville published a travelogue of Egypt, *La Nouvelle Egypt,* a journalist-cum-tourist's account of British Egypt. It enjoyed even greater success than *Au Japon,* and was soon translated into English and German, two nations that along with France were grabbing up colonial holdings in Africa faster than they knew what to do with them. Cheaper editions continued to appear through 1915.

We hear virtually nothing more of de Guerville after his book on Egypt. Save for an article on the "situation in Egypt," he writes no more, at least under that name.[39] After five years of silence a tantalizing notice in *The Times* in the summer of 1911 remarked simply that de Guerville had been seriously ill in London for six weeks.[40] But after this the silence is total. In all likelihood he died of the disease that had so long plagued him, though probably not in London, for his obituary never appears. Perhaps it was in some corner of North Africa, but more likely he was back on the continent, near his mother one hopes and not in the Spartan halls of the Nordach Clinic.

II. THE SINO-JAPANESE WAR AND THE PORT ARTHUR CONTROVERSY

It must always be foul to tell what is false and it can never be safe to suppress what is true.

—Robert Louis Stevenson, *The Art of Writing*

It will be remembered that A. B. de Guerville's second voyage to the Far East was undertaken to cover the Sino-Japanese War as special correspondent for *Leslie's Weekly* and as a freelance contributor to the *New York Herald*. As such, he was in the company of a select handful of other foreign correspondents equally eager to get to the frontlines and make headlines. Most notable among these were James Creelman (*New York World*), Frederic Villiers (*The Black and White*), Thomas Cowen (*The Times* of London), a certain Laguerre (*Le Temps*), and Richard Harding Davis (who arrived too late to see any action).

Late nineteenth century America and Europe were witnessing the emergence of what was then termed "the new journalism"—a more dynamic and more ruthless sort of journalism spurred on by larger urban audiences, faster and more efficient communications, improved technologies, all fed by the development of vast capitalist economies and the concomitant fortunes waiting to be made in advertisement space. Between 1870 and 1900 the number of American dailies increased six fold, from 387 to 2,326 (though it was by no means a uniquely American phenomenon).[41] What this naturally meant was a fierce competition among journals and newspapers to increase circulation numbers by entertaining, shocking, thrilling, and titillating their readers in both words and pictures.

It was perhaps inevitable that the foreign correspondent—and by extension the war correspondent—would be a byproduct of this new industry. The new journalism of the late nineteenth century cannot be fully understood without considering the fact that its emergence paralleled what historians often term the "new imperialism," a second wave of Euro-American colonial expansion that brought with it a period of "dirty little wars" from Venezuela to Cuba, from the Sudan to Korea. In the late nineteenth century the figure of the journalist—particularly the war correspondent—rose to that of public icon, in what one writer later described as "the time of the Great Reporter."[42] Stephen Crane, Jack London, Lincoln Steffens, and even Winston Churchill became household names through their work as journalists, to say nothing of Henry Morton Stanley in Africa or Nellie Bly's very well publicized 1889 journey around the world in seventy-two days. Never before or since have the newspaper and the journalist held such central places in the public consciousness as they did in those brief decades between the emergence of the telegraph and the radio.

Background: The Sino-Japanese War, 1894–1895

Historians still debate the causes and significance of the Sino-Japanese War of 1894–1895. In its most general sense it was a struggle between late imperial China and modernizing Japan over hegemony in Northeast Asia, which came to a head in a contest over Korea. On a more symbolic level, it has been characterized as the final showdown between the traditional political order of East Asia, represented by China, and the modern, Western-oriented international order that Japan was earnestly embracing. Or, to put it in the preferred Western terms of the period, a battle between barbarism and civilization.[43]

For over a millennium China had viewed Korea as a "vassal state." In the traditional geopolitics of China-centered East Asia, this was not as imperialistic as it might ring in modern ears. Rather, it was a relationship both symbiotic and symbolic: Korea, as did other smaller peripheral states to the "Middle Kingdom," acquiesced to China's political and cultural "superiority" in the form of semi-annual tribute missions. In exchange, China was assured of docile and friendly states on its borders. In Korea's case, China not only allowed that state full political autonomy in the domestic realm but even sent armies to its aid when it was threatened by foreign invaders, such as the Japanese in the late sixteenth century.

The arrival of industrialized Western merchants and missionaries in the early nineteenth century, soon backed by the technological and military wizardry of the age, precipitated the rapid collapse of the China-centered traditional international order of East Asia. Western powers were soon dictating at the point of gunboats the terms by which China was to open its doors to a whole range of Western activities—commercial, political, religious, and scientific. It was a reality that soon led by the mid-nineteenth century to China's *de facto* entrance onto the modern geopolitical and diplomatic stage.

The same reality was forced upon Japan with the arrival of the American "black ships" of the American Commodore Matthew C. Perry in Tokyo Bay in 1858. In stark contrast to China, however, Japan soon recognized the need to embrace the brave new world that was greeting them. Soon doing away with the thousand-year-old social and political system of the samurai, Japan began to outwardly remold its society and institutions along more Western lines. The result was that, by 1890, the year of the country's Western-inspired Meiji Constitution, Japan could boast the highest industrial output in Asia, a modern army and respectable navy, a working political system, and a largely independent and thriving press.

From as early as 1874 Japan had even begun to acquire colonies, first Okinawa and then Taiwan, which Japan seized from a virtually helpless China in 1895, in the flush of victory from the Sino-Japanese

War. Thus the Sino-Japanese War was also the result of a Japanese desire to ensure the continuation of its own national development by acquiring sources of raw material beyond its own borders. From early in its drive towards national modernization Japan had begun to take an increasing commercial and political interest in Korea.

Even by the 1890s Korea remained an anomaly, neither fully integrated into the new international order (few Western powers were interested in her), nor completely absolving its traditional tributary relationship with China, a relationship that had ceased to have any meaning outside the ceremonial. As Japan began to industrialize and China seemed only to grow weaker, and as Russia with its Trans-Siberian Railway began to dream bigger dreams of a Russian Far East, in international eyes Korea increasingly seemed less a nation than a geopolitical conundrum: "the Korean question" or "the Korean problem" took hold of policymakers, military strategists, and pundits everywhere. The question was this: could Korea modernize on its own? If not, then in the Social Darwinian international order, where survival was a privilege of the fittest, who would ultimately control Korea?

By the end of the nineteenth century Japan had succeeded remarkably well in modernizing itself within the context of its traditional culture. The singular will that the Japanese applied to simply doing away with outmoded institutions still astounds the modern observer. To Japan's senior policymakers, who through the late nineteenth century watched as Western powers came to control an ever larger share of the world, it became clear that Korea's integrity (to mean its independence from Western control) must be maintained, and that doing so would mean that country's modernization, by whatever means necessary. But China, which itself had set off on a belated attempt at industrialization and modernization as the nineteenth century closed, was no longer willing to sit aside and watch another of its former vassals be taken away. One could say that China attempted to transfer into the power-driven reality of the new international order notions of vassalship that only properly worked in the more symbolic and ceremonial traditional order. Through the late nineteenth century, China stubbornly resisted, and at times openly obstructed, any attempts to give Korea an independent international political identity.

A series of Chinese-Japanese squabbles over Korean politics in the 1880s led to a tense truce over Korea, by the terms of which China and Japan both pledged not to interfere in Korea's internal affairs and

Introduction   xxxv

agreed to quotas on their respective troop numbers there. Japan, however, was merely biding its time. It was still too weak to confront China over hegemony in Korea. But not for long.

In 1894, an armed peasant uprising called the Tonghak Revolt upset again the delicate domestic tranquility of Korea, and even threatened the dynasty. Some rumors circulated that Japan was behind the revolt, just as they had been behind an aborted coup attempt in 1884. Though such rumors proved false, China reacted by sending in its troops. Now better prepared for its long anticipated confrontation with China, Japan recognized the opportunity and immediately dispatched troops of its own. The momentum towards war had begun.

Most historians agree that Japan made only token attempts to stop the coming conflict at a time when China would have done virtually anything to avoid open war. China even agreed to a joint and temporary troop presence until order could be restored. But Japan had moved beyond compromise. The reasons are simple enough. Japan would only be satisfied with the full independence of Korea. More cynical reasons may be inferred from this desire, such as a Japanese design, once Korea was unleashed, to snatch the now-isolated country up for herself (certainly, once the war began Japan was had no interest in seeing it stop until it had carved itself a comfortable sphere of control in Korea and Northeast China). Here is not the place, however, to renew those debates. The facts are simply that no agreement was reached and on August 1, 1894, war was declared on China by Japan's Meiji emperor speaking before a solemn gathering of the new National Diet. Here was Japan's first modern war.[44]

It must be said that *Au Japon* provides us somewhat snapshot and scattered images of de Guerville's Sino-Japanese War experience. Rather than *Au Japon*, it is de Guerville's period writings—for *Leslie's Weekly*, *Munsey's*, the *New York Herald*, and the *Japan Weekly Mail*—that best preserve his impressions of and reactions to the war he covered. This need not be surprising, even if it is a little disappointing. De Guerville was writing in 1904, and there was little need to rehash to his reading public the details of a war that had practically been forgotten, to the extent that it was ever even familiar to a European audience.[45] It is also likely that writing from France, with little documentary residue of his time in the Far East at hand (much, if not most, had been destroyed in the fire at de Guerville's *Illustrated American* in 1898), de Guerville was forced to rely upon a mixture of memory and sentiment.

Secondly, *Au Japon* is meant first and foremost as the author's reflections on a country, people, and culture he greatly admired and the memory of which he cherished, and not primarily as a war memoir. In this respect *Au Japon* is perhaps best seen as a series of anecdotal essays from his time traveling in the Far East. Each chapter is more or less self-contained and self-revealing, rather than forming part of a larger unfurling storyline.

However, as the *Japan Weekly Mail* noted soon upon *Au Japon*'s publication, Port Arthur was one of the few incidents of the war that de Guerville felt it essential, even after a decade, to revisit. It is worthwhile asking why this was so.

De Guerville's Sino-Japanese War Experience

Within weeks of the formal outbreak of hostilities, foreign correspondents were arriving in Yokohama, much as foreign naval vessels crowded into Japanese and Korean ports eager for a view of this historical inter-Asian conflict. Yet even before he had departed Europe for America and then Japan, de Guerville was already penning editorials on the looming conflict, which had yet to break into open fighting. It is fair to say that at this early date most observers in the West anticipated a Chinese victory, despite the fact that Japan had clearly done more in terms of modernization. China's sheer size and numbers seemed enough to ensure it would prevail. De Guerville, however, placed his bets on Japan, with its superior navy and better organized and better equipped army, realities he had witnessed on his trip there in 1892. He also strikes a moral tone that was generally echoed in the Western press and popular opinion of the time: "Japan is fighting in Asia the battle of civilization and it is sincerely to be hoped that she will be victorious, though she will undoubtedly remain in Corea [sic], as the English in Egypt, should she be allowed to gain there a foothold."[46] Indeed, though it does not survive, de Guerville authored a small pamphlet published in Japan in the aftermath of Port Arthur entitled *Civilization and Barbarism* that no doubt dealt with this same theme on a larger scale.[47]

In late August, 1894, de Guerville departed New York City for San Francisco, where he caught passage to Japan aboard the sail-assisted steamer *City of Peking*. From Chicago he shared his journey with his rival correspondent James Creelman of the *New York World*. Though de Guerville may not have realized it, Creelman already harbored a grudge against him, describing the young French-American as "a tall, thin hawk eyed young man with courtly manners and a stupendous faculty for lying."[48] Creelman's obvious animosity is at first glance enigmatic, particularly when one considers that Creelman confesses that in his conversations with de Guerville on the train to San Francisco de Guerville had no idea who Creelman was.[49]

On closer consideration, however, Creelman's feelings can perhaps be better gauged. Creelman had written for Bennett's *New York Herald* before de Guerville had been picked up by that publication, and had in fact left primarily due to Bennett's refusal to put Creelman's name to his stories. That de Guerville was now heading to the Far East as reporter for the *New York Herald* was perhaps an understandable source of resentment.[50] At the very least, the fact that de Guerville was the only other American correspondent to be covering the Sino-Japanese War made for intense competition between the two men.

However, combined with these factors were Creelman's own intimate fears of failure, which come across strongly in his letters to his wife. That de Guerville had the advantage of previous contact with the Far East only compounded such anxieties regarding Creelman's coming tour in Japan and Korea, his first as a war correspondent (almost as if to emphasize this advantage, in San Francisco de Guerville gave Creelman a Korean half-cent piece as a souvenir of his experiences; Creelman promptly sent it to his wife).

Further, Creelman had a reputation as a dandy, one who cultivated an aura of refinement and sophistication in his dress and person. And here was de Guerville, a younger man to whom Creelman himself attributes "courtly manners," a clear talent in the art of conversation (as accounts of his New York lectures testify), and with his intimidating worldly experiences and important contacts in the Far East. De Guerville also stood at six foot compared to Creelman's short and stocky figure, a superficial but not insignificant point. For a man like Creelman, who lamented to his wife his inability to form easy friendships, such a man as de Guerville could naturally be perceived as a rival, both personal and professional, whether de Guerville immediately perceived it or not. As their relationship progressed in Japan and China, de Guerville became increasingly aware of Creelman's very personal hostility towards him.

The *City of Peking* arrived in Yokohama harbor on a stormy evening in early September. A Japanese naval vessel guided it to safe anchorage through two miles of defensive submarine torpedo mines. Arriving at the Grand Hotel in Yokohama, Creelman was greeted with a letter from his wife Alice. "I am so entertained by de Guerville being on the same steamer," she wrote. "I know you will spike his guns nicely if you can possibly do it."[51]

No sooner had de Guerville made landfall in Japan than he was attending formal diplomatic dinners at the French and Russian legations, and if one is to believe his own account, enjoying *tête à têtes* with the highest ranking officials in the Japanese Army and government—including Counts Mutsu and Oyama, the Ministers of Foreign Affairs and War respectively—to the jealousy of the other foreign correspondents gathered in Japan eager to proceed to the front. At first foreign correspondents were not allowed permission to proceed to the front, and frustrated reporters circulated among the Yokohama and Tokyo hotels. However, perhaps seeing the advantage to be got from positive reportage of Japanese victories, the Japanese government soon determined to allow access to properly accredited war correspondents.

In mid-September, and a few days before Creelman, de Guerville received permission to accompany a Japanese troop transport to the battlefront, which was then approaching the Korean city of P'yŏngyang (Pen-Yang). Thus on his return to the Far East as war correspondent, de Guerville served as what we might call today an "embedded reporter." Reasonable charges could be made—and they were—to the objectivity of any reporter whose coverage of the war was limited to the sanction of one of the belligerents. But all journalists covering the Sino-Japanese conflict reached the front only through the permission and assistance of the warring powers, whether that be Japan or China. Further, in the opening weeks of the war the Japanese government issued regulations regarding the dispatch of war reports from the battlefront. They would all have to be cleared by the Japanese government.[52] But further, de Guerville did take the opportunity to strike out on his own initiative once in the field.

And so, while many foreign correspondents found themselves distressfully stranded in Japan during the course of hostilities, de Guerville—thanks in great part to his connections nurtured as Honorary Commissioner for the World's Fair—had an eventful wartime experience. De Guerville was afforded the "privilege" of accompanying the Japanese First Army to P'yŏngyang aboard the troop transport *Nagato Maru*, "the oldest, slowest, dirtiest" of them all.[53] Slow as it may have been, Creelman, who also received permission to accompany Japanese troops to P'yŏngyang, was only allowed to depart after de Gueville and on a later troop transport, as a result arriving there several days after his rival from the *New York Herald*. De Guerville's head start would later give rise to serious accusations on the part of Creelman.

The massive walled city of P'yŏngyang, one of Korea's most important cities, was the primary Chinese stronghold in Korea and its capture was critical to the success of Japanese war plans. At P'yŏngyang, which de Guerville reached following a soggy night's journey up the Taedong River aboard a Korean sampan, the *New York Herald* correspondent encountered death and destruction such as he had never witnessed. Approaching the already fallen city by sampan, his senses were assaulted, and overwhelmed, by the stench of rotting corpses, mostly of the city's fallen Chinese defenders. De Guerville prided himself as the only foreigner to have reported first hand on the fall of P'yŏngyang and took the time to heap almost preternatural praise on the Japanese for the mercy and moderation shown their defeated Chinese counterparts. He also praised the work of the Japanese Red Cross, enthusiastically writing, "If these facts do not call forth the admiration of the world, I am at a loss to know what will do so. I do not see how Japan can be refused the place she rightly claims among the civilized nations of the world." At the same time de Guerville condemned the brutality and ingratitude of the Chinese, who not only left P'yŏngyang a scorched and ravaged shell but were wholly ungrateful to the Japanese for the kind, even pampered, treatment they received as their prisoners.[54]

Following a few days in the city of P'yŏngyang de Guerville turned south, curious to visit the Korean capital of Seoul to see if he might secure an interview with the Korean king, as Creelman had done some weeks previous.[55] In Chemulpo—which the indefatigable travel writer Isabella Bishop Bird had left only weeks earlier, fleeing the approaching war—de Guerville the journalist found himself the object of an interview by a *Japan Weekly Mail* correspondent, likely the result of de Guerville's friendship with that journal's owner Captain Frank Brinkley (something he reveals in *Au Japon*). A few days later, de Guerville related his P'yŏngyang experience in fuller detail in a personal article for the *Japan Weekly Mail*.[56]

THE ADVANCE GUARD OF THE JAPANESE ARMY ENTERING THE MAIN GATE OF PING YANG.

Figure 5. An artist's rendition of the fall of P'yŏngyang that accompanied de Guerville's newspaper account. *San Francisco Chronicle* (19 December 1894).

The *Japan Weekly Mail* was the most respectable of the English papers in Japan. Founded by the Irishman Frank Brinkley—who at times also served as *The Times* (London) correspondent in Japan—it was largely pro-government and its war coverage echoed official policy and accounts. Circulation wars were no less intense in Japan than in America of the period, and the *Japan Weekly Mail* certainly had its rivals and detractors. Prime among these were the *Japan Gazette* and the *Japan Herald* (which actually predated the *Japan Weekly Mail*), whose articles tended to be more sensational and more critical of Japan and its policymakers. Both the *Japan Gazette* and *Japan Herald* were unabashed in their disdain for the Japanese and their support for the maintenance of the unequal treaties between Japan and the Western powers. (56) The wife of one diplomat wrote of the *Gazette* and *Herald*, "I have stopped reading these rags, which always attack us, or the Home Government, or the Emperor, when news is scarce. I can stand intelligent abuse, or good-natured ignorance, but the two nouns in unqualified conjunction make me tired."58

Throughout the Sino-Japanese War the *Japan Weekly Mail*'s writers and editors assailed critics of Japan's wartime policy, all the while praising the Japanese armies' successes in China and Korea and disparaging the barbarity and backwardness of the Chinese troops (on this point at least a view and vocabulary it shared with Western writers). Though de Guerville was never formally employed by the *Japan Weekly Mail*, that his account of the fall of P'yŏngyang was published by that paper effectively demonstrates that his opinions of the Japanese army and its conduct of the war were quite in line with official outlooks, which Brinkley (the paper's owner and editor) was at pains to portray.59 De Guerville himself admitted that he sent a copy of his first *New York Herald* dispatch to Viscount Mutsu, the Japanese foreign minister, so praising was it of Japanese conduct.60

De Guerville was well aware of the danger of a perceived pro-Japanese bias, especially since he was being accommodated on Japanese troop transports to and from the battlefront, while other foreign correspondents ate their hearts out in Tokyo or Nagasaki, so near yet so far from the action. At one point de Guerville is compelled to emphasize that all he relates about the war in his dispatches is "fact, pure and simple, and without the least colouring."61 Such coziness with quasi-official Japanese press organs would prove harmful to de Guerville's reputation later, when de Guerville's detractors would insinuate he had received bribes from Japanese officials in exchange for his relatively glowing praise of the Japanese war effort.62 As we shall see, Creelman would accuse de Guerville of still worse.

If de Guerville was slightly "colored" by his preferential treatment—and a sincere love for Japan and its own *mission civilisatrice* in Asia—we should not consider him a mere pawn of the Japanese. Only days after the fall of P'yŏngyang—and by his account suffering from malaria and dysentery—de Guerville opted to head south to Seoul, the Korean capital, to gauge affairs among the political leaders in Korea. From P'yŏngyang he caught passage to Chemulpo aboard a transport carrying wounded soldiers, and from there by palanquin to Seoul, some thirty miles up the Han River. It was de Guerville's second trip to Seoul (his first trip in 1892 is recounted in rather comic terms in *Au Japon*). As the Korean king was apparently ailing, de Guerville instead met with the Taewŏngun, father of the king and perhaps the most powerful—certainly the most forceful, with the possible exception of Korea's Queen Min—figure in Korean politics, the king himself notwithstanding. With de Guerville, the Taewŏngun exhibited his natural perspicacity. Over cigars the royal patriarch posed many probing questions on the recent military action at P'yŏngyang, not trusting in the reports supplied by the Japanese.[63]

Following the fall of P'yŏngyang and the brief trip to Seoul, de Guerville returned to Japan, again courtesy of a Japanese troop ship. Back in Hiroshima, de Guerville toured a Red Cross hospital (which he recounts in Chapter 18 of *Au Japon*). In early November, de Guerville departed Japan with elements of the Japanese Second Army under the command of General Oyama for the second major offensive of the war: the drive into Chinese Manchuria and the seizure of its crown jewel, Port Arthur.

James Creelman and the Port Arthur Controversy

Port Arthur—modern day Lushun—sits at the very tip of China's Liaodong Peninsula, a triangle of land that juts south from Manchuria into the northern Yellow Sea. Considering its strategic location commanding the sea lanes between China and Korea (a position made more valuable by its linkage to the Russian Trans-Siberian Railway in 1903), its conquest was viewed as essential by Japanese war planners if Chinese—and Russian—influence in Korea was to be decisively checked. In fact, so strategic was the Liaodong Peninsula in the geopolitics of the region that Russian, French, and German pressure after the war would force victorious Japan to retrocede it to China, a check the Japanese would not soon forget nor forgive. Not surprisingly, Port Arthur and the Liaodong Peninsula would play pivotal roles in the Russo-Japanese War a decade later.

In late November. 1894, much of the world was stunned to receive news that the heavily fortified Port Arthur, the "Gibraltar of the East," had fallen within twenty-four hours of its siege and bombardment by the Japanese Second Army under General Oyama. However, word of a massacre of Port Arthur's defenders and inhabitants at the hands of Japanese troops did not follow immediately upon the city's fall on November 21. The dispatches of Creelman first broke this story when they reached the offices of his employer the *New York World* on December 21. The accounts of other correspondents such as Frederic Villiers of the *London Black and White* and Thomas Cowen of *The Times* soon found their own way into Western living rooms.

The reports of Creelman proved the most sensational in their details, and not surprisingly garnered the widest attention. The *New York World* broke the news in alarming headlines: "*Massacre at Port Arthur. At Least Two Thousand Helpless People Butchered by Japanese Soldiers. Streets Chocked with Mutilated Bodies of Men, Women, and Children While the Soldiers Laughed.*"[64] As Creelman described it, "Unarmed men, kneeling in the streets and begging for life, were shot, bayoneted, or beheaded. The town was sacked from end to end, and the inhabitants were butchered in their own houses."[65]

Such accounts were on the whole backed up by Villiers and Cowen, and to a much lesser extent by a few American and British military attachés who also witnessed the fall of the city. Villiers reemphasized the massacre by publishing a long account of it entitled "The Truth about Port Arthur" in an American periodical of March 1895, largely in response to the massacre's detractors, epitomized by de Guerville.[66] The most prominent accounts of a Port Arthur "massacre" are those surviving in Creelman's book of memoirs, *On the Great Highway*, and in the reminiscences (almost certainly specious) of James Allan in his slender tome, *Under the Dragon Flag*. Almost totally forgotten in the debate surrounding the Port Arthur massacre has been the voice of de Guerville, though he was certainly far from silent at the time.

As *Au Japon* tells us, and period records confirm, de Guerville, like Creelman and Villiers, was on the scene at the fall of Port Arthur and its subsequent occupation by Japanese troops. Like Stephen and Cora Crane in Greece in 1897, de Guerville even rescued a dog on the battlefield, a puppy that he duly named "Faithful"—Chiu-ji. A period photograph captured de Guerville comforting the pup on the Chinese front. The dog would go on to play a starring role in de Guerville's New York lectures regarding his Sino-Japanese War experiences.

In sharp contrast to his fellow correspondents, de Guerville steadfastly denied that any massacre had occurred at Port Arthur. De Guerville's defense of Japan did not wait until 1904 and the publication of *Au Japon*. His vocal challenge of the sensationalist accounts of other Western journalists was deferred only by his return passage to America from the now-Japanese Port Arthur in December, 1894.

As soon as he arrived in Vancouver, British Columbia, de Guerville began to hear the stories circulating of Japanese atrocities at Port

Arthur, namely those from the pen of Creelman, Hearst's man in the Far East. De Guerville immediately wired off his own firsthand account of the city's fall to the *San Francisco Chronicle,* which gave it top headline.

Figure 6. De Guerville's headlining account of the fall of Port Arthur in the *San Francisco Chronicle.* 1894.

De Guerville continued his journalistic riposte as soon as he reached New York City: "Great was my surprise when, upon my arrival in New York . . . I read the sensational stories published in some newspapers about the awful atrocities and frightful massacres committed by the Japanese at the capture of the Chinese stronghold [Port Arthur]."[67] De Guerville then proceeded to defend the behavior of the Japanese troops, boldly and emphatically denying that the Japanese "mutilated a single body," much less that "junks loaded with people were sunk." In fact, most Chinese commoners de Guerville witnessed "were so happy, so pleased with the Japanese that they would beg of them to

Introduction

remain and to defend them against the awful oppression of their officials, mandarins, officers, and soldiers." It was a contrast indeed to such accounts as those of Creelman, or even of Villiers, who wrote in March, 1895, of the gratuitous slaughter of innocent civilians, so that all that remained after the Japanese bloodletting were thirty-six Chinese, to be used "in burying their dead comrades or as water-carriers for the [Japanese] troops. Their lives were protected by a slip of white paper stuck in their caps bearing the following inscription in Japanese characters: 'This man is not to be killed.'"[68]

For his part, Creelman later expounded on his account in his book *On the Great Highway*, published in 1901. As a self-professed "witness for civilization," Creelman, whom one contemporary described as a man "made of the clay from which spring crusaders, reformers and martyrs"[69], damned Japan for its gratuitous cruelty at Port Arthur, although qualifying it as "the only lapse of the Japanese from the usages of humane warfare."[70]

Japan denied that any "massacre" had occurred, though it admitted some regrettable transgressions on the part of some lower-class soldiers and coolies. Accounts of the massacre were taken by many in the West as evidence of an atavistic and lingering barbarism beneath Japan's civilized patina, while Japan's denials were interpreted by some as evidence of a collective Japanese puerility. The Japanese, wrote Villiers, "like most young children . . . are very sensitive on being found out, and will tell the most deliberate and unblushing falsehoods to shield themselves."[71]

De Guerville would have none of this. The details of the debate regarding the putative Japanese massacre, which raged intensely in the world press for the six months or so following the fall of Port Arthur, are too numerous to detail here. As a preliminary, suffice it to say that most studies have concluded that excesses did occur, mainly in the killing of Chinese men in the fallen city. However, the extreme accounts manifested best by Creelman were later revealed to be highly exaggerated.[72]

It is important to point out that the major points de Guerville made in his attack against the detractors of Japan is largely repeated in the final chapter of *Au Japon*. One point is worth making, however. In bold words printed in *Leslie's Weekly* (words not repeated in *Au Japon*), de Guerville takes Western critics to task, posing the difficult question of how atrocities by British troops in India during the Sepoy

Revolt of 1858, or American atrocities against Native Americans, differed from the alleged atrocities at Port Arthur, even supposing they had occurred. De Guerville even dared pose the question: "Can the Japanese be expected to be more civilized than the French, English, or—than ourselves?"[73]

De Guerville also took aim at Creelman's integrity as a reporter.[74] He criticized Creelman's earlier account of P'yŏngyang, in which he had intimated he was an eyewitness to the battle when he was not, as well as his various misrepresentations of the size of the Japanese army and the dates of certain engagements.[75] In one article, de Guerville recalled an episode with Creelman in Japan in the weeks before Port Arthur, and suggested that Creelman had arrived at Port Arthur with visions of a sensational story already half-written in his head:

> One day I went to Yokohama with Mr. Creelman. He spent his time there calling on the heads of some banks and newspapers. While in the train returning to Tokyo he told me:
>
> "I have found out why they won't allow us to go the front. The first reason is . . . that the Japanese are being frightfully licked by the Chinese, and the other is that these people, not being yet quite civilized, must act in the battlefield like wild beasts. They must carve each other, prisoners and wounded, into pieces, and we would see the most disgusting sights in the world. On account of the treaty revision the government is anxious that we should not see such sights."[76]

Such attacks against Creelman's integrity and professionalism must have stung the *New York World* reporter to the quick, but perhaps especially so as they came from de Guerville.

De Guerville soon had more damaging, and personal, allegations to deal with. Not long after his return to New York, stories began to circulate, apparently originating with Creelman, that de Guerville had supplied Creelman's name to the Japanese authorities as a spy for the Chinese. Such stories found especially wide coverage in the *Japan Gazette* but were published as well in Creelman's *New York World*. The *Japan Gazette* also made damaging accusations that de Guerville had in fact been bribed by Japanese officials. Naturally, de Guerville denied the charges, and chose the *Japan Weekly Mail* to refute them.

Though there was no evidence ever presented to corroborate such serious assertions, the damage was done. Though he would go on to briefly run *The Illustrated American* during 1897–1898, de Guerville never found work as a regular correspondent. According to a surviving letter by Creelman, de Guerville attributed his failures in this regard to the specious allegations of the *New York World* reporter. In 1897, Creelman encountered de Guerville in a Bologna train station while both were on their way to cover the Greek-Turkish War, de Guerville with his new red-haired bride in tow and still laboring as a freelancer. By Creelman's account, not long into the train journey from Bologna to the port of Brindisi in southern Italy, de Guerville came knocking on his compartment door.

> His voice was broken and his eyes were filled with tears as he told me that the story that he had sought to contrive my death by treachery had ruined him; it had damned his reputation and shut all avenues of journalistic employment.... He [de Guerville] told me that he had never insinuated that I was a Chinese spy in the Japanese army but admitted that he had made a remark which if badly translated . . . might have caused some suspicion.[77]

The precise truth behind such high jinx has been lost to history; in the end one is simply left with the distinct impression that Creelman had succeeded in spiking his competitor's guns after all.

III. *Au Japon* Then and Now

The actual people who live in Japan are not unlike the general run of English people; that is to say, they are extremely commonplace, and have nothing curious or extraordinary about them. In fact the whole of Japan is a pure invention. There is no such country, there are no such people.[77]

—Oscar Wilde, "The Decay of Lying"

Au Japon defies easy categorization. It is part comic portrait, part nostalgic memoir, part apology, and part earnest analysis of political developments in the Far East. All of it is a product of A. B. de Guerville—the man and his environment.

For the first half of the book de Guerville's role as Honorary Commissioner for the World's Columbian Exposition is nearly superfluous, serving only to explain what he was doing in Japan to begin with. This portion of the book is taken up mostly with humorous portraits of people and events in Japan (though some of these should be taken with a grain of salt). Only in the second half does the work change tone as the author discusses his experiences in the Sino-Japanese War in 1894. Then, *Au Japon* becomes more journalistic and analytical, examining such things as the Japanese Red Cross, the character of the *Genro* [elder statesman] Yamagata Aritomo, and the Japanese army's conduct in the Sino-Japanese War, all the while refusing to forsake its sense of irony and somewhat salacious humor.

But if one were to indulge in the dubious exercise of placing *Au Japon*, then perhaps it belongs halfway between two genres: it is in small part a journalistic autobiography along the lines of Frederic Villiers' *Port Arthur: Three Months with the Besiegers,* or James Allan's *Under the Dragon Flag.* More than anything, *Au Japon* seems to echo that work by de Guerville's fellow journalist, and erstwhile rival, Creelman, whose book of reminiscences *On the Great Highway* appeared in 1901. Indeed the lives of these two men seem to parallel one another to an uncanny degree. Creelman was ten years de Guerville's senior, but their two lives were remarkably similar in their particulars: both men were naturalized Americans and self-made journalists; both wrote for a series of New York publications, including the *New York Herald,* and both at one point managed the *The Illustrated American;* both became foreign correspondents and then war correspondents during the Sino-Japanese War. Both men were also fond of boasting of their mutual successes, including interviews with Pope Leo XIII (Creelman beat de Guerville by three years) and kings (they interviewed Korea's King Kojong weeks apart). In the pair's contradictory assertions over the alleged "Port Arthur massacre" their lives at last collide and a thus far unspoken rivalry is made manifest. Though the two men certainly knew one another (and not on pleasant terms), their surviving published writings never mention the other by name.

Au Japon is very much a sentimental and subjective account of travels and impressions of life in the Far East, in the spirit of Sir Edwin Arnold (whom de Guerville admired and with whom he once shared

Introduction   xlix

a jinrikisha) and Lafcadio Hearn (who first arrived in Japan a year before de Guerville). *Au Japon* echoes both Arnold's *Japonica* (1891) and Hearn's *Glimpses of Unfamiliar Japan* (1894). Although de Guerville certainly indulges in some of the sentimental exocitizing of Japan—best manifested by Pierre Loti's *Madame Chrysanthemum*—de Guerville's is also a sympathetic and progressive pen. Though he may poke fun at aspects of the Japanese and life in Japan, he does so in a spirit of good-naturedness and not out of condescension or a sense of superiority, moral or otherwise. De Guerville is as interested in the nation's modern transformation as he is in its traditions. He sees value in Japan's modernization, in the education of women, and in the rise of Japan to equality with the industrialized nations of the west—rather than simply its perpetual relegation to "enchanted bamboo land" of geishas and tea houses. He also takes issue with the then prevalent idea that Japan was, through industrialization and Western influence, only then emerging out of barbarity into civilization.

One should not lose sight of the fact, and indeed it is hard to, that *Au Japon* is foremost a comical look at Japan from a Westerner's perspective. With its risqué and irreverent outlook, *Au Japon* is very much a *French* book of travel writing. *Au Japon* simply does not take itself too seriously, and this in itself is endearing. To be sure, de Guerville records several dialogs that he certainly did not witness, and quite likely never took place. The confusion over the meaning of "Teikoku," for instance, would only be plausible if the Japanese in question had been conversing with de Guerville in French, not something very likely to have occurred. But even these "imaginary" conversations serve not to mislead so much as to entertain. In the end we are to trust in the *Japan Weekly Mail*'s assertion that, delightful as *Au Japon* may be, "to take it seriously from cover to cover would be imbecile."[79]

Au Japon is also simply a humorous account of a foreigner's misadventures in Japan. De Guerville's obvious delight in recounting the creaking of western ladies' corsets as they sat down to an uncomfortable tea *à la Japonaise*, or the flatulence of his Korean "coolies"; his racy account of foreign scandal in the pleasure district of Tokyo, or humorous take on everything from Japanese bathing to firefighting; all these reveal the book's comic quality. One might be reminded of Thomas Raucat's *L'Honorable partie de campagne* (1924), or, even racier still, that same author's *De Shanghai à Canton* (1927).[80] But whereas Raucat's humor is delivered in more of a deadpanned manner, one can almost hear de Guerville laughing out loud, or regaling an audience at New York's Lotus Club, as he recounts his experiences. Indeed, it would come as little surprise for a reader to learn that before his success as a writer de Guerville was an accomplished and popular lecturer during a time when public speaking was a much lauded talent.

Au Japon should also be viewed in the context of the period trend towards travel books in general and Japan in particular. At the time, writing about Japan sold well. Besides de Guerville, there were legions of aspiring authors ready to feed a seemingly insatiable Western curiosity for this intriguing and modernizing island nation. "True it is, 'and pity 'tis 'tis true,' with reference to Japan, that 'of making many books there is no end,'" intoned one period editorial.[81] In the last quarter of the nineteenth century travel books on Japan had become a virtual cottage industry. Between 1875 and 1900 no fewer than two hundred books of travel impressions on Japan appeared in Western languages. Many were the products of journalists like de Guerville, but their authorship ran the gamut from diplomats to adventurers, educators to engineers, and from missionaries to sailors, doctors, general misfits, and the odd man or woman of leisure. In regards to their treatment of Japan, certain trends can be discerned in such works.

Since its forced opening in 1858, and more particularly from the 1870s and its steadfast pursuit of Western-style reforms, Japan had stood apart in Western minds as an anomaly: an Asian nation of strength and will. This only made its traditional culture that much more alluring. On the one hand, there were those Westerners who desperately sought that quaint and traditional Japan, even then being swept away by the very "beastly modernization" (the phrase is Arnold's) that would launch it to Asian dominance. Ironically, perhaps, in lamenting the loss of Japan's traditional national customs to the "beast" of modernization, many Westerners were anticipating Japanese reactions of a generation or so later, as Japan began to reject the wholehearted embrace of the foreign that had fed its modernization, reverting to a chauvinistic nationalism (though certainly nothing unique to Japan). One could say this transition was occurring even as *Au Japon* sold on the streets of Paris.

On the other hand, many Western "Japanophiles" (or "Japan-maniacs" as some described them) sought in the Japanese traditional past those national characteristics that in the last quarter of the nineteenth century were making that nation's modern transformation such a success. While Western writers praised Japan for its triumphant efforts at modernization (a word replete with subtext) and rapid emergence out of "barbarity" into "civilization," they saw such successes as a result of the Japanese character, itself the product of society and history. Many, including de Guerville, were fond of contrasting the hardy, martial, honor-bound Japanese character with the effete, dishonorable, cowardly, and unchanging Chinese. It was a racial profiling that would play into attitudes of the Sino-Japanese War.

Naturally, such sentiments were contradictory: lamenting Japan's vanishing traditions while lauding its efforts at modernization; deriding its crudeness and simplicity while disparaging the modernization that was eradicating it. It is futile to attempt to resolve, or even explain, such contradictions. They find their home in the frustrated and contradictory psychology of humanity itself. Suffice to say that such contradictions are ample in de Guerville as well.

But to give credit where it is due, Japan was far from a passive agent in the promotion of "modernizing and civilizing Japan." Japan in fact became quite adept at what we today might call spin control. From the 1880s or so, Japan began what can only be described as an intense—and very official—effort to influence Western public opinion. This effort intensified in the years leading up to the Sino-Japanese War. One prominent method was to feed stories to the European and American press, or even to resort to bribery to help ensure stories positive of Japan.[82] As already mentioned, Brinkley's *Japan Weekly Mail* also played a useful role in these efforts, especially during the Sino-Japanese War (see Note 59).

The world's fair was another medium for promoting both Japan's modernization and the refined aspects of its traditional culture. Indeed, the world's fairs proved to be a tremendous public relations boon to Japan. Its early participation and lavish expenditures on its national displays (a princely $650,000 at the 1893 Chicago World's Columbian Exposition) ensured it a growing contingent of vociferous admirers in the West. At the World's Columbian Exposition Japan would be acclaimed as "The Light of Asia" (borrowing from Edwin Arnold's sobriquet for the Buddha in his book of that name) or, more complimentary still, the "America of the East." Indeed, it must be said that Japan is perhaps the only non-Western nation during the early decades of the world's fairs to actively use the venue to fashion its own image.

Books, articles, and World's Fair displays aside, by the time *Au Japon* appeared in 1904, Japan had already demonstrated its rise to military and industrial powerhouse in a more concrete way—the triumph of arms. In 1894–1895 it soundly defeated China in a brief land and naval war over Korea, a conflict whose opening months de Guerville witnessed and recollects in *Au Japon*. But if Thomas Carlyle is right, and life is all symbolical, more important still was Japan's participation in 1900 (alongside Western armies) in the siege of Peking that snuffed out the Boxer Uprising. That Japanese troops should join Western armies in crushing an Asian uprising certainly represented Japan's rise to industrial and military parity with the West more aptly than any world's fair display on industrial output ever could.

But in 1904 Japan was on the verge of passing the real test: the actual defeat of a major Western nation in war (in this case Russia). De Guerville had predicted several years earlier Japan's desire to fight and defeat a Western power.[83] In 1904 the crisis brewing between Japan and Russia over control of China's Liaodong Peninsula was about to bring those wishes to fruition.

Japan's domination of the headlines in 1904–1905 (alongside political troubles in Russia) helped ensure brisk sales of *Au Japon,* a factor certainly calculated by de Guerville and his publisher. Why else would de Guerville have waited a decade to write it? He even submitted in his preface to *Au Japon* his own speculations on a Russo-Japanese War, a solid assessment that proved quite accurate. One is even tempted to wonder whether certain official channels between Japan and de Guerville had not been reopened during 1903–1904, in Japan's attempt to promote itself to a European audience. But on this there is no evidence.

The question remains: why should we care about *Au Japon* today?

I don't believe this a difficult question to answer. To begin with, de Guerville's travelogue is more than a collection of those "impressions de voyages" that the author's acquaintance Colonel Tchen-Ki-Tong humorously disparaged. As both a representative of the World's Columbian Exposition and a war correspondent, de Guerville gained access to, and left descriptions of, people and places of historical significance. Westerner encounters with Korea's Queen Min, for example, are quite rare. Though de Guerville's meeting was brief, his recollections bear witness to the headstrong personality of that monarch, who was to die four years later at the hands of the Japanese soldiers de Guerville so often praises. The author's recollections of his meetings with the Emperor and Empress of Japan and Li Hongzhang in Tianjin are also revealing in their way, not to mention the many forgotten episodes that comprise de Guerville's mission to the Far East on behalf of the fair.

De Guerville's observations as a correspondent during the Sino-Japanese War (1894–1895) also contribute significantly to the continued relevance of *Au Japon*. The war caused quite a sensation in the Western press, though not perhaps in the way Japan had intended. Besides more geopolitical motivations, the demonstration of Japan's military skill, coupled with its conformity with the "rules of warfare" (Japan became a signatory to the Geneva Convention in 1886), was meant to sanction that nation's entry into the ranks of the "civilized nations." De Guerville's impressions of the Japanese conduct of the war conform by and large to those of other Western correspondents regarding the honorable behavior and modern methods of the Japanese soldiers and the Japanese Red Cross. Where de Guerville parted ways with his colleagues concerned the siege and capture of Port Arthur in November 1894. His account of what he witnessed is an important and forgotten aspect of the Sino-Japanese War and the debate over the "Port Arthur Massacre." While in late 1894 stories of Japanese atrocities committed against Chinese troops and civilians at Port Arthur circulated widely via the Western press, He stubbornly stood guard over the honorable reputation of Japan. In 1904 he stood there yet.

But most of all *Au Japon* is still worth reading today because it encapsulates one man's late-nineteenth-century impressions of a country that intrigued and beguiled him. This interests not only because of its *sui generis* nature, that is, for the unique experiences and impressions of de Guerville himself. *Au Japon* is valuable because it encapsulates many of the impressions and attitudes of Westerners to Japan of the period, from the bathhouse to the pleasure quarters, from descriptions of Japanese women to the Western obsession with curio hunting. Yet at the same time, discernable below the comic veneer of de Guerville's work, is a critique of Western attitudes toward Japan.

The Sino-Japanese War had relegated Japan to a world power, but in so doing it also served to disabuse the West of its widely and long held notions of Japan as a queer, delicate, and toy-like world in miniature. In fact, for better or worse, it now became clear that Japan was no different than "us," and was driven by the same forces, capable of the same things. Nothing reveals this more than de Guerville's chapter "The Real Madame Chrysanthemum," in which he pokes fun at outmoded—or shall we say quaint—Western notions of Japan that had, in the wake of the Sino-Japanese War, come suddenly to seem naïve and ill-informed at best.They were imaginary stereotypes useful only to those Japanese tour guides eager and willing to exploit them for their own gain. These older ideas are personified by de Guerville's Lord A- (his real identity hardly matters, but de Guerville interestingly makes him an Englishman), who hastens to Hiroshima eager to find the "real" Madame Chrysanthemum of Pierre Loti. No such woman existed; or rather, she existed everywhere and nowhere. If Japan is unique it is also no different.

Quaintness and barbarity are two sides of the same coin. It is not difficult to perceive the parallels between de Guerville's comic approach to this in "The Real Madame Chrysanthemum" and its more immediate manifestations in the Port Arthur controversy. To the likes of Creelman—as well as those who would oppose treaty equality—Japan must be either the Japan she had always been either tranquil and curious or else barbaric and treacherous. To de Guerville, however, Japan's actions at Port Arthur, such as they were, were no different in character—good or bad—than British actions in India, or those of other Western nations along the bumpy road to empire.

In the wake of the Sino-Japanese War, as the Western world struggled to come to terms with the new Japan, one Japanese writer painted in prophetic tones the spirit of this new reality: a nation of "Greeklike quick perception, Tuetonlike simplicity, ready submission to the superior, insatiable ambition for a higher, better life, and chivalric sentiment to which honor is everything and life or wealth nothing."[84]

And yet to the world, the writer continues, "[Japan] has heretofore been known only as a country of curiosity, as a land of the chrysanthemum and the Fuji-san, as a *nidus* of queer arts and petty etiquette. Some would flatter her, as did Sir Edwin Arnold; others would scoff at her malignantly . . . but no one has truly perceived, much less appreciated, her real worthiness."[85] De Guerville—this according to the author—was one notable exception. Calling de Guerville the most trustworthy correspondent to cover the war in the Far East, the author quotes generously from de Guerville's descriptions of noble Japanese behavior on the battlefield, especially when juxtaposed against the "barbarity" of China.

Still, though de Guerville may have praised Japan, he was no mere apologist. He was well aware that Japan's intent was empire and the wellspring of its national efforts, though partly a desire for modernization and international parity, was also a darker and more troubling nationalism. De Guerville recognized that once triumphant in Korea and Manchuria, Japan would not willingly depart. Even as he wrote *Au Japon*, de Guerville sensed the forces tempting his beloved Japan to enter upon the path of militant nationalism, the earliest shadows of the *kurai tanima*—the "dark valley" that would lead ultimately to total war. In the end it is de Guerville's guarded hope that Japan might reject "the laurels won by her young officers on recent battlefields, might turn her intelligence, energy, and perseverance instead towards peaceful projects, there winning laurels just as glorious, which would spread her commerce, industry, and arts throughout the world." Yes, as a friend of Japan he could wish nothing more.

For Further Reading

Allan, James. *Under the Dragon Flag*. London: William Heinemann, 1898.
Arnold, Sir Edwin. *Japonica*. New York: Charles Scribner's Sons, 1891.
Ashmead, John. *The Idea of Japan 1853–1895: Japan as Described by American and other Travelers from the West*. New York: Garland, 1987.
Barr, Pat. *The Deer Cry Pavilion, A Story of Westerners in Japan, 1868–1905*. New York: Macmillan & Co., Ltd., 1968.
Cortazzi, Hugh, and George Webb, eds., *Kipling's Japan: Collected Writings*. London: Athlone Press, 1988.
Creelman, James. *On the Great Highway, the Wanderings and Adventures of a Special Correspondent*. Boston: Lothrop Publishing Company, 1901.
De Becker, J.E. *The Nightless City, or, the History of the Yoshiwara Yukwaku*. Yokohama: Nossler, 1899.
Dorwart, Jeffrey M. "James Creelman, the *New York World* and the Port Arthur Massacre." *Journalism Quarterly* 50.4 (1973): 697–701.
Dorwart, Jeffrey M. *The Pigtail War, American Involvement in the Sino-Japanese War 1894–1895*. Amherst: U of Massachusetts P, 1975.
Hardin, Thomas L. "American Press and Public Opinion in the First Sino-Japanese War." *Journalism Quarterly* 50.1 (1973): 53–59.
Kane, Daniel C. "Each of Us in His Own Way: Factors Behind Conflicting Accounts of the Massacre at Port Arthur." *Journalism History* 31.1 (Spring 2005): 23-33.
Kobre, Sidney. *The Yellow Press and Gilded Age Journalism*. Gainesville: Florida State UP, 1964.

Lehmann, Jean-Pierre. *The Image of Japan: From Feudal Isolation to World Power, 1850–1905*. London: George Allen & Unwin, 1978.
Littlewood, Ian. *The Idea of Japan: Western Images, Western Myths*. London: Martin Secker & Warburg, Ltd., 1996.
Lone, Stewart. *Japan's First Modern War*. London: St. Martin's Press, 1994.
Loti, Pierre. *Madame Chrysanthème*. Paris: Calmann Lévy, 1888.
Milton, Joyce. *Yellow Kids: Foreign Correspondents in the Heyday of Yellow Journalism*. New York: Harper & Row, 1989.
Paine, S. C. M. *The Sino-Japanese War of 1894–1895*. Cambridge: Cambridge UP, 2003.
Valliant, Robert B. "The Selling of Japan: Japanese Manipulation of Western Opinion, 1900–1905." *Monumenta Nipponica* 29.4 (Winter 1974): 415–38.
Williams, H. S. *Tales of the Foreign Settlements in Japan*. Tokyo: Charles E.Tuttle, 1958.
Yokoyama, Toshio. *Japan in the Victorian Mind: A Study of Stereotyped Images of a Nation, 1850–80*. London: Macmillan, 1987.

Notes

1. *Leslie's Illustrated Weekly*, alternately known as *Frank Leslie's Weekly* (hereafter simply *Leslie's Weekly*) (7 February 1895), 82.

2. Tcheng Ki-Tong [Chen Jitong], *Les Chinois Peints par Eux-Mêmes* [The Chinese painted by themselves], (Paris: Calmann-Lévy, 1884), vi-vii.

3. A. B. de Guerville's second volume of travel writing, *La Nouvelle Egypte* published in 1905, fared better. Translated into English (*New Egypt*), German, and even Swedish, it went through various editions through 1915 as an authoritative account of British Egypt. The English translation was recently reprinted in 2002.

4. London Times (1 December 1853), 9.

5. A. B. de Guerville, "France and the Jews," *The Illustrated American* (29 January 1898), 128.

6. *Washington Post* (20 June 1890), 5.

7. *Frank Leslie's Weekly* (22 September 1892), 214.

8. *Japan Weekly Mail* (30 July 1892), 128.

9. Moses P. Handy, ed. *The Official Directory of the World's Columbian Exposition*. Chicago: W.B. Conkey, Co., 1893.

10. Rudyard Kipling's "Letter One" [1892], quoted from Hugh Cortazzi and George Webb, eds., *Kipling's Japan: Collected Writings* (London: The Athlone Press, 1988), 195.

11. Laird McLeod Easton, *The Red Count: The Life and Times of Harry Kessler* (Berkeley: University of California Press), 1–2.

12. Hubert Howe Bancroft, *The Book of the Fair, an Historical and Descriptive presentation of the World's Science, Art and Industry, as Viewed through the Columbian Exposition at Chicago in 1893* (New York: Bounty Books, 1894), xxiv.

13. Horace Allen to Walker Fearn (26 November 1892), Allen MSS, New York

14. Edwin Dun to John W. Foster, Secretary of State (6 May 1892). Department of State, "Despatches from United States Ministers in Japan [DUSMJ]"; *Japan Weekly Mail* (14 May 1892), 4.

15. Edwin Dun to John W. Foster, Secretary of State (6 May 1892). DUSMJ; Horace Allen to Walker Fearn (26 November 1892), Allen MSS.

16. See for example, "Li Hung Chang, the Viceroy and Master of China," *Leslie's Weekly* (15 June 1893), 386; "Li Hung Chang," Leslie's Weekly (10 September 1896), 171; "Li Hung Chang in Pekin," *The Illustrated American* (15 January 1898), 69–71.

17. As quoted in the *Japan Weekly Mail* (23 July 1892), 95–96. For the record, there can be absolutely no doubt, based on diplomatic correspondence, that de Guerville did give a highly lauded magic lantern show for the Japanese Imperial Household as well as the Korean king and queen.

18. *Washington Post* (18 April 1894), 4.

19. *Leslie's Weekly* (5 April 1894), 223.

20. Intentional or not, James Creelman, then of the *New York Herald* (with whom de Guerville would cross horns over Port Arthur), had been the first "non-Catholic" journalist to interview the Pope (Leo XIII) in 1893.

21. "Our Special in Corea," *Leslie's Weekly* (18 October 1894), 244.

22. Ibid.

23. Valerian Gribayedoff, "The Modern War Correspondent," *Munsey's Magazine* 13 (April 1895), 41.

24. *New York Herald* (5 August 1894), section 4, 1. James Creelman's wife wrote to her husband as he was en route to the Far East, "He [de Guerville] had a full page story about his visit to Corea [sic] in last Sunday's Herald with his name in large type in the headlines as 'World's Fair Commissioner' and also signed. It was a right trashy thing." Alice Creelman to James Creelman (16 August 1894), James Creelman MSS, Box I, Folder 4 (1894).

25. *Leslie's Illustrated Weekly* (5 April 1894), 223.

26. *New York Times* (7 February 1896), 12.

27. "Japan and the United States," *New York Times* (7 March 1897), 18.

28. *The Literary World* (27 November 1897), 426.

29. A. B. de Guerville, *La Lutte contre la tuberculose* (Paris: Alphonse Lemerre, 1904), 11.

30. *The Illustrated American* vol. 23, no. 4 (22 January 1898), 101.

31. A. B. de Guerville, *La lutte contre la tuberculose*.

32. *New York Times* (1 September 1900), 12.

33. A. B. de Guerville *La lutte contre la tuberculose*.

34. André Gide, *The Fruits of the Earth* [translated by Dorothy Bussy] (New York: Alfred A. Knopf, 1949), 18,27.

35. Robert B. Valliant, "The Selling of Japan: Japanese Manipulation of Western Opinion, 1900–1905," *Monumenta Nipponica,* vol. 29, no. 4 (Winter 1974), 416.

36. Thomas Dormandy, *The White Death: A History of Tuberculosis* (New York: New York UP, 1999), 153.

37. Ibid., 152.

38. *Der Kampf gegen die Tuberkolose* (Spamer, Leipzig 1907); *The Crusade against Phthisis* (Hugh Rees: London, 1904).

39. "The Situation in Egypt," *Eclectic Magazine of Foreign Literature* 148.4 (April 1907): 312-317.

40. *The Times* (26 August 1911), 9. That de Guerville's illness was noted under "Court News" implies he was of some social standing in the British capital.

41. Sidney Kobre, *The Yellow Press and Gilded Age Journalism* (Gainesville: Florida State University Press, 1964), 3.

42. Charles H. Brown, *The Correspondents' War: Journalists in the Spanish-American War* (New York: Scribners, 1967), 21.

43. A. B. de Guerville, "In Defense of Japan. The Alleged Atrocities at Port Arthur Denied," *Leslie's Weekly* (3 January 1895), 11. De Guerville would in fact later author a small tract entitled "Civilization and Barbarism" (published in Japan) concerning the Sino-Japanese conflict, though such a worldview was anything but unique to de Guerville.

44. Taken from the title of one of the best recent historical examinations of the war. Stewart Lone, *Japan's First Modern War* (London: St. Martin's Press, 1994).

45. France of 1894–1895 had more pressing concerns, such as anarchist violence and the Dreyfus Affair.

46. A. B. de Guerville, "The War between China and Japan," *Leslie's Weekly* (16 August 1894), 108.

47. *The Times* (31 January 1895), 12.

48. James Creelman to Alice Creelman (15 August 1894), James Creelman MSS, Box I, Folder 4 (1894).

49. Ibid.

50. Particularly when one considers that weeks before heading to the Far East—and his first meeting with Creelman—de Guerville had published an account in the *New York Herald* of his 1892 meeting with Li Hongzhang, which prominently displayed de Guerville's name.

51. Alice Creelman to James Creelman (16 August 1894), Box I, Folder 4. James Creelman MSS.

52. This according to a Japanese regulation of July 1894. National Archives of Japan/Cabinet/Kobun Ruishu/Police (31 July 1894).

53. "The War in the East: Embarkation of Japanese Troops for Corea," *Leslie's Weekly* (8 November 1894), 301. There is some confusion on de Guerville's part regarding this. In *Au Japon* he names the *Nagato Maru* as the vessel in which he sailed during the Japanese expedition against Port Arthur in October-November 1894, something that can only be attributed to a lapse of memory.

54. "Letter from Phyong-Yang [P'yŏngyang]," *Japan Weekly Mail* (20 October 1894), 451.

55. Creelman describes his interview with the Korean king in his 1901 memoir *On the Great Highway*.

56. "Letter from Phyong-Yang," 451.

57. On this see Louis G. Perez, *Japan Comes of Age: Mutsu Munemitsu and the Revision of the Unequal Treaties* (London: Associated University Presses, 1999).

58. Quoted in Louis Perez, 82.

59. Frank Brinkley's pro-Japanese stance, though intimately related to Brinkley's own strongly held beliefs in Japan's virtues, was also component of a more formal arrangement with the Japanese government. In 1885 the Japanese government had granted Brinkley a large sum of funds in the form of railway bonds in exchange for Brinkley's agreement to continue publishing the *Japan Weekly Mail* until the Japanese government said otherwise. (Inoue Kaoru to Brinkley [3 October 1885], The Diplomatic Record Office of the Ministry of Foreign Affairs/Records of the Ministry of Foreign Affairs 1/Politics/Category 3/Propaganda). In a later letter of grievance for what he felt were his underappreciated services on Japan's behalf, Brinkley boasted

of having fed pro-Japanese stories during the Sino-Japanese War to both the English and American press (Brinkley to Mutsu [16 November 1895], The Diplomatic Record Office of the Ministry of Foreign Affairs/Records of the Ministry of Foreign Affairs 1/ Politics/Category 3 Propaganda). The western press was not wholly ignorant of such attempts, though they wrote of them through their own strong prejudices. As one period publication expressed it:

> From the beginning of the war, indeed in anticipation of it, the Japanese had laid themselves out to capture the European press, in which they succeeded, as they did in their military campaign, by admirable foresight and organization. They first disarmed criticism by representing that they were engaged in a crusade against darkness and barbarism, and were spreading the light with which they had themselves been illuminated by Christendom. Before their first impression was effaced a fresh one was made by their military successes. These were naturally represented in the brightest colours by ubiquitous Japanese agents ready to supply interesting news as well as enlightened views to newspapers in need of copy. In Japan the Government annexed an important news agency, which transmitted official bulletins on an extensive scale which were received as news coming from independent sources. With few exceptions, indeed, the reports of the campaign were derived exclusively from the Japanese Government—the "war correspondent," notwithstanding the praiseworthy efforts of the leading journal, having neither part nor lot in the matter. ("The Japanese Imbroglio," *Blackwood's Edinburgh Magazine*, v. 158 (Sept. 1895), 313–314).

60. "Interview with the Correspondent of the 'New York Herald,'" *Japan Weekly Mail* (20 October 1894), 441. Though de Guerville is never named as the correspondent in question, the description of him given in the article leaves no room for doubt.

61. Ibid.

62. "Mr. de Guerville and his Accusers," *Japan Weekly Mail* (11 May 1895), 537–538.

63. *Leslie's Weekly* (22 November 1894), 332.

64. *New York World* (21 December 1894), 2.

65. See James Creelman, *On the Great Highway, the Wanderings and Adventures of a Special Correspondent* (Boston: Lothrop Publishing Company, 1901), Chapter Five, "Battle and Massacre of Port Arthur."

66. Frederic Villiers, "The Truth about Port Arthur," *The North American Review* v. 160 no. 460 (March 1895), 325–331.

67. A. B. de Guerville, "In Defense of Japan. The Alleged Atrocities at Port Arthur Denied," *Leslie's Weekly* (3 January 1895), 10–11. Also printed in the *New York Times* (30 December 1894), 9.

68. Frederic Villiers, "The Truth about Port Arthur." 330.

69. Valerian Gribayedoff, "The Modern War Correspondent," *Munsey's Magazine* 13 (April 1895), 41.

70. James Creelman, *On the Great Highway*, Chapter Five "Battle and Massacre of Port Arthur."

71. Frederic Villiers, "The Truth About Port Arthur," 326.

72. See Stewart Lone, *Japan's First Modern War*.

73. "In Defense of Japan, the Alleged Atrocities at Port Arthur Denied," *Leslie's Weekly* (3 January 1895), 11.

74. The general line of argument is the same in each. See for example, *New York Herald* (2 January 1895), 7; "In Defense of Japan," *Leslie's Weekly* (3 January 1895), 10–11.

75. Indeed, in Creelman's later memoirs, *On the Great Highway* (1901), the chapter dedicated to the Battle of P'yŏngyang still reads like a firsthand account.

76. "Messrs. Creelman and Villiers," *Japan Weekly Mail* (11 May 1895), 540.

77. James Creelman to Alice Creelman (26 February 1897), James Creelman MSS, Box I, Folder 7 (1897).

78. Oscar Wilde, "The Decay of Lying: A Dialogue," *The Nineteenth Century* (January 1889).

79. *Japan Weekly Mail* (23 April 1904).

80. First translated into English as *The Honorable Picnic* and widely viewed as a classic western account of Japan. Coincidentally, the narrator of Raucat's book also finds himself in Japan on world's fair business.

81. "Japanese History and Civilization," *The Dial*, vol. XVI, no. 186 (16 March 1894), 181.

82. On these efforts see Robert Valliant, "The Selling of Japan," op. cit.

83. "We must not forget, however, that the military class of Japan would gladly fight any great nation—the greater the better. They have not forgotten that at the time of their victories over China many foreigners exclaimed,

'This is very well; but if, instead of fighting the Chinese the Japanese had been at war with a European nation, it would have been quite different." "Another War Scare," *The Illustrated American* (25 December 1897), 802.

84. Midori Komatz, "Japan: Its Present and Future," *The Arena* 12 (64) (March 1895), 1–2. To be sure, Komatz—or Midori Komatsu—was no neutral observer of events. As an urbane Japanese official, highly westernized and fluent in English, he would go on to serve in the Japanese colonial administration of Korea as Director of Foreign Affairs.

85. Ibid.

Note on the Translation

Though it went through numerous printings, there was only one edition of *Au Japon*—the 1904 edition of Alphonse Lemerre upon which this translation is based. The Italians have an adage, *traduttore, traditore*—"to translate is to betray." Or perhaps more fitting to our subject, in Korean *pŏnyŏk* (translate) is but a vowel away from *panyŏk* (treason). With such things in mind, in attempting to remain as loyal as possible to the original French text, the translator has followed certain guidelines.

A. B. de Guerville spent most of his formative years in America and as such his French is riddled with Americanisms. Where the author slipped into English, italics were used to indicate that those words appear in English in the original. Occasionally a French word or term was encountered which either defied smooth translation or which it was felt should remain in the original French so that the book might retain some of its original Gallic flavor. In such cases, the French has also been italicized, and when necessary accompanied by an explanatory footnote. The Romanization of names and geographical terms in Chinese, Japanese, and Korean also posed a challenge. Again for purposes of fidelity to the original, it was decided to maintain the spelling of these as they appear in the original text rather than to convert them to accepted modern Romanization schemes. However, in all supplementary material Pinyin was used for the Romanization of Chinese, modified Hepburn for Japanese, and McCune-Reischauer for Korean. Where necessary, footnotes translate the differences between names as they appear in the text and their relevant modern Romanization. Also in the supplementary material Chinese, Japanese, and Korean personal names are rendered in the traditional style (i.e. family name first followed by given name). Naturally, the translator takes full responsibility for his work, though I hold out hope the reader might condemn the fault and not the actor of it.

Author's Preface to *Au Japon*

As these pages appear in print events in the Far East have taken a turn for the worse, and war between Russia and Japan now seems possible. General opinion in Europe is that Japan will be easily trounced. However, those accustomed to speak of "colossal Russia" and of "little Japan" have not paused to consider the fact that the Empire of the Rising Sun has a population of forty-five million—greater than that of France—and that its geographical location, an island at the far end of the world, increases its defenses exponentially.

If this war does indeed come, it is impossible to predict the results of its initial engagements. It is a simple task, however, to anticipate the circumstances under which they will occur.

It is estimated that Russia now has from a hundred to a hundred-forty thousand men in Manchuria—let us say a hundred-fifty thousand. Japan could easily throw three hundred thousand men or more into Korea, assuming of course that it enjoyed control of the sea lanes. The first efforts of Admiral Alekseyev[1] will therefore be to prevent the embarkation of Japanese troops in Korea, and to accomplish this, the entire Russian fleet will have to block the passage of the Japanese fleet, which will be covering the movement of its troop transports.

Two scenarios are possible: the victory of Japan or the victory of Russia.

Let us first suppose that the Japanese fleet is victorious. Japan would immediately invade Korea, and two strong armies—each a hundred-fifty to two hundred thousand strong—will advance, one towards Vladivostok and the other towards Manchuria. The harshness of the Siberian winter may very well stop the first army, despite the fact that the Japanese can easily endure even the harshest cold, as they demonstrated in northern Manchuria in 1894.

To establish a solid base in Korea, fortify the frontier, and advance towards Port Arthur will be the goal of the second army. The primary desire of the Japanese General Staff will undoubtedly be to retake from Russia this stronghold [Port Arthur] that it had once conquered by arms, only to be forced to abandon under European diplomatic pressures.[2] But the problems inherent in resupplying such a vast army as it traverses a roadless Manchuria, and in the face of an enemy that will by no means just sit idly by, are so formidable that one wonders if Japan can overcome them.

Therefore, it is likely that Japan will satisfy itself with occupying Korea, and once ensconced there no one will be able to dislodge her. As long as Japan retains its maritime dominance Port Arthur will be threatened with attack, which a landing and advance through Talien[3] would make much simpler. Could this stronghold hold out until the arrival of Russian reinforcements, which in winter could only advance via Siberia with the greatest difficulty?[4] As can be seen, a simple, and very possible, naval victory by Japan will render it master of Korea and put it in a position to threaten Port Arthur and Vladivostok.

Now considering the second possibility, that of a Russian victory.

The loss of its fleet would be a calamity for Japan, not to mention a frightful blow to Japanese self-esteem. Once more they would find themselves isolated on their islands, and their neighbors would have nothing more to fear. Yet, besides the loss of their fleet what else could happen to them? No Russian army, be it a hundred or two hundred thousand strong, could conquer this nation of forty-five million. I know something of Russian valor; I know there are no better soldiers in the world. But man for man, one Japanese is equal to his European counterpart, and when one's motherland is at stake, the prospect of fighting even a million soldiers is nothing. No, be certain of this, Japan has nothing to fear regarding an invasion. Its fleet may be sunk, its ports bombarded, but it will not be vanquished.

So even in the case of Russian victory, Japan will not suffer enormously. The Russians may consider establishing themselves in Korea, but England's likely opposition will prevent them from going that far, and risk throwing England into alliance with Japan. The only advantage Russia may salvage from a victory would be the security of its position in Manchuria, and England will not be opposed to this, for so long as Russia is occupied in the Far East it will not meddle on the Indian frontier.

One final word. If a hundred thousand-man Russian army were to engage an army of a hundred thousand Japanese the result would be the most frightful combat, greater and more horrible than the world has ever seen. The fighting would continue until one was totally annihilated, and God alone knows what would remain of the victor, but it wouldn't be much. Let us hope that the wisdom of the Czar and the intelligence of the Mikado may spare us this bloody and avoidable spectacle!

A. B. De G.

Au Japon

1 To Japan

Au Japon is no profound study of "The Land of the Rising Sun," of its inhabitants or their customs. These are merely one man's recollections—of impressions gained and experiences lived in the course of several lengthy stays among a truly progressive, intelligent, and captivating people. My first visit to Japan was in 1891, when, as a special envoy of the Chicago Exposition,* I was dispatched to Japan, Korea, and China to promote that great enterprise.[1] Received by the emperor and empress, I passed many charming and unforgettable months mingling with some of that country's most influential citizens. My last voyage to Japan was in 1894 during the Sino-Japanese War. I joined the [Japanese] First Army at Pen-Yang[2] , Korea as it was about to enter combat and stayed on there for several days, departing with Marshal Oyama and his Second Army that would go on to conquer Kinchow,[3] the forts of Talien Wan,[4] and then Port Arthur.

At the Imperial Court and in the various salons of peacetime Tokyo, as well as in armed camps en route to Korea and Manchuria, I learned to love and admire the Japanese for their goodness, their gentle nature and civility, their intelligence, energy, perseverance, and indomitable courage.

Hundreds of books have been written in all languages on Japan and its inhabitants, and yet, as incomprehensible as it may seem, there can hardly be a nation that remains so little known and less understood by so many Europeans and Americans.

Even today one encounters men of the world, intelligent and learned men, who speak interchangeably of the Chinese and Japanese, confounding the two with extraordinary ignorance, not understanding that these two people are as different from one another as the Ger-

---

* *Honorary Commissioner for the World's Columbian Exposition to Japan, Corea, and China* [author note]

mans from the Spaniards, or the English from the Turks. No greater insult can be dealt a Japanese than to take him for a Chinese.

Another common error is to speak of the Japanese as a "newly civilized" people that only thirty years ago persisted in a state of semi-barbarity. We are astonished that they should have become "civilized" so quickly. If Japan had indeed passed in thirty-five years from near savagery to being treated as an equal with the world's great powers that would be a most extraordinary miracle surpassing those in the Bible or anywhere else.

But Japanese civilization is anything but recent. It has been formed through centuries of peaceful effort and heroic war; its is a vibrant and glorious national history, of courageous and gallant heroes; of powerful and original artists; of a robust and refined agriculture; of a national literature rich in its social, political, and religious commentary; of a paternal government and a code of conduct that place great value on both male and female honor. Japan possessed all of these things when, after three centuries of isolation, the guns of the foreign powers first came to breech the walls it had built between its civilization and our own.

If by civilization we mean simply an honest and moral people, cultivating the arts and sciences, living happily and at peace in their commerce and agriculture, enjoying equitable laws that protect the weak from the strong, and treating their women and children with kindness and affection—then we me must recognize that Japan possessed all that a civilized nation ought, for it has nothing if not all of these.

Over three hundred years ago, in 1584 to be exact, the city of Rome witnessed the arrival within its city walls of an extraordinary embassy consisting of Japanese princes, led by Father Gonzalez, a Catholic missionary, himself a papal ambassador to the Mikado. These Asians surprised the Romans not only by the richness of their dress, but also by their intelligence, learning and breadth of knowledge.

In presenting them to the Pope, the Catholic missionary gave a discourse upon Japan, describing that country as one "possessing rich and magnificent cities, an intelligent, noble, and courageous populace, disposed to the good, *and far superior to all other Asians,* lacking only the Holy Faith to make it the equal of any great European power."

The Catholic Church had been established in Japan for several years already and had made great progress. Apparently, however, the missionaries had moved too far and too fast: they believed they might become the master of these islands the way they had in the Philippines and on so many other islands, until they came face to face with the inflammable patriotism of the Japanese. As soon as the Japanese realized that the missionaries intended to establish not so much their religion as they did its foreign representatives, a storm of hatred and fury was unleashed. Terrifying and irresistible, it swept all the missionaries, churches, and foreigners before it. Freed again from the meddling of these despised foreigners, Japan severed all contact with the outside world in an isolation that would last several centuries.

In such a manner they proceeded to live tranquilly and at peace, not bothering a soul, until the day we arrived to bombard them under false pretense and force them into unequal treaties. Surprised by the power of the foreign war machines, the Japanese had the intelligence and wisdom not to resist. They soon realized that to counter European incursions, and perhaps invasion, Japan would have to make use of the same technology and means as their adversaries.

With all the energy and perseverance it could muster Japan went to work. Thirty years sufficed, not to become more 'civilized,' but rather to assimilate all of our inventions, to put Japan on the path of progress, to instruct its younger generations in the new ideas, to protect its national treasures behind modern fortifications, and at the head of a formidable and powerful army and navy to be able to declare to the West: "Halt! I wish to be master of my own house; I wish to be respected, I wish to be treated as an equal."

Yes, thirty years was enough to see such results. And what do they think now, those who were so eager to destroy barriers, to pull Japan out of its solitude, to dazzle it with our progress and our discoveries? Do they not regret those cannon shots fired as respite from their spells of lethargy?

For today, in all Asian matters, in all questions touching upon the Pacific, it is necessary to take this new force into consideration, the advance guard of Asian civilization—a truly formidable force made more so by its distance, a force that no European power, acting alone, could ever overcome.

Japan, which first learned to fear us, then to admire us, has never learned to love us. Its pride and patriotism have suffered too much to forgive us the humiliation we caused her while she was weak and defenseless. It was a momentous day for Japan when its national flag flew from atop Chinese fortresses, and the colossal enemy, pleading for mercy, was vanquished.

But yet more beautiful for Japan was the day its troops marched side by side with those of the great European powers towards the relief of the legations in Peking. It was a day the Japanese heart swelled with pride and joy, for here the evidence was clear and undeniable—the foreign officers now recognized the Japanese troops were the equal of their own.[5]

When the Sino-Japanese war broke out detractors proclaimed, "Japan will be destroyed." When it was the Chinese who were destroyed these same people said, "Oh, but it doesn't mean much: the Chinese are easy to defeat. A few European regiments could easily accomplish what it took the entire Japanese army to do."

Finally, when a victorious Japan had obtained from China, Formosa, portions of Manchuria, and Port Arthur, three powers—France, Russia, and Germany—interceded: "This will not be tolerated. We absolutely forbid the seizure of Port Arthur or a single foot of Manchuria. It is necessary for world peace that the Chinese remain in possession of these." The Japanese then withdrew . . . only to have the Russians take their place!

Their anger is understandable. I am convinced that at that time the average Japanese had but one desire, one dream, and that was this: "to engage one of the white powers, and to vanquish it or die in the attempt."

Fortunately, the Japanese statesmen, intellectuals, and other leaders avoided this danger, realizing that in order to complete the task so well begun Japan would need several more years of peace and tranquility, both at home and abroad. All their efforts were geared towards pacifying the masses, to make them understand the benefits of peace, and they succeeded beyond expectations.

That peace might continue to reign in Asia; and that Japan, rejecting the laurels won by her young officers on recent battlefields, might turn her intelligence, energy, and perseverance instead towards peaceful projects, there winning laurels just as glorious, which would spread her commerce, industry, and arts throughout the world—as a friend of Japan I could wish for nothing better.

2 The Ambassador's Wife

It had already been nine days since the steamer *City of Peking* had left San Francisco bound for Yokohama, but the old girl's progress was sluggish as she struggled against stiff winds and high waves, and we still found ourselves only half way to our destination.[1] In fact, so dreadful had the weather been that the passengers had hardly caught a glimpse of one another, the majority refusing to leave their cabins.

On this particular day, however, the sea had calmed, the sun had finally emerged, and the boat's deck was gradually invaded by a motley crew of cosmopolitans—globe-trotters of all nationalities, American naval officers, French and Chinese diplomats, young ladies of light morals off for "flings" in Shanghai or Hong Kong.

Seated next to an old American man, a wealthy tea merchant who had lived in Japan for the last twenty-odd years, and who knew the Far East like the back of his hand, I listened with the keenest interest as he gave me his account of "the land of the rising sun." In the midst of his narration, however, he suddenly stopped to prod me with his finger,

"Quick, look over there," he said. A Japanese couple had just appeared on the bridge, and judging by the prodigious greetings offered them by officers and diplomats, I realized this small stocky man and his young and charming lady companion where persons of some importance. As they passed my new American friend greeted them ceremoniously before turning back to me with a smile. With a wink he continued,

"Now here's an amusing story, and so thoroughly Japanese. That man is Mr. X . . . , the Japanese ambassador to the court of V . . . , and the lady his legal wife.[2] As you can see, she is still quite an attractive woman. Some years ago she was ravishing, but Japanese women wither quickly. Before marrying X . . . she was a dancer . . . that's right, a "geisha." But perhaps you haven't a clear idea of just what is meant by geisha. In Japan there is a whole class of women classified as such. They are dancers, singers, and musicians all wrapped into one, and their job is to entertain men. Every restaurant, every "tea house," every pleasure establishment, has geisha who must be at the continual disposal of their clients. After drinking and eating the Japanese like to have fun; they call for the geisha who come and dance . . . My God! Every sort of dance. Some are quite exquisite and admirable—from an artistic standpoint that is—while others arouse more sensual feelings. In one dance for instance, two geisha perform by removing an article of clothing with each new movement . . . and this continues until they are completely nude! Geisha are generally women of rather light morals, who offer their customers other amusements besides just dancing.

"Their price, like their talent, beauty, and elegance, varies according to the class of the establishment they are attached to. There are also "free geisha," who belong to no house in particular but are generally "maintained" by someone. But I should add that there are some geisha who are perfectly honest and upright. These are usually the ones whose reputation as dancers is so great that they can easily support themselves without having to submit to more degrading tasks.

"Almost all these women are of humble origins. Japanese families tend to be quite large. These people reproduce like rabbits . . . so among poor families, large numbers naturally only aggravate their condition. It is in these families that the Japanese *recruiters* find their conscripts. They offer a certain fixed sum to buy the rights to some promising pretty girl. This obtained, they take her away and train her in the skills she will need: music, singing, dance. Finally, when she is ready they dress her in superb robes for her debut. It goes without saying that nearly every cent she earns will go to her owner. Her life is void of joy. Her master is usually a brute who thinks of nothing but making money, while she is forced to sing, laugh, dance, and . . . well, worse than that, on command.

"Anyhow, my friend, it was as a geisha that Mrs. Ambassador, the woman you see on the far end of the deck, made her debut in Tokyo society. Sold very young to a "manager," she received the geisha education and finally made her grand debut. X . . . , who was at that time a mere deputy, saw her and at once fell madly in love. Not wishing to abandon her to such a fate, he repurchased her, as it were, paying a princely sum to her manager. This done, he gave her a new education and had her learn all the things a woman of the world ought to know. When he judged her ready for the station he wished her to hold, he married her. A short time later he was named the Japanese minister to—, and after a few years was reassigned to V . . . , where Mrs. X enjoyed great popularity. She is a charming woman and a true socialite. But you will hear more of her in Tokyo.

"Mr. X . . . is progressive minded, a diplomat and gifted statesman. When the Japanese parliament reconvenes shortly it is likely he'll be named President of the Chamber.

"But the story I have just recounted is not so unique. Many geisha end up marrying and become devoted wives and mothers. 'But are they faithful?' you wonder. My friend, adultery in Japan is all but unknown. Upper class women are perfectly honest and faithful and quite beyond suspicion."

A few moments later I had myself introduced to Madame X . . . , former geisha, one time wife of an ambassador, and . . . well, more of her later!

3 Teikoku

There were about a dozen Japanese on board, all of them good-natured and well educated. Among them I found Monsieur T..., Commissioner General of the Imperial Japanese Government to Chicago, particularly engaging.[1] He is president of a prestigious government school in Tokyo, a trade school where students study a range of scientific and industrial subjects as well as more scholarly ones. I have since spent several interesting and instructive hours at this school, watching its young students apply themselves with admirable intelligence and motivation. I recall in particular the ceramics department, where the students learned to create and decorate porcelain. They even presented me with a beautiful tea set of white porcelain decorated in a red rose pattern with gold arabesque.

Through my discussions with Monsieur T..., I learned of Tokyo University, where all branches of Japanese higher education are taught—the naval and army schools, the technical and liberal arts schools, the school of mines, as well as trade schools for both men and women, whose strict organization I would later have the chance to observe and admire.

But there were two or three incidents that occurred in the course of my numerous conversations with this well-educated but modest man that struck me as singularly extraordinary and quite incomprehensible.

Once, while discussing these manual training schools, and just as I inquired whether they were government run, we were interrupted by a woman inviting us for a stroll along the ship's deck.

"Yes," he answered, only to add quite calmly as he stood up, "*Tu es cocu . . . !*"[2]

Words could not describe my astonishment, and I was utterly speechless before our lady interlocutor. Later, on the eve of our arrival in Yokohama I approached him on deck to seek his recommendation of a nice hotel in Tokyo. Crossing his arms and raising one hand to his face, he pulled thoughtfully on his thin mustache, as if reflecting deeply over my query. Then once again he slowly uttered those accursed words, "*tu es cocu*"—only this time they seemed muttered more to himself than addressed to me.

"Huh?" was the only response I could muster.

"Well," he replied calmly, "you'd do best to go to the Imperial Hotel, it is unquestionably the finest."

It was with tremendous joy that we discovered upon waking the next morning that *The City of Peking* had at last lowered anchor in Yokohama Bay. Our ship was surrounded by hundreds of small flatboats, all crowded with waving and yelling boatmen and children. It was raining, so they were all covered in odd straw capes that served as sort of mackintoshes. With some difficulty I was finally able to clamber aboard one of these "sampans," all my baggage in tow, and within a few minutes I had disembarked at the customs house. The yelling boatmen were gone by now, to be replaced by hundreds of men clad in nothing but bathing trunks and enormous mushroom-shaped straw hats. They all approached me offering seats in their small rickshaws. I was thoroughly charmed by these vehicles, so much more attractive than our hackney cabs, and they gave me an immediate sense of old Japan. It was just at this moment that I heard an assembly of voices dispensing orders, among which one addressed me in quite excellent English:

Figure 7. A Japanese rickshaw in the 1890s. *Munsey's Magazine* (1895).

"Your bags, sir?" Turning, I found myself face to face with a half dozen officers in European-style uniforms, buttoned up, gloved, trimmed in braids, and in all respects quite sharp. Clearly then this was young Japan I was witnessing. As it turned out, these were customs officers. Pleasant and polite, all their formalities were soon complete.

At last I was comfortably ensconced in one of these rickshaws, and by the hands of two men pulling in tandem I was soon whisked at full speed through the city streets. Part-Japanese, part-European, the city didn't present a very interesting prospect, one might even deem it ugly. But it was the crowds, scurrying through the rainy streets, which really captured my interest. I tell you, what a human spectacle they made!

A TYPICAL STREET SCENE.

Figure 8. A street scene in Yokohama in the period of de Guerville's visit. Frank Brinkley, ed. *Japan* (section 6, p. 128) Tokyo: J.B. Millet, Co., 1897.

From my preliminary observations I divided Japanese men into three categories. First, there are the old-fashioned types, for the most part dressed in large blue jackets covered in white design, or else wearing a longer garment resembling a bathrobe and extending all the way to the feet and usually secured tightly with a belt. Some wear very short and tight fitting pants, but the majority had their legs exposed to the elements. On their feet, they wear either a type of *espradille,* or else high wooden clogs on which they perch rather amusingly.

Then there are the "more or less fashionable" Japanese types . . . European clothes, hats, Wellington half-boots, gloves, canes. Among these there are some that know how to dress, those that have traveled in Europe or America and acquired there a certain fashion sense. But then there are also those who have not gotten the feel for the thing at all, and my Lord, what ridiculous figures they present!

Finally, somewhere between the old and the new fashioned types there are those poor devils, ignorant and simple-minded for the most part, who seem to have been created but for the amusement of us foreigners. I'll offer but one typical example: tall and thin, he sports a four-whiskered mustache, which he tries in vain to fashion into handlebars; he proudly sports a tall and quite threadbare hat that he attempts to protect from the rain with a paper umbrella. His upper body is wrapped in a long black frockcoat, yet he wears neither shirt nor pants. His legs are covered in cotton longjohns. And to finish the picture, he models a pair of rubber boots, but without accompanying socks!

'And what of the women?' you may well ask. With the women the same categories apply. When the Japan of not too long ago first began to adopt European modes and fashions, some ladies completely lost their heads, hoping to become *Parisiennes* overnight. You can discern the effects of this even today. Boats arrive crammed with such outmoded and unfashionable horrors as the Paris and London merchants could never get rid of back home, and the Japanese snatch them up at fabulous, unimaginable prices!

At times you'd think you had walked right into the midst of a masquerade ball. Why, the European *mardi gras* never witnessed such comic scenes. Certainly you would never observe there women robed in garish-colored satin gowns—with nothing beneath—and wearing shirts *over* them, the whole ensemble completed by a corset, which they apparently mistake for a belt by wearing it on the outside! The poor dear things . . .

Thank God the masquerade did not last long. The ridiculous spectacle spent itself fairly quickly and today lower-class Japanese women, as well as most women of the middle class, have all reverted to Japanese dress, a simple, charming, and elegant garb that suits them exquisitely. Among the upper classes, as well as at the court, women dress in the European fashion, but with an irreproachable elegance and taste.

With noses to the wind the two men tied in tandem to my rickshaw soon deposited me at the station, completely dazed by the extraordinary spectacle that had just played before my eyes.

The car we then caught was quite comfortable and reminded me of those "saloon carriages" one finds on English trains. I had three Japanese as traveling companions, one of them a very proper gentleman of recent means. The other two were still unaccustomed to sitting in our western fashion. They removed their shoes, scrambled atop a bench and squatted there facing one another. Gazing out the window I perceived through a fine rain an endless series of small rice paddies punctuated here and there by a picturesque village.

At last we arrived in Tokyo, and following another rickshaw ride I reached the Imperial Hotel, a superb edifice possessing all the modern comforts: an American bar, barber, billiards, baths, electricity, telephones, etc.; it also boasts superb French cuisine and attentive service. It was really quite wonderful to bask in such comfort and civilization.

The following morning I was returning from the legation accompanied by Ayama, my native interpreter. Arriving before the hotel, my eyes were suddenly struck by a series of enormous gilt letters brightening the hotel's facade. I read them:

TEIKOKU-HOTEL

I was a bit taken aback to read such an awful sounding name and asked Ayama for an explanation.[3] It was then that he informed me,

"In Japanese, *teikoku* means 'imperial.'"

So that explained it!

But a few days later I was paid a visit by a most distinctive French-Canadian, Monsieur B . . . , former mayor of Montreal, and his family.[4] Naturally, the gilt letters drew his attention as well. He took me by the arm and drew me aside,

"My friend, tell me, aren't you a bit ashamed to live under such . . . a sign?"

"What the devil else was I to do?"

"That'll do, that'll do . . . my goodness, it's no great matter . . . you're only a young man after all. But when you invite married couples over, well then, do be careful."

4 A Tokyo "Five O'Clock"

It was Madame X . . . , wife of the former ambassador to V . . . , who threw the reception I won't ever forget! No sooner had she and her husband set foot in Tokyo than the entire city, recognizing in the former ambassador a rising political force, rushed to their doorstep: ministers, senators, deputies, diplomats, officers, and missionaries, all wished to pay homage to a statesman whose star suddenly seemed to blaze brilliantly in the official sky. Overwhelmed, and not knowing where to turn, Monsieur and Madame X decided to hold an *at home* on a certain afternoon so they might receive all of their friends—new and old—at one time. The only problem, however, was that their furniture had not yet arrived from V . . . , and their Tokyo home was furnished in the Japanese style, that is to say, the floor had some lovely mats, here and there a *kakemono* graced the wall, and in the corner sat the odd vase or some other such ornament; but not a single table or chair was to be found. The Japanese fancy this sort of living, preferring a simple cushion on the floor to the best armchair in the world. But ministers, officials, men of wealth and influence, in short anybody who is somebody, have at least a portion of their home furnished in European fashion. It is there that they entertain their guests, while living in the other part.

So the Xs announced a simple reception, with tea to be taken *à la japonaise*. I arrived with a charming young German gentleman, Count Harry de K . . . , whose mother is well known in her adopted Paris.[1] Currently attached to the German diplomatic service, he was taking advantage of some official leave to make a world tour.

Upon descending from our rickshaws in front of the X residence, we were quite surprised to notice there a mass of shoes of all styles and sizes. Our surprise turned to chagrin when a smartly dressed page kindly requested we remove our own boots before entering. Though we may have been fresh off the boat, we were well aware that in Japan one was required to remove one's shoes before entering a temple or a traditional Japanese residence; but at a five o'clock given by Madame X . . . at the ambassador's . . . no, now this had certainly never occurred to us!

Highly amused nonetheless, we sat down on the front steps and graciously acquiesced. I could not stifle my laughter, however, when I saw de K . . . , so "stylish" in his frockcoat of perfect cut, step forward sheepishly, one foot in front of the other, both covered in red silk, and my lord what red!

Finally we entered the salon, and if I live to be a hundred I will never forget the irrepressible urge to laugh that came upon me at the sight of so many ladies made up in their *grande toilette* and men in their dinner jackets, gloved hands grasping their top hats and canes—all those ministers, senators, deputies—and in *socks!* And what socks! Silk ones and lace, cotton and fiber, red ones, blue ones, black and white ones, some embroidered, some striped; some appearing much too large, others ready to tear under the strain of feet too big or too fat. It was in a word profoundly absurd. All inclination to laugh vanished, however, when upon meeting our hostess I realized I had put one of my socks on inside out! *Vanitas vanitatum!* Though my embarrassment was extreme, among the other guests I was quite a success. Meeting Countess B . . . , wife of the Minister of War, a charming Japanese woman educated in Europe, I said wistfully, pointing to my sock, "Can you believe this?"

"Oh," she smiled, "just be thankful that's the extent of your worries," which just goes to prove that one can be Japanese and still know the song of King Dagobert.[2]

Tea and crackers made their appearance, set on small tables on the floor; along the walls of each room were also placed brocaded silk cushions, while all of us—Europeans and Americans—gazed at one another with undisguised discomfort. Alas! Such worries were only too well founded. We realized this as we watched the senior diplomat of the foreign diplomatic corps enter escorting the evening's hostess to one of the cushions. While she gracefully took her seat, the diplomat, losing a good part of his balance and all of his official dignity, proceeded to flop himself down on the cushion beside her.

Naturally we were now required to take our own places on the floor. At first this may seem the simplest thing in the world, but for those of you who were not present, just try to do this gracefully without looking like a complete oaf when, to make matters worse, you are wearing a long frockcoat and balancing a silk hat, gloves, and cane in your hands! It's a veritable tour de force! As for the women, a series of discrete crackling sounds gave me to believe that their corsets, laces, and clasps were not made for such maneuvers, and I could read in the expression of more than one of them, "Oh Lord, will it still hold together when I stand up?"

The worst thing about all this was that the Japanese believe it ill-mannered to sit on the floor with one's legs *extended in front,* with one's posture any which way that is comfortable; Japanese fold their feet *underneath.* This may seem simple enough, but for those not used to it, it is genuine torture. To get into the correct position one need only place the knees on the cushion and then continue to descend until you find's yourself sitting on your heels! A Japanese can remain in this position for hours; for him it is the most comfortable position in the world. I was once invited to a Japanese dinner that went on for over two hours, during which time not a single Japanese altered his position. It was at this dinner that the Countess B . . . , the one who knew the song of King Dagobert, gave me an answer that bears repeating.

The meal was comprised of dishes that were not to my taste—a fish soup, seaweed omelet, a stir-fry of chicken and bamboo shoots, etc.—but still, the meal went off fairly smoothly. There was one dish, however, that I was simply unable to look in the face, much less taste, and this was the raw fish. For this dish the fish is carried still alive into the room adjoining the dining area and at the moment it is to be served it is taken from the water tank, its skin torn off, and then sliced into small pieces that are immediately placed before you: it always seemed to me the thing was still moving! The evening in question, when I expressed my distaste for this particular dish, Countess B . . . responded calmly,

"I really cannot understand your attitude."

"How is that, madam?" I replied. "You who have lived in Europe must . . ."

She interrupted me shaking her head. "No, no, I cannot understand your disgust because you eat much worse than this in Paris and London, and especially in New York."

"And what is that, Countess?" I asked.

"Why, your oysters!" And she added for good measure, "Not only are they raw, they're alive."

The evening of Madame X's five o'clock I was scheduled to dine with Harry de K . . . , whom I had left plopped on the floor near a small stove, and nearer still to a ravishing young blond. When at seven o'clock I met him in the lobby of the hotel he addressed me quite coldly,

"My boy, that is absolutely the last time that we go out together. I did not realize until today that you are very ill-bred."

Shocked and speechless, I did not know how to respond. He continued in his glacial tone, "A man absolutely deprived of good manners and with all the bearing of a stable boy . . ."

Trembling with fury I'd lifted my hand to slap his face when he added with a scornful tone, "How could you drink your tea in the manner you demonstrated at the home of Madame X . . . ?"

Suddenly I was crestfallen. Dropping my hand I could only stammer, "My tea? How . . . ?"

"Why you ignorant savage. You drank your tea simply and gracefully, as if you were in Paris or Rome . . ."

"Yes, of course."

"Well my good man, from the Japanese standpoint that is an odious habit. Here, when one takes tea one sniffs the cup, snorts, makes a frightful smacking sound with the lips and tongue with interjections of 'hai, hai'! All of which demonstrates to the hostess that you appreciate her tea!"

Dear Harry de K . . . ! It was his revenge for my mocking his red socks, yet he was perfectly correct all the same. In taking tea at my second Japanese five o'clock I was in top form, and my steam engine imitation was a resounding success!

5 The Yoshiwara

In Tokyo, so-called "houses of pleasure," recognized in such places as Paris and elsewhere as essential to the public good, are not authorized. It's not that the Japanese are more virtuous than other mortals, it goes without saying that temples dedicated to Venus and Love exist there as they did over twenty centuries ago in Pompeii, and in the large cities of our own day. It's simply that police ordinances forbid their existence within the city proper, and so such establishments have taken collective refuge a few kilometers away, forming in themselves one large city—a city of pleasure, of vice, of love, and even of marriage. This extraordinary place is called the Yoshiwara.

The Yoshiwara is comprised of numerous avenues and narrow streets, lined on each side by houses whose ground floors have neither walls nor enclosures, and are thus exposed for all to see. It is here, in their "showroom," that the women come to display themselves—painted, made up, hair glittering and robed in exquisite dresses of embroidered silk. Every evening the gaily-lighted streets are invaded by an immense crowd from Tokyo, arriving on foot or by rickshaw and comprised not only of those on "private business" but also of a fair quantity of curious spectators, the majority of whom consists of Europeans and Americans.

In fact, a visit to the Yoshiwara comprises part of any Japan itinerary, like a visit to Uyeno Park, the giant Buddha statue, or to any number of temples. Whether ambassador, consul, globe-trotter, or missionary, none wishes to neglect the smallest portion of this circuit. Even women don't pass up a chance to glimpse this city whose social utility they may not always appreciate, though generally of course they don't "visit" such establishments but content themselves with an outside view.

In the history of the Yoshiwara (shall it ever be written?)[1] , there are two events above all that caused such a stir they shall not soon be forgotten. The heroes of the first of these two adventures were the American minister and his wife; and of the second a charming Spaniard, the wife of a high-ranking official, and a certain secretary of the Italian legation.

Mr. D . . . , minister plenipotentiary and envoy of the United States, was a stout Californian, a good man, extremely affable and always ready with a smile.[2] Having spent most of his life in a small California town he was somewhat naïve to the ways of the world, to say nothing of courtly etiquette and diplomatic protocol. One day the minister committed so formidable a gaff as would have ended the career of any other minister, but he committed it so naturally, frankly, and with such innocent goodwill that nobody could really take offense by it. In the end they all shrugged their shoulders and laughed, "*Only an American could do that.*"

One evening Mr. and Mrs. D . . . , finding themselves alone and without engagements, decided the best way to kill some time in an instructive fashion would be to go and see the Yoshiwara. The legation's young Japanese interpreter was summoned and Mr. D . . . explained to him his plans, asking if there would be any problem with his wife accompanying them.

"None at all your Excellency, all the foreign ladies in Tokyo go to see it," the interpreter informed him.

"Even the wives of ministers?"

"Oh, certainly. I've accompanied two of them myself."

"Very well," was the minister's response. "We leave in half an hour. Go harness the landau."[3]

At this the interpreter scratched his head awkwardly and said, "Only . . . usually we go there by rickshaw."

"Rickshaw? They're very uncomfortable those contraptions. And how long does it take to get there?"

"About two hours your Excellency. It's quite far."

"Two hours in a rickshaw? Not on your life! No, no, prepare the landau."

The interpreter retired to give the orders. Like most Japanese employees he was timid before "the master" and didn't dare explain that ministers, as other important persons, when compelled by curiosity to visit the Yoshiwara did so incognito, journeying there by rickshaw like everyone else. As there are literally thousands of these little vehicles on the streets, one can travel in them unperceived. However, there were very few carriages in Tokyo and only foreign ambassadors or members of the government or court used them. This being the case, one can imagine the sensation caused by the arrival of a carriage whose coachman wore the official livery of the legation and which was preceded by a runner whose hat and uniform were embroidered with the United States insignia and who yelled out as he ran,

"Make way! Make way for his Excellence the American minister!"

"This marks the first time," remarked one Japanese newspaper the following day, "that the Yoshiwara has received an official visit."

The other adventure had more serious consequences.

Señora . . . , wife of the governor of the most important of the Spanish colonies in Asia, came to spend a few weeks in Japan with an English lady friend, whose red tresses and pale and delicate complexion only accentuated the stunning jet black hair and fiery complexion of her companion. These two were received and feted by everyone and it was whispered that *la señora* left behind many a broken heart when she departed Tokyo.

For one reason or other the English lady steadfastly refused to visit the Yoshiwara, something that vexed the governor's wife to no end as she was dying to go see it. Unable to stand it any longer, she finally made her wishes known to a certain rogue named C . . . , secretary of the Italian legation. Always ready for an adventure, he was delighted by such a stroke of good fortune and naturally offered himself up as an escort.

The following evening, after an excellent champagne dinner, C . . . escorted the señora to the Yoshiwara. Amused and enchanted with their little escapade, they explored the most intriguing streets on foot, leaving their rickshaws waiting at the city entrance. Suddenly, however, a storm broke the evening sky and within moments the rain was falling in torrents, soaking them to the skin. Not keeping their surroundings in mind, they ran for shelter in the first building they could find. Entering, they soon discovered there a number of women painted and made up, whose company the governor's wife certainly did not approve of.

"The only thing to do then," submitted C . . ."is to request a private room. It's only a rainstorm and we can leave once it has passed." He then went out in search of the establishment's patroness.

At this moment four Japanese soldiers, so drunk they could hardly stand, burst into the establishment roaring like wild beasts. Astonished to find a beautiful foreign woman in such a place they soon surrounded her. Convinced (quite rightly) that she could not understand a word of Japanese, they proceeded to berate her in the most insulting manner. Unfortunately for them, Signor C . . . , who had served as his legation's interpreter for several years, spoke perfect Japanese. From behind the house's thin paper partitions he heard the insults being heaped upon his companion. Out of his mind with fury, he fell upon the soldiers. Endowed with Herculean strength, he seized a chair and gave them all a thorough thrashing, destroying the house's partition walls in the process. The uproar was frightful and the police soon arrived on the scene, dragging off the four Japanese soldiers as well as the Italian secretary and the lady who had accompanied him!

At the station everything was explained, and C . . . was apologetically released as soon as it was realized he was a diplomat. On the return trip to Tokyo C . . . assured Señora . . . that the whole business would have no adverse consequences of any sort. Alas! The very next day a Japanese newspaper published a full account of the case down to the smallest details, and the whole city soon discovered that the wife of the governor of . . . and the secretary of the Italian legation had been arrested, apparently for causing a disturbance in a Yoshiwara establishment, where they had requested a private room!

That same day the señora left Tokyo. I was in Korea when all this took place but upon my return the whole affair was explained to me at the Tokyo Club by General L . . . ,[4] who added,

"In any case, the governor should thank his stars, he had a near escape!"

"How is that?" I asked.

"How is that? Why, do you think a rascal like this C . . . , left alone in a room with a beautiful woman, would be content to pass the time playing tiddlywinks? No my friend, from the governor's perspective it is fortunate she was arrested before having gone deeper into that house . . . of pleasure!"

Poor C . . . ! *So near and yet so far!*

6 A Socialite

As in all true stories, she was young and charming. She is still young and will always be charming. Her husband, the Count I . . . , is currently the ambassador to one of the three imperial courts in Europe and my only reason for not writing out his full name is that Japanese diplomats do not like seeing their names in print, much less those of their spouses.[1]

The scene took place in an immense Tokyo park, one of the most beautiful in Japan and belonging to the president of the chamber of commerce. On the day in question he was throwing a "garden party" in honor of several foreign visitors, among whom he wished to include myself. Besides these special guests, the invited included foreign ambassadors and Japanese ministers, artists and university professors, all told about a hundred guests.

Our host received us on a large open lawn, where we gathered, chatting and laughing. Once he had determined we had all, or nearly all, arrived, he removed his top hat, made several deep bows, and gave us a charming welcoming address. In the course of this speech my attention was drawn to a fence before which a carriage had come to a stop. An extremely elegant young lady descended and headed our way. With creased brow I examined her carefully, but the only conclusion I could come to was that I did not know her. I was nonplussed, for I really thought I knew all the ladies of the diplomatic corps, as well those other foreign ladies who might be invited to such an exclusive gathering.

As she approached us from a distance, I admired her stunning dress of crepe and grey silk, a Parisian masterpiece, and her hat that could only have been crafted on the rue de la Paix. I was bowled over, however, when this *Parisienne* approaching us with such unaffected grace turned out to be Japanese! What's more, I did not know her!

Touching the arm of Baron Sannomiya, Master of Court Ceremonies, I inquired:

"Tell me, who is this charming lady?"

"It is the Countess I . . . , daughter-in-law of the Minister of the Interior. Her husband who you see over there, next to X . . . , is one of our up-and-coming diplomats. He has only just returned from Europe. Would you like me to introduce you to the Countess?"

Did I indeed!

Heavens, the lady spoke French, English, and even German. Simple, personable, and kind, she could prattle off in any one of these languages at the drop of a hat:

"Really, this speech is endless, why it's enough to put one to sleep. Would you like me to show you the park? It is superb!"

Breaking away from the crowd of guests, we followed a shaded alley lined with superb chrysanthemums. We skirted miniature lakes and ventured across fanciful bridges, finally stopping at a spot where our host had gathered a myriad of small diversions. There was a theater for pantomime; there were musicians, dancers, wrestlers, jugglers, and a buffet tent where they were serving up delicious champagne.

We chatted as she guided me over. She said to me in English,

"I've heard you spoken of and I also understand that besides your official mission you intend on writing something about Japan. Is this true?"

"So true in fact that I've already begun writing it."

"What? Already? But you've been among us for such a short while. What could you possible have to say now?"

"You'll laugh and make fun of me, but I'm writing a piece called *Japanese Women*."[2]

"Japanese women! Well then, you presume to know us?"

"Oh no, I don't pretend to know you at all, these are only impressions . . . the impressions of a traveler."

"My, how I would like to read this article! Quickly, tell me something you wrote . . . anything."

"Well, among other things I said that Japanese women know nothing of kissing . . ."

At this she laughed and clapped her hands: "Bravo! Bravo! But you are right. In Japan we know nothing of kissing, why we don't even hug! And tell me, how did you discover this?"

"My goodness . . . but Countess, you being Japanese, you must be ignorant of kissing as well, or do you by chance know what is meant by the word . . ."

"*You bet I do!*" was her response, exploding out of her like a bolt of lightening. But ever the diplomat's wife, she smiled and changed the topic by asking me,

"Will you be attending the ball tomorrow evening?"

I'd discovered that the following day was the emperor's birthday and that every year on this day the Minister of Foreign Affairs played host to a grand ball, which everyone naturally sought to attend.

"Certainly. And you Countess?"

"Ah, yes, but I'm afraid I won't be having any fun as I'm not permitted to dance. You see, at this ball the princess represents the emperor and I must accompany her as a lady in waiting. Since the princess does not dance I'll have to remain at her side the entire evening."

"Why in the devil hasn't she learned how to dance then? She must be bored as well?"

"But she dances very well."

"Well then . . . ?"

"Well there will be a dilemma at this ball. There won't be a Japanese prince in attendance, and the princess can only dance with a very high ranking foreigner, and such foreigners would never think of asking her to dance. Perhaps they think she does not enjoy it."

Meanwhile we had arrived at the buffet. While fully appreciative of the foie gras, candied chestnuts, and champagne, I silently nurtured an idea that was now taking shape in my head.

At the moment Countess I . . . was preparing to leave I briefly took her aside.

"Countess, I think I've discovered a way to allow the princess to dance . . . Don't look so incredulous, I really think this may work. But for now Countess, a favor to ask . . . if the princess dances, would you do me the honor . . ."

"Of dancing with you? . . . Ah! Now that would be my pleasure. I think you will have well deserved it."

The ball, the first major event of the season, was held at the Imperial Hotel. At the end of the immense ballroom, and facing the large doors, formal chairs and seats had been arranged for the princess and her suite. The day of the ball I had asked General L . . . , who knew everything, who would be the highest ranking person at the ball.

"Why Admiral U . . . [3], my boy. The Commander-in-chief of French naval forces in the Far East will be attending with his entire general staff."

I was a bit taken aback by this response as I didn't know the admiral, who in fact had only just arrived in Tokyo that very morning.

Leaving my rooms for the ball, I caught sight of the admiral and his officers leaving the rooms of the Viscount de L . . . ,[4] the French military attaché, who like me resided at the hotel. He approached me and said,

"Quick, come with me. I'll introduce you to the admiral."

As succinctly as possible I briefed him on my current situation, pleading with him to help me convince the admiral to invite the princess to dance. The admiral was charming. However, after having heard us out he replied,

"Terribly sorry messieurs, but . . . old wounds you see, rheumatism . . . in short, I can't dance."

And so with a bit of contempt I gave up on this soldier who refused to march, and set off in search of the doyen of the diplomatic corps, who turned out to be the minister from Mexico, Señor R . . . [5], a charming man of great intelligence, who possessed both a vast fortune and a beautiful wife, two things that helped ensure his renown. However, Señor R . . . wasn't exactly striking to behold. He was small—quite small, thin, had jaundiced and very wrinkled skin and one eye nearly extinguished with cataracts. With his stature and complexion he could easily have passed for Japanese.

I caught sight of him near the ballroom's large entrance doors. Pulling him aside I said,

"I have some news for you. Fancy this, but the princess would like to dance."

"Well then! And with whom will she be dancing?"

"What do you mean with whom? Why, who else but you, the doyen of the diplomatic corps, the most important of all the foreigners!"

The minister began to glow. His eye—the good one—twinkled.

"And the admiral?"

"He never dances."

"Por Dios! Then it is *me!*"

But he still had his doubts and, fearing some sort of joke at his expense, he asked who had informed me of this.

"The Countess I . . . , lady in waiting to Her Highness," I replied dryly.

Giving his waistcoat a tug and twigging his moustache, with all eyes upon him the Mexican minister advanced majestically across the length of the grand ballroom. Standing tall, chin up, his chest extended, he suddenly seemed larger, more handsome than ever. He made three deep bows before the princess, upon which she arose, smiling and enchanted, to take his arm. It was a sensation!

Nobody, I can assure you, had the time to consider requesting the Countess I . . . to dance; the princess had hardly put her hand in the arm of the minister then she and I were already spinning in a mad waltz.

I was young after all, and quite proud of my little success.

"Well then, countess," I said, once she had again taken her seat, "you see I have triumphed."

"Yes, you certainly have. You have drive. You'll go far."

Alas, countess! Your prediction never came to pass . . . I am still at your feet!

7 Tokyo

The Japanese capital sits only three quarters of an hour from Yokohama, the major port of entry for foreigners. The city covers an immense area, but from a distance its appearance is less than impressive: a sea of roofs, low and somber, amidst which absolutely nothing captures the eye of the visitor. No twenty-five story monuments as in New York, no Eiffel Tower, no domes or houses of six or seven stories as in Paris, not even any chimneys are visible.

Earthquakes are so frequent and violent there that Japanese architects never consider building structures elevated far off the ground. Japanese buildings are rarely over a story high, and two at the most.

For several years now the residences of the imperial family and ministers, hotels, and some schools have been built in the European fashion, but far from adding to the beauty of the city, they are mostly abominable creations resembling nothing more than barracks. One can only hope that some violent earthquake might one day topple them to the ground.

Japan is without a doubt the country of earthquakes par excellence. Not a day passes without some corner of the empire feeling a shake, and in Tokyo you can count on such about once a fortnight.

The celebrated English professor Milne[1], who was for many years a member of the faculty of the University of Tokyo, took the opportunity of his sojourn there to study earthquakes. With government assistance he established "observation stations" throughout the country, at which extremely delicate instruments placed at the bottom of shafts registered all of the earth's movements, jolts, and palpitations.

Milne is a charming man, intimately familiar with Japan and its people, and I shall never forget the several hours I spent in his company.

At the time of my first voyage to Japan as a representative of that country to the international exposition at Chicago, Milne—whom I had just met—remarked to me one afternoon at the club:

"I have a proposition to make regarding your exposition. When shall we be able to talk?"

"This evening. Do give me the pleasure of dining with me at the Imperial Hotel."

He accepted, and that same evening as we were taking our coffee he expounded on his idea:

"You know, my dear boy, how much the civilized people of Europe—and America even more—love extreme thrills, fearsome jolts. At past fairs, when one wanted to be roused one made do with riding spinning wooden horses or swings that cut through the air. In the last few years, however, we've been looking for some new contrivances. In place of wooden horses you now find boats, which not only turn but reproduce all the movements of rolling and pitching. We've constructed twisting slides and immense wheels that roll people around at dizzying heights. In America there are boats launched on rails from high scaffolding that shoot like balls from a cannon to be hurled into a lake. They call this *"to shoot the chutes."* I'm told the sensation quite defies description. Why, I've even heard that at certain Paris fairs there are enormous tunnels open on both ends and containing benches upon which the thrill-seekers sit, and they then spin the tunnel! They call this the *"tunnel of love"* because it makes one's heart ache.

"So you see my boy, all these examples demonstrate the tastes of the civilized. They love to be shaken and stirred. And so, I, Milne, am now proposing a wholly new thrill. In a word, I want to reproduce at Chicago the most celebrated Japanese earthquake."

His words gave me a shock.

"But that's quite mad!" I cried.

"Oh no, not at all. I can assure you it would be very simple."

"Very simple! But it's not a question of simplicity. Do you imagine that we would amuse ourselves with constructing a palace at enormous expense in labor and money only to allow you to collapse it with your earthquakes?"

"Easy, easy, slow down. Now hear me out. I won't be collapsing anything. Well, perhaps the occasional individual with poor balance, but they won't be harmed. On the contrary, they'll be quite amused. No, no, I will not be demolishing any palace. A large platform that can carry several hundred persons can be set up, either in a special building or in the open air. This platform would be constructed over powerful machines built in such a manner as to allow them to create at will all the movements and jolts of a real earthquake.

"We have in fact recorded on diagrams the movements of the largest Japanese earthquakes of the last ten years. We could reproduce them at Chicago. People would mount the platform and we would announce: 'the quake you are about to experience is the exact same as that which hit the Tokyo district in August 1888, destroying five thousand homes and killing 8,500 people."

The mad professor went on to detail for me all the most celebrated quakes until my head spun. As I escorted him to the door of the hotel I remarked laughing, "It looks like I'll be dreaming of earthquakes all night."

"Oh, don't bother with dreaming. Perhaps we'll have a small earthquake, a real one, and that'll give you some idea of what they're like!"

We never realized just how right he was! That very night I was suddenly awoken from a sound asleep by the sensation of my bed dancing a wild saraband. As I had recently arrived from a fifteen day journey across the Pacific, my first thought—thinking I was still aboard ship—was "Damn! The sea is getting rough!" A moment later, realizing I was now in Tokyo, I suddenly recalled Milne and his earthquakes and leapt out of bed.

"That idiot," I thought. "Now I'm dreaming of earthquakes. I suppose it was inevitable." I peacefully went back to sleep.

Imagine my surprise when the following morning I learned there had been a strong earthquake during the night. One of the hotel's wings had been severely damaged, the walls on that side exhibiting some sinister cracks.

"The alarm was quite serious," the hotel manager informed me. "Men, women, and children were led out of the hotel in their nightshirts and pajamas. What a spectacle! You were the only person to remain inside. You were lucky!"

Ah, is this what he called lucky? . . . What I would have given to have seen all the beauties and horrors of the hotel under the moonlight, and in my nightshirt! . . .

Japanese city dwellers have another enemy, perhaps more terrifying than the earthquake: fire. A conflagration, once ignited in the midst of all these houses built entirely of paper and wood, spreads with frightening speed, soon devouring entire districts. During the time I was in Tokyo the means to combat such fires were still utterly inadequate. There were only two or three modern steam-driven fire pumps, but whether from a lack of water or insufficient pressure, you could be certain their performance would be less than satisfactory. There were also a number of small manual pumps, nothing more than toys really, but which were apparently taken seriously.

Once a fire alarm is given the entire population heads for the site of the blaze, driven in some very laudable part by a desire to be useful, but also by a certain indescribable and puerile curiosity that consumes all Japanese. And as there is no overall command the confusion is extreme.

Two or three days after my arrival in Tokyo, a violent conflagration broke out around seven in the evening in one of the city's most populous areas.[2] Curious to witness the event up close, I made my way on foot to the area of the fire. The avenue leading there had been invaded by an enormous mass of men, women, and children, all running as fast as their little legs would carry them, some laughing, others crying, and all making extraordinary sounds evidently reserved for just such important occasions.

Into this avenue every street and alley emptied its running, shouting human tide.

From time to time a squad of volunteer firemen, yelling in rivalry as they dragged along a small manual pump on its belly, flew through the mob like a cannon ball sending several dozens flying.

At one point from two separate roads came galloping on their little legs two different squads, only to smack right into another. The shock was dreadful and there was a score or more injured. I myself was knocked over and trampled on, and it was in a pitiful state that I finally arrived at the site of the disaster.

The impression I got was of a total absence of any common and intelligent effort to regain control of the fire. Everyone did whatever came into his head, and here and there one observed a courageous man standing on his roof as he tried in vain to save it by dashing it with a few bowlfuls of water while the rest of the house burned. Most of the people were thinking of only one thing: to save whatever they could. In the midst of this incredible and indescribable confusion, men, women and children were emerging from their homes carrying their furniture and belongings on their heads and screaming at the top of their lungs. They threw themselves into the mob, but since the mob was heading towards the very blaze they were attempting to flee, the confusion became yet more dreadful. They were all knocking each other over, but the most incredible thing was that instead of getting angry, hitting or hurting each other, they found release in explosions of laughter— delighted, tickled and finding the whole affair wonderfully amusing.

Figure 9. Japanese firefighters in the late 19th century. Private Collection of Mr. Christophe Schwarzenbach, Switzerland. From: M.Winkel, *Souvenirs From Japan*, 1991, p. 43. Used by permission.

No race in the world has a better character than the Japanese. If the French are *badauds*[3], the Japanese are a thousand times more so. In Japan the most insignificant event becomes an excuse for congregating, chitchatting, joking, and prank-playing. Everyone you meet, scurrying along in high wooden clogs, smiles and wears the expression of one about to have a good joke at his neighbor's expense.

Only the village sergeants have a serious manner about them; the devil himself couldn't make them smile. Wrapped in large, dark woolen uniforms in winter, and in white clothe in summer, gloved, long sabers hanging at their side, they are the very personification of both punishment and—think upon this you Parisian *sergots*—politesse.[4] However difficult the task, they carry out their duty with energy and firmness, but without brutality, insult, or injury. They are in two words, perfect gentlemen.

Tokyo

Tokyo presents an extraordinary mix of old and new, of Japan of yesteryear and today. European style buildings arise amidst palaces and wooden shanties; people in kimonos brush up against others in frock coats; here and there businesses have replaced signs in Japanese letters with others written in wretched English; electric lights now illuminate the avenues, but have not completely chased away the traditional paper lanterns; and finally, the famed jinrikisha has found a formidable rival in the electric tram. The Japanese seem to take an extreme joy in riding this tram, which is always jam-packed with riders, and whose shareholders are reaping a fortune.

The shops of Tokyo are all extremely small, and even the most important among them are mere dwarves compared to French, English, or American firms. Colossi like the Louvre or the Bon-Marché are simply unknown in Japan.

Women of the upper classes are not in the habit of making their purchases at the shops. When they desire to purchase silk, wool, or linen, they contact the shopkeeper, who then arranges a complete assortment of goods and spends a whole day, or even longer if need be, at their home. There he has them try on his merchandise until either they have found something they like or until he is forced to concede, with much regret and apology, that he has nothing worthy of the tastes of such noble ladies.

The majority of boutiques are very basic affairs, open in the front with neither doors nor windows. The customer would never even consider entering into such restricted space, but rather takes a seat on the outside portion of the floor while the merchant shows him the merchandise, trying his hardest to fleece him with forced smiles, bows, and graciousness. The price of each object varies according to the importance of the buyer, the elegance of his clothing, or his ignorance of the value of the item being sold.

The very evening of my arrival in Tokyo I took a stroll along the Ginza, the commercial street par excellence. There in the front window of a small boutique I saw a charming little vase and inquired as to the price.

"Five *yen**," the merchant responded, bowing politely.

I hesitated. I liked the vase, but I found the price really too steep and I began to walk away. Bounding from the shop, the Japanese shopkeeper pursued me crying,

---

* Nominally the *yen* corresponds to the dollar and should have the value of five francs. At the time it was barely worth three francs fifty [author note].

"How much? How much?"

Hoping to get rid of him, I responded with what I thought a ridiculous price.

"Fifty *sen*.*"

I expected he would simply dismiss my offer with a disdainful sneer. To my great astonishment, however, he held out the vase saying, "Very well, fifty *sen!*"

I felt rather embarrassed that the merchant should have lowered himself so much for my sake. Upon my return to the hotel, however, the manager, after examining my vase, told me,

"If I'd sold this to you for twenty-five *sen* . . . I think I'd have gotten the better part of the bargain!"

The majority of foreigners who have been to Japan, and who have had similar experiences with the country's shopkeepers, will tell you that the Japanese are all thieves and bandits and that honesty is a stranger in that country. They are a bit like that Englishman who, having passed through a European village where he noticed only two women, both of them redheads, then recorded in his journal, "All the women of X . . . have red hair."

For not all Japanese are scoundrels, far from it. However, it is undeniable that the class of petty merchants doesn't make a shining example of honesty. This is apparently tied to the fact that throughout history the merchant has been scorned as the most vile, base, and humiliating of occupations, taken up only by the dregs of society. Until only a few years ago no member of the great warrior class of samurai, no artisan or artist, not even a peasant, would ever so demean themselves as to become a merchant. For that reason the trade remained in the hands of the lowest class, individuals who did not consider the trade to be about honest and loyal transactions but a perilous game, where one party must win and the other lose, and where each party to the deal had to be on their guard against and get the better of the other.

"Horrible and shameful!" cries the globe-trotter like me who has paid twice as much for his vase as it is worth. But honestly now, is it only in Japan that such things occur? How many Frenchmen have been had in Spain, in Italy, in Greece? How many foreigners have been fleeced in Paris? Let us leave it at that.

Within the past few years more respectable Japanese have taken up the commercial trades, and there are now a number of stores in that country that clearly mark their prices so that no bargaining occurs.

---

* About one franc seventy-five centimes [author note].

There are a number of very important bazaars and shops in Tokyo—those where silk is sold, for example. One of these large stores impresses the foreign visitor as being nothing but an immense roofed platform with only blue cotton curtains for walls. On the mat-covered platform countless workers sit crouched on their knees displaying their wares to their clients, likewise elegantly crouched before them. Atop the mats are innumerable cups of tea, for Japanese etiquette demands that any customer, even if only there to inquire on prices, be offered several small cups of this beverage.

The merchandise isn't kept on hand: it is protected from fire and theft within a special structure, a veritable commercial fortress, and a swarm of children runs continuously from the platform to this building to retrieve the items the sellers wish to present and for which they provide the children with specially numbered tags.

In Japan major manufacturers are scarce, and the silks, bronzes, cloisonné, etc. are mostly made in humble workshops by two or three artisans working fifteen and eighteen hour days, contenting themselves with the slimmest of profits.

A friend of mine who knew Japan intimately had his own pet theory on the subject of merchants.

"You see," he told me. "These people are misunderstood. When they demand a hundred francs for some item that's not worth ten it isn't with the intention of robbing you. They don't take you for a complete fool. They're well aware you'll never pay such a price. Rather, they're attempting to stress the beauty and value of the item, and so they take tremendous pleasure in performing an act of generosity, of emphasizing through their own exquisite courtesy the enormous sacrifice they're making in giving you the piece at your price, simply to make you happy, to have the distinguished honor of having sold you an object of such value for such a trifle, a trifle . . ."

Very beautiful theory that, and *si non è vero* . . .

8 A Few Silhouettes

Tokyo, for those who dwell there year-round, is not exactly a rollicking place. The winter set is composed of members of the diplomatic corps, a handful of Japanese who have lived in Europe or who are attached to the imperial court or the ministries, a few foreign professors from the university, and finally, a select group of travelers so enamored by the country's charms that they've lingered on even after the chrysanthemum season.

The Tokyo Club is a major meeting place for the men. There, between six and seven in the evening, they gather for cocktails and to enjoy a superb dinner. Foreigners who are passing through Japan meet with the greatest hospitality there, and besides foreign diplomats and Japanese of rank, one can encounter at the Club some very interesting personalities. Among the first rank of these is an Englishman, Captain Brinkley, who has lived in Japan upwards of thirty years.[1] Arriving as a military instructor in the early days of reform, he developed such an abiding affection for the country, and such an interest in its inhabitants, and love for its art and artisans, that he stayed on for good, even marrying a Japanese woman of quality. He has established a large newspaper there, the most important in Japan: *The Japan Daily Mail.*

Captain Brinkley is an exceptional and reputed connoisseur of Japanese art and possesses some marvelous collections. Unlike other English papers in Japan, which on numerous occasions have sought only to sow discord between Japanese and foreigners, his paper has only one aim: to make Japan, its arts and industries, known and loved, and to cultivate between its sensitive and charming people and the rest of the world feelings of sympathy, goodwill, and mutual admiration.

Naturally, the captain is quite sought after at the Club, and those who have had the opportunity of hearing him discuss Japanese issues with Kipling or Sir Edwin Arnold will never forget those captivating occasions.

Sir Edwin Arnold, the great English poet, was in Tokyo during the period of my sojourn. Enchanted by the country, seduced by its charming inhabitants, which he covered with his verse, he could not bring himself to give up what he viewed as the ideal life.

The day of my departure he accompanied me as far as Yokohama, where we dined together at the Grand Hotel. Having asked him when he was considering returning to England, he exclaimed:

"Don't speak of such things! How could I leave this earthly paradise . . . it would be the death of me." In effect, Sir Edwin had found in this paradise a charming Japanese Eve, whom I believe he ended up making his wife.

One of the most interesting figures at that time was General Legendre, who had arrived in Tokyo on a special mission for the king of Korea. He was French by birth but a naturalized American and had played a brilliant role in the United States Civil War, commanding a regiment with great valor. A little later he was dispatched as American consul to China.

He passed through Japan en route back to the United States at the time of the revolution that preceded imperial restoration.[2] He ended up staying on and held several high positions as a private advisor to the emperor. After several years of service he had gone into a well-deserved retirement when he was offered the position of private advisor to the king of Korea. The situation in Korea at the time was complicated, and a determined fighter, he couldn't resist the temptation to throw himself into the fray, made triply interesting by Japanese, Russian, and Chinese intrigues. He later died on the field of honor, in Seoul.

He was a charming man, and having taken a liking to me, he aided me with his wealth of experience and offered me valuable advice. In Tokyo he had numerous friends and one 'enemy.' This latter was the Viscountess de B . . . of the French Legation, a delightful lady, blond and aerial, who seemed to harbor for the general a genuine antipathy. Between the two there was never an encounter that did not leave its scar.

One evening at a farewell dinner hosted by the Italian military attaché, the Marquis Rudini, the Viscountess de B . . . found herself seated next to the general. From where I was seated I observed her suddenly pale, whereupon the general called to a servant, "Madame has caught a chill. Quickly, fetch her a shawl."

Since the dining room was oppressively hot, and judging by the style of her dress, it was impossible to imagine she was cold, or at least not unduly discomforted. As soon as the dinner had ended I approached her to ask how she was feeling.

"Quickly come closer, I'll tell you all about it. It's horrid! I'm still upset."

Once we were seated off to the side she continued, "Would you believe that from the very start of the dinner I noticed the general gazing at me in the most extraordinary fashion. I can't say he was doing so through his spectacles, but just through one of the eyepieces of those spectacles—the eye on the other side seemed to remain indifferent, dead. It was only with the one eye that he looked at me, so that he was obliged to turn his whole head toward me. Compared to the other one, one eye had an extraordinary glimmer to it. The whole thing was baffling and towards the middle of dinner I couldn't resist staring for a second at those two eyes—one that spoke while the other remained silent.

"Well the general noticed this and became very upset. Pushing himself practically against me, he asked menacingly,

'What is it madame? What is so curious?'

"His manner was so angry and frightening that I became terrified. I could only mumble, 'But nothing, general, only . . . the eye.' All of a sudden he became calm and said softly,

'The eye? Oh my goodness, Countess, tell me quickly, is it crooked?'

'What do you mean crooked?'

'But of course, so it's turned.'

"I thought he was quite mad and drew back a bit. 'How can your eye turn general? I don't understand.'

'Ah, you don't understand?' he said, more and more excited. 'Well, evidently madame you are unaware . . . '

"While talking he had removed his glasses, and taking hold of a four-pronged fork he then made a series of small taps on the pupil of his eye, adding, 'Evidently you are unaware that this is a glass eye!'

"Now the porcelain like sound of the fork tapping his eye had such an effect on me that I felt like fainting. He noticed this, ceased his tapping and asked if I were all right. Unable to reply, 'You have nauseated me,' I just told him I had caught a chill. That's when he called for a shawl.

"Oh, I'll never forget that horrid incident for the rest of my life. I'll never, never be able to forget it!"

Charming Viscountess! Not a quarter of an hour later she was seated at the piano singing gaily,

> *Un baiser est bien douce chose,*
> *Tu le sais sur leurs lèvres roses*[3]

Among those Japanese in more or less regular contact with foreigners of mark, I would cite Count Ito, Marshal Count Oyama, Mr. Mutsu, the Minister of Foreign Affairs, Marquis Hijikata, Minister of the Imperial Household, Baron Sannomiya, Master of Court Ceremonies, Count Inouye, Count Matsukata, and Count Okuma.[4]

This last gentleman, former Minister of Finance, former Minister-President of Council, and today chief of the opposition party, is without doubt the greatest orator Japan possesses. All his influence, all his talent, and all his energies are continually placed in the service of progress and civilization. In fact, so receptive has he been to new ideas that his enemies spread the word that he is nothing but a traitor, eager to sell his country to foreigners.

In a country where patriotism is the first of virtues, that's all it takes to rouse the fanatics. In 1889 one of these tossed a dynamite bomb under Count Okuma's carriage. The coachman, a servant, and the horse were all killed. The Count escaped with a shattered leg. It was amputated and only after a period of great suffering and despair did the man reemerge.

Outside of politics, the Count also takes the greatest interest in questions of scholarship and the universities. He has established two large schools in Tokyo, one for the higher education of young men, and the other for the higher education of young women. These are both model institutions, well organized and which do the greatest honor to their founder.

Count Inouye, one of the most influential men in Japan, has been in the vanguard of affairs for some forty years now. Even before the revolution that would restore power to the Mikado, he had visited Europe, obtaining his passage there by disguising himself as a common sailor. He returned to Japan at the dawn of the new era and was named Vice-minister of Finance. Since then he has filled virtually all of the higher government offices and was named Minister of Foreign Affairs.

The Baron Sannomiya is without doubt one of the most charming Japanese I have ever encountered. Having traveled much, witnessed much, read much and retained much, fluent in several foreign languages, and having been in contact, due to his high position at court, with the elite of the world, he is the perfect type of Japanese gentleman. He married an Englishwoman, a woman of high character and lofty qualities. The Baron and Baroness were precious friends to me and I will never forget all the kindness they showed me.

The Minister of War, the Marshal Count Oyama, who had to abandon his functions as minister to assume command of the Japanese Second Army, is a most distinguished officer. He undertook all his higher studies in France, where he maintains several friendships. The Countess Oyama is one of the loveliest, most charming women at the imperial court. Educated at an American college in the United States, she speaks English and French perfectly and represents the feminine progressive element at the palace. She is the perfect example of the great Japanese lady educated abroad, imbued with our principles of civilization, polished by contact with the great American thinkers and high European nobility.

It would require an entire volume to do justice to Count Ito, the greatest statesman of modern Japan. The history of Count Ito is the history of Japan, of its modern civilization, its progress, its trials and tribulations, its sufferings and its glory over the last four decades. Four times Minister-President of the State Council, friend and confidant of the Emperor, and leader in everything the Japanese consider the most intelligent and brilliant. It is Ito who decided the Japanese should abandon their feudal ideas, their hair buns and their sabers; it is Ito who always represents Japan in its discussions with Europe, which still refuses to accord the empire the position it merits in the great family of civilized nations. It is to Ito's credit that Japan has its new "Constitution," a profound piece of work which has won the admiration of statesmen the world over. The impressive Japanese fleet is also his work, for it was Ito who forced Parliament to vote through the act known as the *Ito Program of Shipbuilding*. Following the accomplishments of the army, it was also Ito who negotiated the peace conditions with Li Hung-chang[5] and then signed the Treaty of Shimonoseki.[6] Finally, it was Ito who proudly denounced the treaties with the foreign powers in the wake of that war, treaties which for more than thirty years had humiliated Japan, and then Ito who signed new treaties which finally placed his country on an absolute equal footing with the great powers.

In conclusion, an anecdote about Count—now Marquis—Ito. A certain American diplomat was discussing with Ito the issue of marriage and the relative condition of women in Japan and the United States. Carried away by his superb rhetoric, the American detailed all the advantages and attractions of feminine freedom, as it is understood in America. Retaining his reserve, Ito received the barrage of his interlocutor's formidable arguments without flinching. When the American had concluded, the Marquis, his small eyes sparkling mischievously, replied quite calmly in his soft voice,

"Yes, yes, I understand perfectly. There is, in effect, a great difference.—*When I marry I take a head servant, when you marry you become one!*"

9 Their Women

"How is it," I asked a Japanese one day, "that even those among you who most closely follow European ways persist in treating women as inferiors?"

The question visibly annoyed him. In this respect the Japanese is very oriental; he does not like to discuss his mother, sister, wife or daughter with strangers. But we were good friends and had discussed many other such thorny issues. He decided to answer me frankly.

"You touch on a very delicate point there. As you know, our women enjoy the greatest freedom. We treat them as cherished friends and they are certainly happy. I seriously doubt that the women of any other country can claim as much. We now find ourselves in a singular position vis à vis our women. In short, for forty years the men of Japan have covered tremendous ground along the path of progress and civilization. We have taken some gigantic strides. And along this rapid and incredible journey we have carried along with us our army, navy, universities, government, everything in fact *except our women!*"

"Oh, come now."

"I speak in all seriousness. While we males ran about Europe and America with minds wide open; while we launched army, naval, and other state schools; while we established arsenals, railroads, and western tailor shops; our women stayed home, peaceful and content amidst their children. As a result, one fine day we men realized that we were at least a century ahead of them, and they were, in a manner of speaking, inhabiting another world. In short, they remain on the bottom rung, whereas we men are about halfway to the top. How in the devil are we to get them back?"

He said this in such a despondent tone that I could not help but smile.

"Look here my friend, maybe things aren't as serious as all that?"

"Oh but they are, nothing could be more so. You simply don't perceive it because you judge our women based upon the exception, based upon the women of court and high society, those who have traveled and been brought up in Europe and America and who are in daily contact—even here in Japan—with foreigners of distinction.

"But I am speaking of the millions of Japanese women who represent the bourgeoisie and the common people, and it's the ignorance of these that frightens me! Fortunately they're not the ones running the country. And yet, I can't help but wonder if they may not be the source of our strength as well."

The next day I recounted this conversation to a person at court, a very elderly man of wide experience.

"There's truth there, in what the man told you, much truth. In effect, we have taken giant strides while our women with their shorter legs have been unable to follow. But we will no longer run so fast. We are familiar with the Italian saying, *chi va piano va sano*.[1] We have slackened our pace so as to be sure of our progress. Our women can now take the opportunity to catch up.

"We men have been very preoccupied with this question in recent years, and a number of schools and institutions of all sorts have been opened. But to be quite frank, we are in no way eager to make bluestockings, doctors, lawyers, free-thinkers or Socialists of our wives and daughters. In this respect we prefer more amiable company, sufficiently educated to be sure, and capable of running a household; in a word, good mothers and devoted and faithful wives."

"Certainly," I reflected upon returning to my lodgings, "these Japanese are quite extraordinary. They've found the means of molding a race of perfect women, who do precisely what the men desire while never impeding them in any way . . ."

To resume, everything there is to say about those millions of bourgeoisie and commoner women my friend spoke of so dejectedly may be briefly summarized as follows: young Japanese girls are almost all pretty, more or less kind, gracious, friendly, charming, gay and spirited; they love their toilette, bright colors, music, and the noise of crowds and festivals. Young ladies make model spouses and have a good many children. Old women . . . oh, now they are quite hideous. The Japanese wither quickly, and once withered they are generally frightful to behold! Yet they must still retain hidden charms for there are millions of babies who simply adore their grandmothers. Amongst the peasantry and petit bourgeoisie, women labor tirelessly, following the example of the men, for among these energetic and diligent people the loafer is a being more or less unknown.

To whichever class she belongs, the Japanese woman is a coquette. I was on the point of writing that in this she might flatter herself a true "daughter of Eve" . . . But it may very well be that all the diverse and various colored races alike are descended from Eve!

It is because she is a coquette that the Japanese woman quickly abandons any notion of dressing *à l'européenne.* She realizes immediately that she would look ridiculous, because Parisian dresses in no way flatter her type of beauty, nor her manner of walking or sitting. It may work fine for court ladies and ladies of high society who inhabit fully furnished palaces, but not for those simple little dolls that live in paper houses and sit on the ground upon well bleached mats.

Without doubt the Japanese woman is the cleanest woman in the world. Rich or poor, she has her daily—if not twice daily—bath. For the very poor there are the public bathhouses, free of charge, which are very frequented at all hours of the day and night. There everyone bathes *ensemble,* and the curious foreigner can witness some extraordinary scenes between the joints of the paper partitions that form its walls and doors. I say the foreigner because it would never occur to a Japanese to peep on such a scene. To the Japanese the nude body is nothing, and to expose either a portion or the whole of it does not strike them as the least indecent.

"After all," says the Japanese, "it's only the human body, and we are all of us made in the same image. If your body is clean and healthy, then why should one fear being seen undressed? Rather, shouldn't one fear to display it when it is sick and dirty?"

It was but a few years ago that the Japanese—whose homes are very small—still had the habit of carrying their baths into the street, and to bathe there in full view of passersby—men, women, and children. With the invasion of European civilization, however, the bathers were forced back into their little paper houses, and policemen—a new species that—with their gold-buttoned blue uniforms then went only so far as to permit people to leave their doors open while they bathed . . . an Englishman had only to pass by . . . oh! *Shocking!*

There was even a time when a lady of the upper classes felt it perfectly natural to receive visitors from her bath.

Honni soit qui mal y pense!

Their Women 45

Two Japanese Belles.

Figure 10. "Two Japanese Belles," an illustration from Frank Brinkley's guidebook. Frank Brinkley, ed. *Japan*. Tokyo: J.B. Millet, Co., 1897.

In a small village between Yokohama and Kobe, where I spent several days, I found a fairly comfortable hotel—half-Japanese and half-European—whose name now escapes me. While undressing on the evening of my arrival, a young maidservant entered by room to inform me the hotel owned an English "tub," which they would bring to my room in the morning.

Indeed, I was awoken around seven o'clock by the appearance of this same *musume*[3] accompanied by an equally attractive girl who was helping her carry in the tub. After depositing it in the middle of the room they went to fetch the water. When my bath had been prepared they came rushing to my bedside (I'd been feigning sleep), grabbed hold of my covers and laughing wildly flung them off my bed.

"Come quick, quick, your bath is ready!"

It was pointless to ask them to leave . . . they would not have understood . . . and wasn't it their duty after all to serve and assist me? They unfolded some large towels and placed them down near the tub. Smiling, they then waited for me to finish, and still laughing proceeded to wipe, rub, and dry me, one concentrating on my lower body, and the other, standing on a chair, on my upper.

Dear little Japanese ladies, you are all charming, enchanting . . . don't change. There is nothing for you to envy in your Occidental sisters, for you already possess what so few of them do: happiness!

10 Their Children

Chubby and round with large black eyes at once cheerful and dumbfounded, with their shaved heads sporting here and there an ornamental pigtail, they are charming and adorable those Japanese babies. They've been described as delightful little dolls dressed as for a costumed ball. These are the happiest children on earth. Born in a country where anger is all but unknown, where gentleness, politesse, and good manners are, alongside courage, the most admired of traits, Japanese children are never scolded or hit, and never, ever do their parents stoop so low as to harm them. They possess a gentle temper, and are not crybabies, bullies, nor brats. It would never occur to them to bite, scratch or kick—they are patience, calm, and wisdom personified.

The Japanese mother nurses her own children and during their first few years never lets them leave her side. Regardless of her social position, she cares for them herself night and day. Those poor women who must work all day, unwilling and unable to separate themselves from their children, attach their babies to their backs with a large belt or type of shawl.

The mother can attend to all her daily chores while the baby sleeps peacefully astride her back or gazes about curiously at the goings on around him, its small head shaking and rolling to the left and right with each movement. We foreigners may pity its fate, afraid lest its tiny neck be unable to endure such intense gymnastics. But the neck of a Japanese baby is made of well tempered steel: it yields but it does not break.

A certain English lady desired one day to try out the weight of a child carried in this manner, and of the fatigue that would result from it.

"Can you imagine," she recounted afterwards, "the experience really defies description. You might naturally think the baby would be so much dead weight on your back, but not at all. As young as it is, the baby takes hold of you tight . . . one gets the impression he's really stuck to you, holding on with all the strength in his small body. He becomes one with the person carrying him, and just like a skilled horseman conforms himself to all the movements of his mount, the little Japanese baby seems able to sense your movements even before you make them, and refuses to be dislodged no matter how abrupt they are."

Children of the upper classes are not carried on the back, and the middle classes as well have in the last few years come to adopt our baby carriages. Japanese families are large, and from the age of six or seven the eldest daughter replaces her mother as guardian of the youngest baby, which she carries bravely on her small back. Her new charge, however, in no way prevents her from going out with her friends—or of scampering about, jumping, running, or playing.

Figure 11. Japanese children in the 1890s. Private Collection of Mr. Christophe Schwarzenbach, Switzerland. From: M.Winkel, *Souvenirs From Japan*, 1991, p. 43. Used by permission.

Their Children

It is an unforgettable sight to see these pretty Japanese children of seven to twelve years, dressed in kimonos of striking colors, each one carrying on her back a little brother or sister while engrossed in their favorite games. They jump, run, yell and laugh with all their heart while the baby, perched on her back, follows the action with extraordinary joy, laughing and yelling as strongly as its little lungs allow. There can be nothing so picturesque as a Japanese park filled with such frolicking children.

To a Japanese man the prospect of not having children is a dreadful one. If a man's wife remains childless after a year or two of marriage he divorces her or takes a concubine who, though she may end up being the mother of his children, will maintain her status below that of the legitimate wife, whom she must always obey.

Great is the joy in a Japanese house when a child is born, especially if that child is a boy. Every Japanese family owns a large pole set up in their courtyard, which rises three or four times as high as the house. At certain times of the year large painted fish, inflated like balloons, float gaily above the pole, their numbers indicating how many boys the house can boast. The Japanese have chosen the carp pendant to indicate the number of boys. This animal, which always chooses to ascend the most violent currents, is for the Japanese a symbol of courage and perseverance. Following the example of the Chinese and Koreans, small Japanese lads once sported queues, but these have lately disappeared with the adoption of western values and ideas.

One curious custom has parents, family friends, and acquaintances visiting a newborn with gifts and well wishes.

There is a quarter of Tokyo composed entirely of children's toy merchants. It is a perpetual carnival and the source of immeasurable happiness and indescribable joy. What's more, Japan is a country of children's festivals; and there are as many for girls as there are for boys.

In mid-November all children flock to their neighborhood temple to thank the gods for having thus far watched over them. This annual visit to the temple is the occasion for a charming parade, the children all dressed up in colorful new clothes.

The New Year's festival is the most important of them all. For an entire week, children, parents, and grandparents let themselves go in a surfeit of celebration. In the afternoon they visit others or receive visitors, exchange numerous gifts, stuff the children with small cakes and candies and give them every imaginable sort of toy. They take aimless rides in jinrikisha or on the electric tram, and in the evening, after a veritable feast, the entire family loses itself in lively games.

The most important festival for young girls is the "Doll Festival." On this day families bring all of their prized dolls out from their cabinets. Some families possess dolls over a century old, all dressed up in the costumes of their epoch. Every doll comes with its trousseau, its lacquered furniture, silverware, porcelain, crockery, musical instruments, and precious mother of pearl boxes. Some are dressed in rich and fabulous costumes representing the Emperor and Empress, or celebrated men and women honored by Japan. The celebration lasts three days, three unforgettable days for a girl, during which all these marvelous dolls are hers; she can play with them, dress and undress them, change their toilette, throw tea parties or hold receptions, and in short, enjoy a happiness not to be equaled.

For the boys, the doll festival is replaced with the "Flag Festival," which takes place in May. On this occasion gifts are presented just as on New Year's Day, consisting mostly of toys. Sabers, rifles, pistols, cannons, drums, trumpets, and military helmets are the gifts most cherished by the martial-spirited Japanese boys. In each Japanese house a small alter is built upon which are placed small figurines representing all the heroes of Japan. Behind each of these is a flag with the person's coat of arms and at its feet all sort of miniature weaponry.

The clothing of the Japanese baby is simplicity itself: a single long open robe which can in no way injure the baby or hinder its movement. Quickly put on and taken off, in this way the baby is not burdened or annoyed by that old and cumbersome custom of placing it on its back or stomach so as to wrap it in the linen, tape, and clothing which will hold it prisoner and restrict all its movements.

When a Japanese baby cries it is not rocked, or taken for a stroll, or told to be quiet, or soothed; it is simply left to cry, and as a result it quickly loses the taste for it. When it neither annoys nor elicits concern, there remain few reasons to cry.

As extraordinary as it may seem to us, the Japanese child has an instinctive and striking fear of we foreigners. Is it because we appear in their eyes so different from their parents (this conclusion seems quite possible since the blonder the foreigner the greater the Japanese child's terror)? Is it because when they misbehave they are threatened (but oh so gently!) with the prospect of the foreign devil, just like we talk in the west of goblins? I don't know, but what is certain is that they find us all frightfully ugly and to them we are just so many bogeymen.

11 At the Imperial Court

Before the momentous events of forty years ago that sent the empire into upheaval and then marked its embarkation along the path of civilization and progress, Japan was a nation of dual courts.

In the ancient capital of Kyoto, surrounded by a few loyal courtesans, the Mikado lived a modest, even impoverished, existence—scorned, forgotten, and voiceless in the management of state affairs.

At Yedo, now become the capital as Tokyo, the shogun lived a life of unrestrained luxury. He was a usurper whose base of support was the nation's nobility. These latter could be divided into two large groups, composed of the samurai, or lesser nobility, who held the right to carry a sword (sometimes even two), and the *daimyo*, great and powerful lords who controlled the land and its fortified castles.

As everyone knows, one fine day the young Mikado (the actual emperor), exhausted and disgusted with the idle and dishonorable life that had been imposed upon him, resolved to reclaim his throne. With a poignant appeal to his people and the nobility, and surrounded by his partisans, he quit the ancient palace of Kyoto and headed for Yedo determined to offer battle to the shogun.

His appeal echoed among the thousands of *daimyo* and samurai: abandon the usurper and gather round the banner of your true sovereign. The struggle was horrendous and bloody, for in battle the Japanese have the courage of lions and do not pale before death.

In the end victory fell to the young Mikado, who established himself at Yedo, changing its name to Tokyo and himself assuming the title of emperor. His ministers, the very same men who had criticized the shogun for his initiatives towards progress, now signed treaties of commerce and amity with the foreign powers, and overnight Japan found itself inoculated with the desire to civilize itself, and to accept in mass all the ideas, customs, and progress of the Occident. This was a second revolution, from which Japan emerged stronger, healthier, and more vigorous than it had ever been and from which were born all the country's most estimable institutions—the army, navy, ministries, parliament, senate, and universities.

The time and care to which it dedicated to creating this new reality did not stop the emperor from dreaming of his own court, nor of repaying those without whose support he could never have triumphed. The titles of the samurai and *daimyo* vanished to be replaced by a new nobility comprised of princes, marquises, counts, viscounts, and barons. If in naval matters Japan imitated England, for its court the Tuileries was its inspiration, namely the glorious reign of Napoleon III and the Empress Eugénie.

Who would have thought that thirty odd years later the Tuileries would cease to exist, while the court at Tokyo, growing more brilliant by the day, would be the equal in every manner to the great European courts, and would even extend its hand across Asia to partner with the court of St. James?[1]

The new imperial palace in Tokyo is a beautiful structure equipped with the latest comforts. I had the opportunity to view Their Majesties on several occasions. The first was on the occasion of a small presentation the emperor desired me to give one evening at the palace. This presentation—illustrated by numerous electric slide projections—was given in a large impressive hall, whose lacquered doors alone were worth a fortune.[2]

In the first row two large armchairs had been arranged for Their Majesties, and behind them chairs had been set up for the ladies, gentlemen, and officials of the court. I was presented by the Minister of the Imperial Household, the Viscount Hijikata.

The emperor kept his hair fairly long and had a moustache as well as an imperial.[3] He wore a dark uniform that resembled those worn by senior officers of the French artillery. The empress was dressed very elegantly in the European style, as were all the court ladies.

The two sovereigns took the keenest interest in everything I said and all the images I displayed, and by their numerous queries demonstrated to me they were thoroughly abreast of European and American affairs. Having thanked me—the emperor with a few words, and the empress with a charming smile—Their Majesties retired and I was then escorted by the Viscount Hijikata, Baron Kido, and Baron Sannomiya to another large hall where I found a large table covered in flowers and gold and crystal settings. Servants in embroidered uniforms, knee-breeches, and silk stockings (as I said, the Tuileries!) then served us a marvelous dinner. The chef was a Frenchman, the wines and liquors of the best vintage and the cigars fine Havanas.

Figure 12. Mutsuhito, the Emperor Meiji, around 1895. *L'Illustration* (29 December 1894).

Not long afterwards, I had the honor of again seeing Their Majesties on the occasion of a garden party that they hosted as part of the annual "cherry blossom festival." As lovers of beauty, and therefore of nature, the Japanese hold festivals to celebrate the seasons and different flowers. The most celebrated are the cherry blossoms in spring and chrysanthemums in autumn.

In my opinion, the cherry blossoms are the more beautiful. There are thousands of such trees in Japan. In Tokyo immense cherry trees line some avenues and fill certain parks, and in the spring they are covered in enormous white and pink blooms. (While these colossal trees produce large flowers they do not bear any fruit.) At these times the city has an unforgettable fairytale quality to it.

At Uyeno Park, one of the largest parks in the capital, there is a veritable forest of cherry trees, whose white and pink blossoms contrast nicely with the darker foliage of the other trees. Under these cherry trees hundreds of flat tables are set up and covered in red cloth to await the tea drinkers—men, women, and children—who arrive in droves. There are no chairs, however, for the Japanese don't make use of these tables the way we would: they take off their shoes and climb on top of them!

Figure 13. Cherry Blossoms in Tokyo's Uyeno Park (1890s). Private Collection of Mr. Christophe Schwarzenbach, Switzerland. From: M.Winkel, *Souvenirs From Japan*, 1991, p. 125.

At the Imperial Court

Now, at the time these cherry blossoms were in bloom the emperor and empress threw a garden party in one of the imperial parks. The invitees included the court, certain prominent individuals then in view, and members of the government and diplomatic corps. These latter enjoyed the privilege of bringing along foreign guests, persons of distinction then passing through Tokyo. For the men, a uniform or frock coat was de rigueur, and no lady dared show herself without being made up in the most elegant fashion. This always poses a challenge for the globe-trotter, for as distinguished as he might be it doesn't always occur to him to pack a frock coat and full dress before setting off on an Asian tour.

I recall a Madame D.G.S . . . in particular, a charming American lady, well known in Paris and Cannes, whom I accompanied on a mad dash through all the city's Chinese and Japanese tailor shops, while her husband and brother turned Tokyo inside out in search of two silk hats. They eventually succeeded in finding what they were after and appeared at the garden party. She was deliciously elegant, *in spite of all* . . . as for the men . . . oh lord! Yes, they got their hats, but they must have dated back to the time of Robespierre and had as likely witnessed the Revolution!

The guests at the garden party gathered in the park near the entrance gate to await the arrival of the sovereigns. They finally appeared, followed by members of the court and all the invitees. The emperor wore a general's uniform and the empress a stunning dress of grey silk. We then took a small tour of the park, which was scattered with several military bands. Arriving at a large tent where a buffet was being served, Their Majesties stopped at the entrance to receive the respects of the diplomatic corps, the Japanese ministers, and the like. After having a bit to eat the sovereigns departed by carriage, whereupon the invitees—Japanese and foreigner—uncorked the champagne and let it flow.

The cherry blossoms were gone and it was frightfully cold when I saw the emperor for the third time. This was at a military review that took place in honor of his birthday—at seven in the morning in the month of November! I had to leave my hotel at five-thirty in the morning and dress coat, yes, in evening dress, since I did not possess a uniform! Only members of the diplomatic corps and those having an official mission had been invited.

The emperor had us waiting quite a while and we were all shivering with cold by the time he arrived, followed by marshals and generals and a brilliant General Staff, among which I was pleased to notice the light cavalry uniform of the French military attaché.

The procession of twenty thousand select troops of such admirable bearing and discipline was truly a spectacle to behold. The entire Chinese embassy was there, watching without much apparent interest and scorning these troops which a little later would crush their country!

I had the occasion to be of some service to the ladies of the court. At my request, Her Majesty the Empress had desired to form a committee of ladies in charge of organizing an exposition about women's work in Japan for the exposition at Chicago. Her Majesty pledged to cover the expenses of the undertaking herself and named Princess Mori president of the committee which also included Marquise Oyama, Marquise Nabeshima, Countess Inouye, Viscountess Hijikata, Madame Mutsu, and Baroness Sannomiya. In short, the most intelligent and influential lades of the court and government.

A little bit later the Marquis Kido, Master of the Empress's Court, informed me that these ladies wished to discuss their work with me. Thus it was decided that the members of the commission would meet at the imperial palace where I then went to join them.

The meeting, held under the direction of the Princess Mori, went on for four hours—from three to seven o'clock—in a most animated manner. There were several dozen ladies present—to the very tips of their toes, venerable ladies all. Nearly all of them spoke one foreign language, and often several, and in the course of the meeting all the questions under discussion were discussed, adopted or rejected with the utmost intelligence and efficiency.

At seven o'clock, thinking these ladies as fatigued as myself, I wished to take my leave of the princess.

"Oh, but no!" she cried. "Why you must be dying of hunger, and we won't allow you to leave like that."

She stood up and taking my arm guided me towards the large lacquered doors, the rest of the ladies following. The doors opened before her to reveal in the adjoining room a fully set table where I then had the honor of taking my place besides all these charming ladies, the most illustrious in Japan.

The meal was delicious, but it got better.

A few months later, just before my departure, the Marquis Kido paid me a call to pass on the following communication:

"Princess Mori and the ladies of the Commission are deeply grateful for the help you have given them. To demonstrate their gratitude, as well as the commitment they have to their work, Her Highness wishes to invite you, as well as Mr. W . . . [4], director of the exposition, and his wife, who are now en route to Tokyo, to a banquet. Her Highness has a genuine Japanese dinner in mind, such as the princes traditionally enjoyed. She thinks it would be of greater interest to you than a European style dinner now so routine at court."

The banquet was held as planned and I will be eternally grateful to Princess Mori and her friends for the absolutely delightful evening they gave me.

None of the ladies were dressed in European fashion as I'd always seen them before, and at first it was difficult to recognize them. Now they all were decked in magnificent Japanese court dresses such as were traditionally worn and whose beauty and extravagance are really beyond my abilities to describe.

What colors! What a tableau for the brush of a great artist! Alas! It is truly regrettable to think that all of these admirable costumes worthy of a queen, of a museum, are disappearing . . . what am I saying? . . . have disappeared to be replaced by the monstrosities coming out of Paris and London!

The dining room was quite large indeed, and longer than it was wide. At one end, silk cushions on the floor provided places for the princess and her three invited guests. The other ladies (there were no Japanese men) were all seated along one side for the length of the room. Each course—and they were innumerable—was carried separately to each guest upon small platformed plates which also served as tables.

All the dishes were excellent, and none of them resembled any of the dishes you typically find in a Japanese restaurant. To my great surprise, following each Japanese dish came a plate prepared by the court's French chef: poultry, pâté, etc. Clearly the princess had feared the national dishes might not be to our tastes.

Towards the end of the meal a number of court dancers dressed in fantastically opulent costumes performed a series of very beautiful dances and scenes. One of these dances, called "Butterflies," involved dancers with silk and gauze embroidered wings, which they opened and closed in cadence. It was quite stunning.

At the end of the banquet the princess was brought three packages wrapped in embroidered silk. Turning towards us, she spoke:

"Formerly there was a tradition among the princely families of Japan to drink from a silver cup to the health of any family member about to depart on a voyage. Friends were invited to a farewell dinner, at the conclusion of which the silver cup filled with wine was passed around to all those present, concluding with the one departing on the voyage. This evening we want to revive this old custom, and before saying farewell—for you are leaving us—drink to your health!"

The princess then opened the silken packages, which contained stunning silver sake cups with the royal coat of arms in relief. She drank, and then the little cup was passed around to each one of these charming ladies, who wetted their lips with the wine and expressed a wish for our continued happiness. And after I had drunk in my turn the princess wrapped one of these cups back into the embroidered silk:

"Take it," she said. "To remember! . . ."

12 The Real Madame Chrysanthemum

To Pierre Loti

This story was recounted to me by a young Englishman. It's none the worse for that, and may even bring a smile to the face of that renowned academic.[1]

After pulling out of Nagasaki, our boat, a vessel of the Japanese steamer company Nippon Yusen Kaisha, was heading full-steam towards the Inland Sea. I was enjoying a smoke on deck with a certain Lord A . . . , a large young man of twenty years, strong as an ox, stubborn as a mule, and as simple as a school girl . . . but to the point.

We were discussing the beauties of Nagasaki when I remarked that it had been "admirably described by Loti." At the mention of this name he gave a sudden start, his face reddening, and exclaimed,

"Ah yes, Loti! Now there's a laugh. And his Madame Chrysanthemum . . . What a joke!"

He muttered a few 'damns' between his teeth before turning to me. "I must tell you of an extraordinary adventure I had at Nagasaki, and one which should be made known around the world, because this Loti, he's a fake! Yes, and a liar!

"You see, between Shanghai and Nagasaki I had reread *Madame Chrysanthemum,* a book I admired above all others, and I thought to myself, 'If she is still alive, this Madame Chrysanthemum, I absolutely must track her down and have a talk with her. That's it, I'll interview her. We all know what Loti thought of her, he still hasn't tired of relating and publishing his account. What remains to be discovered is what *she* thinks of *him.* Ah yes, mister naval officer, we know your opinions, now we want to know hers.'

"And so, as soon as I'd arrived in Nagasaki and secured a hotel room, I found the best guide available and inquired:

'Have you ever heard of a Madame Chrysanthemum?'
'Hai! Hai!' he said grimacing.
'The one of Pierre Loti?'
'Hai! Hai!'
'And do you know her?'
'Hai! Hai!'
'You know where she lives then?'
'Hai! Hai!'
'Very well, take me to her.'

"Well, this rascal, smiling even wider, cried out, 'Nay, nay,' and I was given to understand eventually that this Madame Chrysanthemum had become so annoyed by tourists of all sorts hoping to see her, that she had taken refuge in the countryside so that it had become very difficult, if not impossible, to meet her.

"However, now the brute told me he was willing to make some efforts to obtain me an interview with her that very day, but this was only possible through several intermediaries, all of whom it would be necessary to pay, so that the total cost would be something like fifty dollars.

'I'll go for fifty dollars,' I said, thinking it was a cheap price for obtaining something I had desired so dearly. While he was engaged with the arrangements I went and lunched with the consul. Over dessert the consul invited me to spend the afternoon with one of his colleagues. I responded that I would gladly go but only for half an hour, being obliged to return to my hotel, where I hoped to find Madame Chrysanthemum prepared to meet me.

"With a dumbfounded look the consul asked, 'What do you mean Madame Chrysanthemum?' I recounted to him the arrangements I had made with my guide, after which he replied in a most calm manner, 'Ah! Perfect.'

"Arriving at the home of the other consul, we found on the terrace a dozen or so guests, smoking and enjoying iced drinks. I took a seat, had a smoke and a drink, and at the end of half an hour got up to leave. Some of the guests tried convincing me to stay.

'No, no,' the consul said smiling. 'Let him go, it's important. He has a rendezvous with Madame Chrysanthemum.'

"As soon as these words left his lips the whole group exploded in laughter so loud it shook the house. They had tears in their eyes and twisted in their chairs like epileptics.

"Naturally, I was furious, all the more so since the cause of their amusement completely escaped me. Finally, the laughing stopped, and the consul addressed the gathering,

'My friends, Lord A . . . is a jolly good fellow, who was very warmly recommended to me, and I think it my duty to put an end to this and give him the entire truth.' All the others approving this sentiment, he turned towards me,

'Please forgive our laughter. It was impossible to hold it back. You'll understand better when I tell you that there are hundreds of Chrysanthemums in Nagasaki, it's a common enough name. The one you are seeking, the Chrysanthemum of Loti, does not and never has existed except in the mind of that charming writer.'

'Impossible!' I cried. 'So the house and the marriage and all the rest?'

'All the rest, my good man,' the consul continued, 'exists in one corner or other of Japan. It is our life, more or less, as Loti *saw,* but not *lived,* it. As for the house, there are numerous others just like it up in the hills. He observed and described things from the naval vessel on which he served—his marriage, the women, his house, all these things were born of his own imagination.'

"Not yet prepared to admit defeat, I cried out, 'But I've encountered many globe-trotters who claimed to have seen Madame Chrysanthemum!'"

'Ah!' the consul exclaimed. 'I don't doubt that at all. Introducing Madame Chrysanthemum to globe-trotters has become a very lucrative business for Nagasaki guides in recent years. When they realized all these foreigners disembarking with copies of Loti's novel under their arms were prepared to pay for the privilege of meeting his heroine, they naturally didn't refuse the money. All the guides, much like your own, are ready to introduce her in exchange for some dollars; to them it's always the *true* Chrysanthemum, it's just not always the *same* Chrysanthemum. As for the price of the interview, that varies from five to a hundred dollars, according to the quality of your baggage.'

"And there you have my adventure," continued Lord A . . . , "and the more I think about it the more extraordinary it seems."

He settled back into his chair, took two or three puffs on his cigar, and, with the most satisfied air in the world, added,

"That Loti! But I found him out—what a fraud!"

13 A Visit with His Excellency, the Governor of O . . .

To Madame Melba[1]

In the large towns and cities of Japan, such as Yokohama, Tokyo, or Kobe, the European traveler can find all the comforts of home. There the hotels are first-rate and thoroughly modern, the cuisine and the service perfect, and with prices that could hardly be more reasonable. The Grand Hotel of Yokohama, and above all the Imperial in Tokyo, can compare in every aspect to their finest European counterparts. The history of the Imperial is particularly interesting.

During the period when the Japanese were setting out to adopt the ideas and manners of the Occident, they sent a number of delegations to Europe and America in order to study a given subject in detail and to draw up a comprehensive report for the emperor upon their return. In this manner, year after year special commissioners were sent abroad to study naval, military, university matters, and the like. The commissioners rarely failed—though I wouldn't say never—the result being that Japan's universities were inspired by those of Germany, its navy by that of England, and its army by that of France. This was all prior to 1870. The Franco-Prussian War dealt them a severe shock. Thereupon a military mission was immediately dispatched to Berlin and the round Prussian helmet was not long in replacing the French kepi atop the heads of Japanese soldiers. The army was Germanized. A few years later, however, and Germany too lost some ground, and now one sees clearly the influence of different nations on different branches of service. The artillery has been inspired by France, the cavalry by Russia, and the infantry by the German general staff. Since the war with China the Japanese army has undergone a *japanization* of sorts.[2] With extensive battlefield experience, Japanese officers have been able to improve their armed forces, without allowing them to fall under the influence of European ideas.

After having "adopted" our senates and parliaments, our ministries and titles of nobility, our frock coats and evening tails, one day the Japanese asked themselves if they oughtn't to adopt one of the Occidental religions as well. In short, they decided to treat themselves to an official religion, a state religion. Without further delay a commission was formed with the intent of investigating this question throughout the world. It fell to this commission to decide whether Japan should be Catholic or Protestant! But the final report of the commission threw cold water on the plan. According to them, adopting an official religion would be exceedingly expensive while bringing little benefit, least of all on questions of morality—for the commission had discovered as many vices among those having a state religion as those without! And so Japan remained Buddhist, Shinto, and above all, free-thinking.

But to return to the Imperial Hotel. Formerly Tokyo had only insignificant little inns, so uncomfortable that whenever an important ambassador or visitor arrived the government was obliged to offer them rooms in one of the imperial palaces. Needless to say this became quite expensive and troublesome. For these two very good reasons, it was decided that a first class hotel, a true modern "palace," should be built in Tokyo. A committee was formed comprised of members of the court and government. The emperor himself underwrote a good part of the capital, and a certain Mr. Yokoyama, a Japanese of first rate intelligence who had traveled through many of the countries of the world, was delegated to head up the enterprise. He made one more trip, this time returning with plans, and it is to him that we owe the Imperial, a magnificent hotel that combines American comfort, English service, and French cuisine!

However, if excellent hotels exist in the large cities, the traveler to small villages and countryside will find only traditional Japanese inns. These establishments are always meticulously clean and their owners and staff friendly and courteous, but the food agrees neither with our tastes nor our stomachs, and the comforts we are accustomed to are nowhere to be had. Chairs are replaced by small flat cushions placed on the floor and the bed consists of padded blankets also placed on the floor—one underneath you and the other on top.

The mission upon which I was sent to Japan led me in the month of June to O . . . , a small village known for its baths where the Japanese inns had such a poor reputation that I was more than happy to accept the invitation of the village governor when offered his hospitality. Naturally, he also lived in the Japanese style.

Our dinner on the evening of my arrival was as gay as can be imagined, with excellent sake (rice brandy that is drunk warm), to which the governor, his wife and daughters did great honor. The little housemaids that served us were as delightful as dolls, and the geishas, whose music, singing, and dancing enlivened the evening, were most spirited and engaging.

At seven the next morning I was awakened by my domestic Arai informing me,

"Sir, your bath is ready."

"Very good, Arai. Where is the washroom?" I asked, jumping out of bed.

But Arai just shook his head.

"There isn't one, sir."

"Well then Arai, where is the tub?"

He pointed his yellow finger in the direction of my paper windows:

"Why over there, sir!"

A bit chagrined, I headed towards the partition I knew opened up on to the garden. I pushed open one of the screens and was amazed by the site—as extraordinary as it was unexpected—which then greeted me.

On this splendid June morning, the garden with its fabricated streams and lakes, its bridges and lanterns of stone, and its radiant flowers, was truly a wondrous, idyllic spot. But if this sunlit and fragrant scene charmed me, the scene that animated it had quite the opposite effect. A few meters from the house, in the midst of flowers, I could make out a wooden Japanese "tub" looking like a large barrel, encircled by the governor, his wife and daughters, and the little servant girls, all dressed up . . . well, like Adam and Eve. Thinking that they had just finished their bathing and not wishing to disturb them, as well as being—shall I confess?—a bit shy myself, I shut the partition and turned towards my servant.

"Well Arai," I asked. "Are they finished now?"

"Oh no sir, on the contrary. They wait for you."

"What? Waiting for me? What on earth for?"

"Why, to take bath with you, sir. In Japan the polite way says you must take bath the first. After you, then come the governor and wife, then daughters, then servants. It is great honor for them to be there to help you . . . you, most honorable and distinguished guest!"

"Arai," I replied with all seriousness. "There is only one problem. I don't have a bathing outfit."

Arai smiled modestly, "Oh, they don't have also sir."

"Yes, but they are accustomed to it and I am not. Arai, how about I decline my bath this morning."

"Oh sir," he replied, vigorously shaking his head. "Impossible. After that you will be taken as dirty man. In Japan nothing is worse. It will be disaster for your mission."

There was nothing left to be said then. My modesty had to be sacrificed for duty.

"Very well then, Arai," I said resolutely, making my way towards the door. "I'll go."

But he stopped me, and to comprehend what follows one must first understand that everything in Japan is *small:* plants as well as men. I, however, had the misfortune of being rather tall.

"Sir," Arai said. "You should take off pajamas here. There is nothing in the garden large enough to hang them from."

Alas, so take them off I did. Arai then opened the door and I advanced through flowerbeds towards the "tub" as majestically as possible . . .

The governor and his family rushed towards me and we exchanged a number of greetings, and then his Excellency fell into raptures over the straightness of my legs, something quite rare among Japanese. He asked permission to touch my knees which to him appeared quite different than his own, something the women wished to do likewise . . .

Finally I reached the tub and dunked my right leg in first . . . But with a cry of pain I immediately snatched it out . . . the water was *boiling!* The Japanese take their baths at a temperature we simply cannot tolerate.

Furious, I turned on Arai:

"You brute! You know very well I take my baths *cold.*"

"Yes, sir, and I tell them yesterday evening. But they don't want to believe me. They think it is joke . . ."

The bath, as large as three large barrels, then had to be emptied and refilled. This all took three quarters of an hour, during which, "draped in my majesty," I stood like a marble statue; the others, they were more like statues of bronze, and it really seemed to me as if they were less naked than myself!

When I was finally able to take my cold bath, and after the charming little housemaids had dried me off, the governor announced with a series of deep bows that his turn had come. Poor Excellency! Japanese etiquette demanded that he bathe in my water,* and for him, accustomed to boiling water, it was a frightful torture to have to plunge into this cold bath. But he suffered it bravely with little guttural cries and grimaces. Then it was the turn of his wife, of his daughters, and then the housemaids, all of whom shrieked as they plunged into the icy pool and emerged with teeth chattering.

I left O . . . that same day, fearing that all these misfortunes could lead only to pleurisy or pneumonia. Ah, Japanese politesse!!!

Famille japonaise au bain.

Figure 14. Japanese women enjoying a traditional bath, late 19th century. *La Revue Hébdomadaire* (1902).

---

* One does not lather up before taking a hot bath, but merely plunges in [author note].

14 The Missionary

Though apparently a woman I can assure you there was nothing of the weaker sex about her save her name. Oh Lord, I can still recall the fearsome punch to the face she dealt me, a brutal cure for my sea sickness that had me seeing a million stars.

I first made her acquaintance during my second Pacific crossing aboard an old steamer whose name now escapes me. We were six passengers in all: two American journalists who must have had Gascon ancestors,[1] another American who suffered from attacks of delirium tremens, a fourth American on his way to sell the Chinese (a prolific race) an extraordinary remedy—which apparently would curb the fecundity of both Chinese and rabbits—the missionary, and myself.

She was large, very large, boney, and as broad shouldered as a grenadier. Her inordinately long arms were finished off by enormous hands. Her face was extremely long and covered with a yellow, parchment-like skin. On her crooked nose perched a pair of huge spectacles. Her lips were so thin that her mouth, enormous when it opened to reveal a set of yellowed teeth, was practically invisible when shut.

She clashed with every one of the passengers, with the captain, even with the Chinese servants.

"Mam," the man suffering from delirium tremens exclaimed to her one day, "in the United States there are five hundred thousand drunkards like me and at least three hundred thousand women who tip the bottle on a daily basis; there must be about ten million human beings who believe neither in god nor the devil; there are thieves, pimps, murderers, and blackguards of every sort and degree. That's not to mention the hundreds of thousands who suffer from cold, hunger, and sickness. Why then, in the name of the God you claim to represent, don't you occupy yourself with all these wretches instead of going to pester the Chinese and Japanese who want nothing to do with you and are quite fed up with you?"

When traveling to Japan via the Pacific you lose an entire day. We went to bed one Saturday evening to awake not on Sunday but on Monday morning. When our brave missionary discovered that the captain had pilfered Sunday she practically fell into apoplectic fits. She stormed the captain's bridge with such fury, demanding by what right he had stolen "The Lord's Day," that he decided to switch the dates back. The breakfast menu had read Monday, but the lunch and dinner menus now read Sunday. The missionary was pacified, but soon the male passengers had their turn at rebellion.

About our only distraction aboard ship was poker, and on this particular American steamer line card playing was strictly forbidden on Sunday. We were seated in the smoking room and ready to play a hand when the steward stepped in to announce,

"Sirs, no card playing on Sunday."

We now fell upon the bridge, making a series of bitter and furious complaints to the captain.

"Well, captain," we cried. "Is it Sunday or is it Monday? If it was Monday an hour ago at breakfast, as the menu states, then how in the devil can it now be Sunday?"

Thoroughly torn between the missionary who refused to give up the Lord's Day and the other passengers who refused to give up their cards, the brave captain suddenly hit upon a brilliant idea:

"Well one must please the good Lord as well as the gamblers. It will be Sunday before noon and then Monday after." Enraged, our missionary finally gave way.

A few weeks later she and I were again passengers aboard a Japanese steamer with service between Korea and northeast China. It was an old style ship, with a long and narrow galley lighted from above. The cabins were all arranged around the galley and opened on to it. At night this room was lighted by lamps which also illuminated the cabin interiors as the doors on these latter had glass portholes.

We departed Nagasaki under a horrible gale and the passengers immediately vanished into their respective cabins. Having tolerably good sea legs, I remained on the bridge. With nightfall, however, the storm's furor worsened and a horrible smell of oil and garlic now emanated from the galley. Suddenly I felt deathly ill and I headed for my cabin. Apparently the steward responsible for lighting up the galley was likewise sick, for the lamps had not been illuminated making the place as dark as the grave. Groping along, I managed to find the door to my cabin, within which it was equally dark. Entering, I dropped down on the stool next to the toilet and began undressing as quickly as possible in the hope of getting to bed before having to pay my tribute to Neptune. Tossing my clothes haphazardly on the upper bunk, I then groped on the bottom bunk trying to locate my nightshirt when suddenly I was compelled to stick my head in the washbasin.

Anyone who has ever been seasick knows the effect it can have and just how ill it can make you. They will also easily appreciate how utterly indifferent I was to my nudity when the priority was proximity to the toilet. In fact, I never even considered it. I had only one idea: "my bed," and I threw myself upon it.

What happened next almost defies description. Rather than falling upon my mattress, I dropped on top of the soundly sleeping missionary! She awoke screaming:

"Thief! Murderer!" Attempting to lift myself up on my hands, two of my fingers then became lodged in her mouth, and now half smothered she bit into them furiously. She then landed a formidable punch to my face that sent me reeling from the bed.

At the same moment the lamps in the galley were suddenly illuminated and when she saw my naked state her cries turned to shrieks. From the top bunk I grabbed the first piece of clothing available and wrapped it around my body. Alas! This particular piece of clothing didn't belong to me . . . it was a pair of woman's knickers which opened up in the very place they should have been closed! However, as she looked like she were ready to attack me, and because her first punch still had me smarting, I opted to rush from the cabin—her cabin I must confess, her knickers in hand. Exiting the cabin I ran into the captain and purser who had naturally arrived in alarm upon hearing the woman's screams. As soon as they saw me they were overcome with fits of laughter, and became positively delirious when the missionary appeared in her hatchway screaming, "My knickers you villain! Give me back my knickers!"

I returned them in exchange for my own clothes, and now completely recovered from my attack of sea sickness, I recounted what had happened to the captain and how in the darkness I had entered the wrong cabin. The next day we arrived at Fusan.[2] The missionary went immediately to her consul and tried to have me arrested for indecency. She wanted ten thousand francs in damages for the danger that had been posed . . . to her virtue.

It is not my intention to pass off "my missionary" as the typical missionary type. She was ugly, old and cantankerous; and I admit I have encountered any number of female missionaries who were friendly, intelligent, interesting, and dedicated to their work. Among American female missionaries I have encountered many that were quite young, gracious and indeed pretty. It is difficult to judge the work being done by Catholic and Protestant missionaries in Asia. From a purely religious standpoint, that is to say "conversion" and the "salvation of souls," those most informed in the matter say the result has been nil.

The Asiatic becomes Christian not because he has been convinced by the missionary, not because he senses himself touched by divine grace, not because he believes in our religion and in our God, but simply because he finds in conversion a material advantage, particularly in the case of Protestantism. I would even venture that in discussing this issue one must distinguish between Catholic and Protestant missionaries.

The former are animated by nothing but the triumph of the Faith. They live simply and modestly in the manner of the natives. By contrast, the Protestant missionaries live in relative luxury. Over there they are people of consequence, veritable lords of the manor.

A married Protestant missionary receives 7,500 francs a year; he is lodged for free, usually in one of the best homes in the area; he is furnished with all sorts of medications free of charge and he receives, I believe, an extra 1,000 francs or more per year for each of his children. In a country where commodities cost next to nothing, where servant wages are absurdly low, a missionary can live like a prince and still set aside the bulk of his salary. If taking up missionary work in the Chinese interior calls for a certain amount of courage and self-abnegation in light of the dangers encountered, this is in no way the case with Japan, where representatives of foreign religions are completely protected.

It would be difficult to imagine a more calm, comfortable, or idyllic life than that of a Protestant missionary in Japan.

What then have they accomplished? From a purely religious standpoint, nothing I'm afraid. I repeat, a number of Japanese are Christians simply for its numerous advantages. They receive a thorough education free of charge, they learn foreign languages, they have the libraries of the missionaries at their disposal to continue their studies, and they are cared for during sickness and receive all the medication they need without paying a cent. For these reasons and still others, a number of Japanese are baptized, attend church, and seem to lead respectable Christian lives. But how many among them live and die as true and complete Christians in their hearts?—Not even five percent! From the purely Japanese standpoint, the missions are an excellent thing, for they have allowed thousands of them to get educated and begin to understand our civilization.

One must also recognize the fact that though the missionaries may fail at their task regarding the soul of the so-called converted, they nevertheless render services for civilization in Japan, their efforts generally resulting in the education of thousands of individuals in our ideas and values. Any effort that tends to bring people closer together in mutual understanding is a commendable one.

By contrast, in China the results have been disastrous. The extreme hatred of the foreigner the Chinese demonstrate today is due in great part to the missionaries.[3] One should not believe the Chinese detest the missionaries because they represent a God different from their own—nothing could be less true. In matters of religion the Chinese are perfectly tolerant, or at least they were before the word "Christian" became a byword for "reclamation, intervention, bombardment, indemnities, and loss of territory."

One must admit it is a thorny business! Had the missionaries in China been content to preach the gospel and tend the sick there would never have been any massacres. But as the Chinese might so aptly put it, "We happy, missionary come with bible, behind missionary come gunship, foreign devil follow with opium.* Mandarin say: 'Opium, no.' Then officers cry: "Opium, yes,' and they bombard, villages burning, men, women, children dead. Chinese say: 'Enough!' Later, foreign agent come and say: 'Buy guns, buy cannon, chase out devils.' Chinese buy at high cost and want take back stolen land. But guns no good, cannon too old. Foreign devil kill Chinese and take more land. Always like this." It's been no picnic, that's for certain.

Another complaint—and not the least of them—the Chinese have is the following: When a Chinese of bad character wishes to evade the laws of his country he has himself baptized. If after that the authorities have the misfortune of laying their hands on him, he calls for the missionary, who then summons a council and immediately threatens to call in a gunship!

---

* This was the British [author note].

The Chinese, like the Japanese of yesteryear, give a number or reasons why they cannot take our religion seriously. We will never succeed in making them believe that a man could have "stopped the sun in its course" and that the "good Lord" allowed him to continue to exterminate his enemies! It is also impossible for them to accept the idea of the flood. They will show you documents which certainly must predate the flood yet show no evidence of having taken a dunk.

What seems to them, for just reason, to be the height of contradiction is that all the foreigners—French, English, American, German, Spanish, and Italian—who come and preach neighborly love are full of mutual contempt and never lose a single opportunity of impeding or vilifying one another, and competing—by legitimate means or otherwise—in *saving* the most souls and making the most money!

To crown this edifice of hypocrisy and lies, these foreigners cannot even be understood to have the same God! For never, not until the crack of doom, could you ever make a Japanese or Chinese believe that the God of the Catholics, Presbyterians, Jews, Greeks, or Methodists is the same God.

And now Japan is invaded by the Salvation Army! But how in the devil will she recognize it amongst so many diverse religions, each one of whose representatives assures that, "mine is the only, the one, and the true!"

For the Japanese, who have an essentially critical nature and relish analysis, the difference between the doctrines of Christ and the manner in which they are understood by modern Christians is simply incomprehensible. Didn't Christ say, "Love thine enemies"?

A few years ago Mrs. S . . . , the wife of an American senator, went with her charming daughter to spend several months in Japan. Upon her arrival she hired the services of a young Japanese woman as her chamber maid. This Japanese woman was a Christian, had been baptized by the missionaries, and spoke tolerably good English. She carried out her duties admirably and her mistress was enchanted with her—until she began to notice the disappearance of several personal articles. At first these were mere trifles, but they were followed by others of more value, and eventually by silver and jewelry.

The thief was eventually uncovered and ended up being the Christian chamber maid. I can still recall how all the long-time foreign residents, those intimately familiar with the country, told Mrs. S . . . , "You were quite mistaken to hire a Japanese convert. The majority of these overnight Christians are disreputable young women, hypocrites, and pretend virgins. One simply cannot trust any Japanese that would debase themselves so far as to embrace a foreign religion."

That's one side of things, here is another: according to those who support the work of missionaries, their efforts in Japan are bearing fruit. Even if converts among all religious sects number no more than a hundred twenty thousand—about one third of one percent of the total population—their influence is nonetheless great. One finds Christians among members of Parliament, army and naval officers, and ministers. Young Christians are in great demand, businessmen and industrialists put great confidence in them. Finally, according to missionary leaders, Japanese Christians make the best husbands and treat their wives as absolute equals.

I cannot conclude this chapter without mentioning some truly admirable work accomplished by the Salvation Army not too long ago.

Previously I have discussed the Yoshiwara, but perhaps I did not make sufficiently clear that the unfortunate young women sold by their parents into the hands of brothel keepers became virtual slaves, and though it may have been their ardent desire to lead some other sort of life, they were utterly incapable of escaping. Their only hope was to be repurchased, but this occurred only rarely.

One can imagine the horrible position of these young girls, sold at an age when it would have been impossible for them to either understand what was happening or defend themselves.

The sale of young women has been illegal for some thirty years now, but flesh merchants can evade this difficulty by calling their sales "loans." To such loans, however, are added the costs of feeding, lodging, educating, and dressing these unfortunates, until the debt reaches such proportions that the poor girl can count only on death for her deliverance.

Japanese Christians have labored over the last fifteen years or so to foster a popular movement sympathetic to the plight of these girls, but without the least success.

In its turn, the Salvation Army has taken up the struggle. A special Japanese edition of its journal, *The War Cry,* was published and distributed in the streets of the Yoshiwara. It addressed itself to all these unfortunate women, advising them to abandon their life of vice and shame at once, while offering to take them in and protect them. Naturally, the brothel keepers and their employees attacked these "soldiers" of the Salvation Army, and after a frightful battle drove them out of the Yoshiwara.

Figure 15. An issue of *Toki no koe* (*The War Cry*), the Salvation Army's newspaper in Japan (1897). The Salvation Army.

But the battle so begun did not end there. The Tokyo press took up sides with the "Salvationists" and a vigorous campaign began which soon spread throughout Japan.

The government was eventually moved to promulgate new police ordinances, according to which brothel owners could no longer hold young women against their will. They now had to be paid in silver in either their own name or that of their family, and a simple request submitted to the police was all that was required to release them from their employment.

A few weeks after the publication of these new laws, fifteen percent of Tokyo prostitutes had quit the Yoshiwara, either to return to their families or to seek refuge with the Salvation Army.

It was a promising start.

15 From Tokyo to Tientsin

It proved a most interesting voyage. We were made quite comfortable aboard a vessel of the Japanese steamer company *Nippon Yusen Kaisha*. From Yokohama the boat makes its first leg to Kobe from whence it follows the Inland Sea past Shimonoseki and Nagasaki. There is nothing more strikingly picturesque than this Inland Sea, dotted with precipitous forest-enshrouded islands, bordered by well-cultivated fields and charming little villages. From Nagasaki the steamer steers for Fusan,[1] a large Korean port city, where the traveler finds himself suddenly transported to another world.

The Korean natives are tall, slender, and solidly built, and they dress all in white. The men wear immense pants *à la Zouave* that float from their hips to their ankles where they are tucked into large quilted cotton socks. With this they wear a small vest, sometimes pink rather than the usual white, over which is worn a long robe with several tails, four I believe—two in front and two behind. The entire ensemble is made of white cloth resembling calico but the quality of which varies according to the wearer's station.

But the visitor to Korea cannot help but be struck by the Koreans' extraordinary headgear. They have their small hats, rounded like the crest of a rooster with two small wings in the back; then their medium-sized ones, somewhat resembling our own silk top hats back when they sported flat brims; and finally the immense variety made of straw, under which a man can completely disappear to the shoulders. If I'm not mistaken, only those in mourning wear this last type.

All Korean men carry a supply of tobacco in a pouch hung about their waist, along with something I first took to be a fan but which in fact is nothing more than a length of waterproofed linen used to cover their precious headgear when it rains. They all possess long pipes, some so long that a man cannot light it by his own hand as his arms are not long enough.

The only women one spots on the streets are those of the lowest classes. They dress in short white petticoats attached high under the breasts so that they seem to cover only half the body. Below them protrude long, yellow, enormous legs. Women of quality hardly ever leave their homes and do so only with their heads concealed by a silk cloak, completely hiding them from the curiosity of passersby. The men have a tendency to lower their heads or turn away when passing a woman.

It would be difficult to imagine a country more poor or miserable than Korea. Disgusting, mud-covered hovels, foul and noxious side streets where pigs, dogs, and children wallow in filth, everywhere a frightful asphyxiating stench: these are the things that really strike the visitor to Korea. The country is as ugly as the curious costumes of its people are picturesque. But Korea, which today has nothing—not arts, commerce, industry, or agriculture—was rich and prosperous only a few centuries ago, boasting a civilization far superior to that of China or Japan.

It is Korea's admirable geographic situation that has proven the source of its ruin. Hemmed in by Japan, China, and Siberia, it has always been the coveted object of powerful neighbors. Violated in turn by China and Japan in a constant series of wars, ruined and stripped bare, she ended up becoming a tributary not just to one but to both empires at the same time. Though only China may claim Korea as its vassal, Japan exhorts from her a hefty annual tribute. How can an estimated ten to twelve million Koreans resist the Chinese and Japanese hordes?

The Koreans do not resemble their neighbors in any way. They are a race apart. The Korean king exercises absolute power and just below him is a class of nobles (both civilian and military) who enjoy such privileges as allow them to impose crushing taxes and corvée duties on the commoner classes.

But this nation, which has only in recent years sunk to the lowest level of degradation, boasts a brilliant history, and Japan owes much of its civilization to her. It was the Koreans who taught the Japanese the use of written characters, wood and metalworking, and the distillation of rice wine; and it was the Koreans who taught their neighbors the art of firing and decorating porcelain.

By the eleventh century the Japanese had already invaded Korea in an effort to conquer her, something repeated a hundred times since. From a 1615 treaty Korea recognized Japan's right to use the port of

Fusan. As a result, it is not surprising to discover there a significant Japanese colony comprised of merchants and fishermen numbering from twelve to fourteen thousand.

From Fusan the steamer heads for Chemulpo[2], the port serving the royal capital of Seoul. This latter city is located a bit over thirty kilometers from Chemulpo, and ten years ago a miserable little trail was all that linked the two by land. The journey was made on the backs of small Korean horses no higher than a large Newfoundland dog. It was also possible to make the journey by small boat trip up the Han River. These small vessels can take you the four to five kilometers up river to the city walls. This was how I reached the capital, in the company of four friends (including two American ladies). We took a launch belonging to a Mr. Townsend, a courteous gentleman and important Chemulpo merchant representing *The American Trading Company.* The voyage was rather dreary. Nothing but flat and monotonous riverbanks, mud as far as the eye could see. At one spot where the river was still quite wide and its two banks only just discernable, I noticed the nearer bank seemed to undulate slightly. Peering through my binoculars I was astonished at the sight that greeted me: ducks and wild birds blanketed the earth to the horizon. Seizing our rifles, my companions and I took aim. With the crackle of our gunshots an unforgettable scene unfolded before us. On all sides and with an awesome noise the riverbanks seemed suddenly to come to life. To our right and left two dense masses rose up in unison only to as suddenly break up into innumerable flocks, some dark, others entirely white, and all shooting off in different directions like so many brilliant comets.

Night had fallen by the time we arrived at the disembarking point, where sedan chairs sent by the United States minister already awaited us. Each of these chairs was carried on the shoulders of four vigorous Korean runners, who sped off in a barrage of savage cries. This would have been fine enough had not the devils, who clearly subsisted on a special diet, taken the liberty to let loose with some very disagreeable noises under our very noses. But if only they'd been satisfied with simply making noise! Oh no, from time to time one of them would shout something, whereupon his companions would halt, allowing the one who had cried out to satisfy some natural need or other right before our eyes.

Figure 16. A view of Seoul at the time of de Guerville's visit. *L'Illustration* (4 August 1894).

The city of Seoul has a population of about two hundred and fifty thousand and is encircled by immense walls punctuated here and there by monumental gates. At nightfall these gates are shut, not to be reopened under any pretense until the following morning. So that we would not have to spend the night under the stars, the minister had sent his servants to a convenient spot atop the wall. From there they threw down ropes by which means we were able to scramble over the walls. This was difficult enough for us men, but even more complicated and dangerous for the ladies, one of whom was large and robust, and as a result quite heavy.

During my first stay in Korea I had an interpreter named Pak, who must have been one of his country's wiliest characters. Regardless of the situation, Pak, who spoke tolerably good English, was a crafty fellow and could make do, and he made a fine servant and interpreter. Apparently one of his uncles was a figure of some consequence, for one evening Pak proceeded to describe to me and my two American lady friends the entourage that always accompanied this high-placed relation whenever he went out.

"First," Pak said, "There are the soldiers, and after them the servants. After the servants come more soldiers and then slaves to carry the hats, slaves for the clothing, slaves for the food, slaves carrying pipes, then eunuchs who guard the concubines, and then slaves to carry the pot used for p . . ."

"Oh the dreadful man! Stop!" cried the shocked ladies, and poor Pak, not understanding his offense, fell into a vexed and humiliated silence.

One day, when I was refused entrance to a certain temple, Pak flushed with anger and declared I was none other than the son of the formidable 'King of America,' and if he ever learned how his son had been so insulted he wouldn't hesitate in his righteous wrath to dispatch a powerful gunboat to let slip a fury of fire and blood! The threat (whose meaning at the time was lost on me as it was given in Korean) had the desired effect; the doors were opened wide and I was afforded a royal welcome.

Figure 17. Korea's fainthearted King Kojong. *L'Illustration* (2 November 1894).

La reine de Corée.

Figure 18. King Kojong's strong-willed wife Queen Min. There is doubt concerning the authenticity of the Queen Min image. *L'Illustration* (2 November 1894).

I had the honor of being received by King Li-Hong himself, son of the famous Tai-Wan-Kun and adopted child of the dowager queen.[3] His Majesty was charming and very interested in my mission. He assured me that Korea would be officially represented at Chicago.

I passed an evening at the palace, a small city unto itself comprised of innumerable structures and courtyards, presenting the king and queen with views of the planned exposition as well as of some of the most celebrated scenes in North America. They also saw a number of views of the 1889 Paris Exposition, whose marvels they had all heard about already. The queen and several court ladies were seated behind a screen so as not to be seen by foreigners. But after I'd projected the first electronic images the queen became very animated and unable to contain herself quitted her hiding placed to approach the white curtain on which the images were being illuminated. She touched it with

Le Taï Wen Koun.

Figure 19. King Kojong's father, the headstrong and wily Taewŏngun (Tai-Wan-Kun). *L'Illustration* (2 November 189).

her finger, asking a thousand questions. She struck me as a woman of exceptional intelligence and will.[4]

At this time, and for several years previous, the court had been the scene of bloody factional struggles, crass intrigues during which the contending factions supported either Japan or China, the politics of the Tai-Wan-Kun—the king's father—or those of the queen. Such rivalries, supported and encouraged by Korea's enemies, did not shrink even from assassination, and before long the country found itself embroiled in indescribable anarchy. It was this anarchy that furnished the pretext for intervention by Japan. Viewing Korea as its own vassal, China strongly resented the Japanese interference, and the war came.

Thanks to the eminent "Pak," I departed Korea in the possession of an extraordinary Korean general's uniform. According to Pak, this marvelous outfit was courtesy of the Korean king, but considering how His Majesty's tailors footed me with the bill, I have reason to doubt its royal origins. Whatever the case, I came upon this suit in the following manner.

SÉOUL. — Entrée du palais.

Figure 20. Main gate of one of the Korean royal palaces in Seoul (1894). *L'Illustration* (4 August 1894).

A few days following my royal audience I learned of a special procession to take place that was to include the king, queen, and all the court officials. I immediately expressed my desire to participate, only to be informed that this would be quite impossible as the ceremony in question was a religious one that would take place at a sacred locale, and it was feared that the Koreans would not suffer a foreigner—and pagan—in such a place. I made no effort to conceal my extreme disappointment from Pak. Pak mulled over the matter a long time while tugging at the four strands of hair that served as his mustache, and finally announced he had come up with a solution whereby I could assist in the ceremony. He then exclaimed he was off to submit his plan to the proper authorities at the palace: I was to participate in the ceremony in Korean dress. Two hours later Pak returned to tell me that everything was arranged and that the king had already given orders for the official tailors to take my measurements.

The tailors soon arrived and at once began a series of perplexing procedures along with taking some quite extraordinary measurements of my body, all of which took up nearly an hour. Two days later I was duly presented with a round hat with large brim adorned in front with a peacock feather and in back with a long tail of red and yellow bristles. A cord made of large red and yellow balls passed beneath my chin to keep this remarkable headgear in place. The outfit also included a charming little pink vest, a larger white vest, and a pair of equally white trousers that were so large I could easily have vanished completely into one of their legs.

"With all the time they took those idiot tailors still got my measurements wrong," I remarked to Pak.

Pak shook his head and explained that since the material would shrink with washing, very scientific calculations were required to ensure the pants were sufficiently loose to withstand fifty washings and still fit me.

They've still not had so many washings, though I've displayed them in nearly every country on earth. They have always, however, enjoyed great popularity, but nowhere so much as at the Court of Spain.

The Madrid Geographical Society, of which I have the honor of being a corresponding member, invited me one day to present a lecture on the subject of my recent travels in the Far East.[5] As this enjoyed some success, Her Majesty the Queen Regent then invited me to repeat the presentation at the palace.

Thanks to the deference and interest shown me by the Duke of Sotomayor all the arrangements were soon made and Her Majesty along with the Princess of Asturias and the ladies and gentlemen of the court were intensely interested in the account of my travels, as well as with the magnificent electric projections that accompanied it.

Korea seemed to interest Her Majesty in particular, and at the end of the presentation I showed her a few objects brought back from the "Hermit Nation." Among them was the general's uniform and I endeavored to explain to the queen the long and complex procedure of the royal tailors in procuring my measurements.

"Well then," she said, "this uniform must fit to perfection."

"'Perfection' is not the word." I replied, "As Your Majesty may readily judge for herself. Here are the pants . . ." And with a snap of my wrists I unfurled the things.

At the sight of such enormous white pants everyone present exploded in laughter. It was in the midst of the general merriment that the Duke of Medina Sedonia leaned over and whispered in my ear, "Try them on."

Without hesitating I slipped one leg and then another into the impossible things. Next came the little pink vest followed by the large white one and then the feathered hat, and the overall effect was greatly admired.

While proceeding to respond to Her Majesty's numerous questions I managed to gradually get out of all these garments, which were becoming quite hot since I had put them on over my own clothes. Getting the trousers off modestly and gracefully proved particularly challenging.

After Her Majesty had retired the Duke of Medina Sedonia, who had escorted her to her private apartments, returned to me and said in the most serious manner,

"You can boast, monsieur, of having done something no other man has done."

"And what would that be, your excellence?"

"Monsieur, you can boast being the only man in the world to ever put on and take off his pants in the presence of the Queen of Spain!"

One final note before leaving Korea behind . . . One morning Pak entered my room to announce:

"Today big festival, very big national festival in all Korea!"

"What sort of festival, Pak?"

"A national festival."

"Yes, I understand that. But of what sort?"

"The women are going to wash themselves . . ."

"What?"

"Yes, Korean women take bath one time every year. In cities, villages, they meet and together go to river and take bath."

"And what of the men, Pak?"

"The men, they watch but from far away."

"Then the men don't bathe?"

Pak took on a mysterious air and responded, "That's different."

I couldn't get any more out of him, nor figure out if the men bathed more or less than the women.

I was fed up with Pak and his stories when, only a few minutes later, an attaché from a foreign legation stopped by. I asked him whether the annual bath was really a Korean tradition.

"Oh yes," he responded. "And the worse thing is that for the three months following the ritual you can't eat fish!"

Having recounted this story to Mr. Reick, the talented and energetic director of the *New York Herald,* I was surprised to hear him remark,

"Well, it sounds like the Korean people are remarkably clean."

"You think?"

"Certainly! You say all the women there bathe once a year? Well think about it. Among the lower classes of Paris, London, Berlin, and New York, there are thousands of women who have never bathed in their life!"

All the same, I am still unprepared to bestow on Korean women, much less Korean men, any certificate of cleanliness.

From Chemulpo the Japanese steamer proceeds, either directly or in stages, to Chefoo at the mouth of the Pei River. Here are found the famous Taku Forts, which so resolutely resisted the French and English fleets, and perhaps would never have fallen at all had the allied admirals not landed a force to attack the enemy from the rear. With that strike the Chinese turned tail.[6] The strategy of the rear attack, which cuts off the line of retreat, is something the Chinese could never stomach and which they consider extremely base and cowardly.

The Pei River between Taku and Tientsin[7] is a foul river of dirty yellow water flowing between banks of yellow mud. For five or six months of the year it is unnavigable due to ice, and for another four or five months due to a lack of water. Today the Taku-Tientsin[7] railway has simplified things, but only a few years ago a voyage along this ignoble river was an unattractive prospect indeed.

At Tientsin lives the famous Li Hung-chang, Viceroy of Pechili, Admiral of the Fleet, Tutor to the Imperial Prince, Superintendent of Commerce, High Commissioner of the Armed Forces, etc., etc. At this time he was the master of China. He was in the complete sense of the word, a "self-made man." Son of a humble scholar, he first distinguished himself as an official during the Taiping Rebellion. Following this, all the positions and honors he accrued one upon the other were due to his hard work, intelligence, strength of character, fine diplomatic skills, tremendous courage, and—to believe his enemies—his skillful machinations. And yet, as remarkable as he was, he failed to grasp the power of Japan right up until it had destroyed his army and fleet at Port Arthur and Weihaiwei was occupied by those he referred to with scorn as, "little monkeys."

From my arrival in Tientsin he greeted me with the utmost cordiality. China, furious over measures taken by the American authorities against Chinese immigrants, had yet to respond to the invitation extended her to participate in the Chicago exposition.[8] When in the course of our interview I delicately broached this subject, the viceroy exclaimed,

"Send an exposition to America! Hah! I'll tell you what I'm going to send. I'm going to send a fleet of warships to teach the Americans how to respect China."

Figure 21. A depiction of Li Hongzhang (Li Hung-chang), his son, and grandsons. *L'Illustration* (6 October 1894).

I smiled and the great man, now calmer, asked me, "Well what do you think of that?"

"Just this your Excellency. We Americans are a very hospitable people. If you send this fleet I'm certain we shall throw it such a reception that it won't ever go home."

Li Hung-chang enjoyed butting heads. My response amused him and he let down his guard, at least towards me.[9]

One evening at the viceroy's official residence, in the course of giving a magic lantern presentation of those scenes already admired by both the emperor of Japan and the king of Korea, I made the acquaintance of a certain Lofengluh,[10] whom I believe held the position corresponding to that of naval minister. If I am not mistaken he even served at one time as ambassador to England. The next day the fellow paid me a visit at my hotel.

"Do you think," he asked me, "you could possibly show your splendid scenes again at my residence tomorrow? There will be some high officials present, members of the government from Peking, who may be of the greatest service to you. I would of course be happy to introduce them you to."

Naturally, I accepted his invitation and I soon found myself within the immense salon of Mr. Lofengluh, and surrounded by persons of rank. Soon upon my arrival a Chinese man dressed in the European style veritably threw himself upon me with the greatest enthusiasm.

"My god, but how good it is to finally talk with a man of culture," he said in most excellent French. "Do you know Paris? Do tell me about Paris. Paris . . . how I love her! To say nothing of the Parisian ladies . . ." However, my assistant's signal that all was ready for the magic lantern display to commence prevented me from responding to this guest, and the show was soon underway.

After views of the United States and the future exposition at Chicago, came images of Paris and the 1889 exposition. Hardly had these last images appeared then violent and shaking sobs broke out across the darkened salon. Intrigued, I pointed my desk lamp (which was arranged so as to illuminate only my notes) towards the source of the outbreak and I noticed, seated next to the Chinese man who had recently spoken to me in French, a young and charming European woman balling her eyes out. A few moments later this Chinese Parisian escorted the lady from the salon. I never saw either of them again.

Now quite intrigued, I made inquiries and did some research and this is what I discovered. The Chinese man was none other than the famous general Tchen-Ki-Tung, former Chinese ambassador to France.[11] One may recall his social and literary, not to mention financial, successes while in Paris. Accused of having swindled several millions from large French banking houses he was arrested by Chinese officials and hustled back to China. The government in Peking pretended to have punished him severely, to the effect of locking him in a cell and throwing away the key. This "cell," as it turned out, was the comfortable and luxurious home of his friend the naval minister.

"And the weeping woman?" you ask.

Now that is more mysterious. The noble general had married a French woman, but I don't believe that was her in Tientsin. His legitimate wife, with all the dignity and devotion afforded a good cause, had shown up in Tientsin accompanied by her mother, and had beseeched the Chinese authorities to allow her to share her husband's fate. The authorities told her such a thing was impossible, as he was then languishing in some forgotten cell. As she was at the end of her means, the Chinese repatriated her and her mother by third class passage.

During all this time our brave general was passing his days in his friend's palace, in the company of a little lady who had followed him all the way from Paris—an unknown lady, but one who had obviously had her fill of China and the Chinese, for upon seeing images of her beloved Paris she was overcome with tears!

16 Ayama

Valet, interpreter, and secretary, Ayama played all these roles for me, and accomplished it all with intelligence and devotion.

He was around twenty years old when I took him on as my servant through a friend's recommendation. He didn't strike me as particularly clever at the time—the little English he knew was difficult to comprehend, and anywhere besides Japan his manner (he dressed in the European style) would have seemed a bit absurd.

"But blast it!" I concluded, "For preparing my bath, polishing my boots, and brushing my garments, he'll do."

Ayama, my friend, I want to proffer some well-deserved apologies. I was wrong. Blind. You were a true *"rough and uncut diamond."*

If you'll excuse my lack of modesty, Ayama transformed quickly through his contact with me and my friends. His deportment took on a remarkable new ease, and his manner finally began to harmonize with his personality. He made astonishing progress in the language of Shakespeare, and while remaining a valet, became an invaluable interpreter as well.

I soon realized that he was very much abreast of events in his own country, and the world of pretty *musume* held no secrets from him either. I even believe he was a veritable Don Juan among those young ladies, with whom he enjoyed a renowned success. In his casual way he often even proposed to introduce me to some ravishing geishas, but I always declined. It seemed to me he was on very familiar terms with those ladies, and the thought of becoming the rival to my valet, as attractive as that may sound from a Japanese perspective, did not appeal to me.

I did, however, make use of Ayama's numerous contacts and information in a different manner. I had him tell me all about the curious traits and customs of the Japanese, and he often made some very interesting points on questions of the day in his own country. I was no more curious than most, but I swear I could spend many delicious hours with Ayama and his stories. Over my morning shave he would routinely go over the day's—and the night's—gossip.

He knew everything. Everything. Not just what went on in our hotel—the Imperial—but in the ministries, embassies, and pleasure quarters. How many times, in shaking a stranger's hand at the hotel or in greeting a beautiful lady at an embassy reception, did I have to bite my lip to stifle a laugh in recalling that person's latest misadventure, as related to me that very morning by Ayama.

There were two older American gentlemen at the hotel, Mr. F. S. W. and Mr. C. S. X., both holding important offices back in the United States.[1] Their wives had accompanied them to Japan.

"Old misters, very crafty," Ayama related to me one morning. "Last night make good time. After dinner, they look worry and tell wives, 'Very tired but must go out, so bothersome. Have important meeting, two ministers in Chamber of Commerce. Come back late.' Old misters, they leave like they annoy and wives say, 'Poor things. Business is business. Careful no catch cold.' Old misters, they laugh quietly and get rickshaw. Quick, quick, they go by small dark street to beautiful geisha!"

Ayama paused to wink and lick his lips; he then made a clack-clacking noise with his tongue.

"Very beautiful geisha . . . four . . . and music too. Old misters, they want to kiss but geisha, they say 'No! No like old beards.' Well, so they tell geisha, 'Dance!' and geisha say 'What kind?' Old misters, they say, 'Something *shocking!*' So geisha do making love dance, and when they take off all clothes the old misters they want have fun but geisha say, 'No. Too old.' They return to hotel very angry and wives ask, 'No catch cold?' More old mister, he say, 'No catch anything, those Japanese ministers, no work.'"

Ayama then convulsed with laughter.

Between my first and second voyage to Japan I received many letters from Ayama. His style was taking form and his fortunes had met with unanticipated success. He was no longer a valet, nor an interpreter, nor a secretary. He was a broker, involved in the establishment of new companies, dealing in textiles, and Buddha knows what else.

Upon my return to Tokyo I inquired of Ayama. The hotel porter responded, with the air of a monk speaking of the Pope, that he would "request *Monsieur* Ayama kindly stop by my rooms." Late the next morning I was handed an elegantly engraved calling card bearing the name: A. AYAMA.

I hardly recognized him when he entered. He was now a dandy in every sense. Polished boots, butter-hued gloves, shirt of pink and white, and a complete and perfect copy—in fabric and cut—of a masterpiece by my own tailor. Mimicked as well were my waistcoat, the tie of my cravat, and even my occasional habit of giving a sharp pull on my sleeves.

The entire ensemble was admirable, bewildering even, but not so agreeable in the details. He reeked of expensive cologne. The handkerchief in his vest pocket protruded too much and was not properly arranged. His skin seemed to fade into the color of his sleeves, and the pomade with which he'd saturated his hair, in the hopes of imitating my own coiffure, had run down on to his collar.

Figure 22. Japanese in western dress (late 19th century). Société Géographique de Paris. Used with permission.

And yet despite all this, for a former Japanese valet Ayama was extraordinarily stylish. I could imagine how he must have been ravishing the hearts of Japanese women. After all, what's to astonish? In London, adorned with a prince's title, he could quite possibly woo and marry a beautiful English countess. It's been known to happen, though perhaps not every day.

Previously, while in my service as a valet Ayama had accompanied me to China where we had stayed a fairly long time in Tientsin. The Japanese are brave by nature, and I have no reason to doubt Ayama was any different, though at times he hid his valor in the large pocket of prudence.

Tientsin had nothing to offer Ayama. He recalled the massacres that had occurred there and threatened to come again.[2] The northern Chinese are large, strong, and well-built, giving to Ayama the impression of giant devils and filling him with unspeakable terror. He never set foot outside the hotel unless compelled to accompany me. Even then he was close on my heels, always fearful lest he become separated from me and my protective revolver. He never went out alone. I later learned that rather than carry out the errands I had given him he paid a Chinese servant to do them with money out of his own pocket. One day something happened that nearly killed the poor fellow with fear and had me believing I'd seen my last as well.

Feeling very stiff one morning after a previous day's riding excursion, I called for a masseur, one of those Chinese masseurs of whose wonders I'd heard. They sent a veritable colossus to my room, a giant whose enormous head nearly brushed the ceiling. Ayama later claimed this giant's skin, rather than yellow like that of other Celestials, was a fiery red, and that his body effused the odor of sulfur. Whoever he was—son of heaven or hell—he gave me a very tortuous quarter hour. After ordering me to remove my pajamas and lie down on the bed, he plunged his enormous hands into a basin of oil he had brought along with him and then threw himself upon me.

In no country could you call this a massage. The sensations are impossible to describe. At first I thought he intended to flay me alive, and then that he meant to thrust his gigantic fists into my poor little chest, and then that he had every intention of dismembering me, or was it only to snap my bones? While he pounded away at my body his chest let loose with terrible groans and he breathed like a steam locomotive. His long queue whipped through the air with a whistle while a cascade of sweat, originating on his shaved head, first drenched his demonic form before dripping on to me, where it mixed with the oil he had used to lather my body. It was horrible. I wanted to cry for help but lacked the strength.

Just as I thought I was done for he suddenly stopped, and grabbing me under one of his arms with the other he snatched a stool and set it down in the center of the room. He then plopped me on the stool like a sack, my torso on the seat with my legs and head dangling off either end. Taking me by the throat with one hand, with the other he grasped my shins and with a sudden push bent me so that my head and feet touched the floor at the same time. He then yanked me back to a sitting position and amused himself by corkscrewing my legs around the chair's legs. This done, he picked me up and tossed me back on my bed. He then said quite calmly, "Pay two francs." And you must admit, that is rather cheap!

Ayama meanwhile had vanished. Some time later I discovered him squeezed into a corner behind a large piece of furniture. He was pale with terror, eyes bulging, hugging my Winchester, which thank god he hadn't dared to use. It took me forty-eight hours to recover from this extraordinary massage. A week later Ayama was still feeling its effects.

A few days later I was sitting in the garden when I caught the sound of music coming from the nearby Tientsin Park. Ayama, busy arranging my photographic slides, seemed to take an interest in the music and so I gave him the name of the piece being played.

"The waltz from *Faust*."

He looked up at me in surprise. "How do you know?"

"Because I know the piece," I replied.

A few minutes later I remarked, "This here is an English piece, *Home, Sweet Home*."

He now appeared even more surprised. "But how do you know?"

"And this," I said a bit later, "is the *Marseillaise*, the French national song."

For the third time Ayama repeated his question and now I answered impatiently, "But I know these tunes, and when you know them the difference . . ."

Here Ayama interrupted, "But me no hear difference, all same!"

He then explained that to him, as to all Japanese (with the exception of those of some education or who have seen something of the world), all of our music is nothing but a horrible cacophony of which they can make no sense. Wagner? Noise. Berlioz? Noise. Rossini? Noise. Meyerbeer? Noise—*Faust*, the *Marseillaise, Home, Sweet Home*, all nothing but noise, more or less agreeable to be sure but all resembling each other such that they cannot tell one from the other.

Now if the Japanese ear cannot analyze our music I have learned as well that their palate is no better able to appreciate our cuisine. One morning I asked Ayama what he had had for breakfast and he answered,

"Beefsteak, very good, all red, with egg."

I was a bit surprised as the hotel manager had assured me there was no beefsteak.

"And what about yesterday evening, Ayama? What did you have for dinner?"

"Good beef with beans."

"No Ayama, that was lamb."

"No, no," he insisted, shaking his head. "That was beef."

"Let's see then, can you describe this morning's beefsteak?"

"Very good, red, with egg half cook."

"How half-cooked?"

"Yes, half cook. One side cook other not."

Unable to understand, I summoned a waiter and asked him to go find out from the kitchen what Ayama had eaten for breakfast. The waiter answered right off,

"Ham and eggs, sir!"

Ayama's half-cooked egg was a fried egg and his beefsteak was ham!

Ayama explained that he knew the difference between cows, sheep, pigs, chicken, and ducks. Certainly, living he could distinguish them, but killed and prepared *à l'européenne* they were just so many ingredients in one big stew, all with the same taste. Moreover, our food gave him—as it does all Japanese unaccustomed to it—violent stomachaches.

Ayama could not understand our music because his ear was not accustomed to it, had not been "trained" from childhood like ours. He could not appreciate our food as he had never even tasted it before he was twenty, and even then only on rare occasions that left his intestines in horrible pain. The Japanese eat very little meat and are incapable of distinguishing the taste of one meat from another. Everything in this world is a question of education: education of the eye, the nose, the tongue, etc.

One day I was showing photographic views of twenty-story Chicago buildings to Li Hung-chang. They had absolutely no effect on him for the very simple reason that he could not grasp the idea of the things. They were too large, even for the greatest of Chinamen.

On this topic Monsieur P . . . ,[3] the former French minister to Korea, recounted to me how he had once received the king's prime minister at the embassy. He came upon the prime minister in the lobby where he was admiring a bust of the Republic.

"Who is this?" he asked curiously.

"That your Excellency, is the French Republic."

No sooner had he said this than the prime minister bowed deeply to the bust exclaiming, "How beautiful she is! Please extend to her my most humble respects."

For him, as for nearly all others, the Republic could only be a sovereign of flesh and blood, an empress of some sort. There are some things no Asiatic will ever comprehend, no, never, not even one so clever as Ayama.

17 Marshal Yamagata

A very curious and interesting figure, this Marshal Yamagata.[1] Many consider him the Moltke of Japan, and he is without doubt the most illustrious of all the nation's generals.

This is due not to the marshal's command of Japanese troops in the field, for in fact he did not take part in a single important combat in the last war with China.[2] Yet it is thanks to his untiring efforts that the Japanese army was elevated to the position of supremacy it now enjoys.

It was Yamagata who created and directed the admirable Japanese General Staff, and it is apparently he who developed the war plans against China; and never were plans more thorough. For several years before the outbreak of hostilities, the provinces of Manchuria and Pechili were pervaded by Japanese spies. These included disguised army officers, bankers, and financiers who affected to be studying questions of railway lines and the establishment of industries, etc. There were even some Japanese with shaved heads and sporting real or false queues who passed themselves off as local inhabitants, whose language they could speak to perfection; there were those disguised as Buddhist monks and missionaries, who wandered about, infiltrating everywhere and taking notes, photos, and measurements, the result being that Marshal Yamagata's General Staff knew the Chinese provinces as intimately as if they comprised part of the Japanese empire itself.

By the outset of the war many of these spies had infiltrated into the Chinese army itself, and from Pen-Yang[3], Port Arthur, and Weihaiwei they provided the Japanese with precious intelligence, while within the Chinese army and the besieged towns they fomented discord, disaffection, and fear, often alarming people with fantastic accounts of the awesome cannons supposedly possessed by the Japanese, and of the powerful gods which were aiding them and who had decided to destroy the Chinese. A few of these spies were discovered and massacred, but the majority of them were able to escape upon the arrival of the Japanese army, and I had the occasion to witness several.

Japanese preparations were so thorough that they had pontoon bridges prepared that were specifically adapted for all river crossings they would encounter in enemy territory.

Figure 23. Marshal Yamagata Aritomo at the time of the Sino-Japanese War. *L'Illustration* (29 September 1894).

The Sino-Japanese War was inevitable. On the one hand the immense empire of China had always treated the Japanese with the most profound contempt. The famous Li Hung-chang himself once spoke to me disdainfully of the Japanese, commenting, "They are not men, but the offspring of monkeys!"

The extraordinary progress accomplished by the Japanese, far from inspiring Chinese respect, only made them look at the Japanese as contemptuously as ever. "The Japanese monkeys amuse themselves by playing like western devils," they remarked. They were convinced that these little soldiers dressed up *à l'européenne,* this army that mimicked ours in the west, would collapse like a house of cards at the appearance of the army of the Son of Heaven. On the other hand, Japan, proud of its new organization, convinced of the invincibility of its army and fleet, was eager to demonstrate all this to the world by some brilliant feats of arms, while no less desirous of testing its new power against its hereditary enemy, loathed down the centuries. Yet besides these motives Japan had two primary reasons for wanting this war.

First, in 1894 the major powers were still treating Japan like a semi-barbarous country—an oriental country. Foreign settlers in the open ports of Yokohama, Kobe, and Nagasaki had established their own small communities, which they considered practically as conquered territory. They treated the Japanese like dogs and spoke of them as if they were their masters. By the terms of the then existing treaties, no matter what crime or misdemeanor the foreigner committed, he would not fall under the jurisdiction of Japanese law. Foreigners had their own consular courts where they were judged by their own consuls. Japan, which had adopted a very equitable law code and boasted perfectly sound tribunals, bitterly resented this humiliating state of affairs. For this reason—among many others—they harbored but one thought, one sole desire: to denounce the old treaties and draw up new ones.

These same treaties that had been imposed upon Japan forty years previous prohibited them from imposing a customs duty of more than five percent on foreign products, a figure thoroughly inadequate to protect certain native industries and further, which did not provide the government with sufficient means for national administration. One can easily see how such a situation became intolerable, and what amazes is that the Japanese had the patience to endure this for some thirty years.

On several occasions the government in Tokyo had wanted to denounce the treaties, but each time the major powers responded: "No, no, you are not yet civilized enough." The foreigners established in the open ports did whatever was in their power to maintain the status quo and to make the world believe that Japan was still a half-barbarous country. Their motives are easy enough to comprehend. First of all, they wished to continue to receive European and American products at much lower prices, knowing full well that the moment new treaties were passed Japan would impose much higher duties on many of these items. But more fundamentally, for many years these foreigners had been the masters of their "concessions" at Yokohama, Kobe, and Nagasaki, and they could not suffer the thought that they might become subject to Japanese laws and that their actions would be judged and punished by those same Japanese they had flouted, riled, and insulted. With a single voice they opposed treaty revision and their newspapers competed with one another to conceal from the world the true state of affairs in Japan. All this invoked from the depth of the collective soul of Japan's forty million inhabitants the resounding event that fixed the attention of the world upon them, and convinced the major powers that they had at last acquired the degree of civilization that would allow them to become masters of their own house, if not more. This event was the war with China.

Can you recall the sentiments of pity and derision with which the foreign papers greeted the news that Japan was going to war? Colossal China will have Japan for lunch, they said. This would be the end of the little men of the Land of the Rising Sun and their pretty little *musume;* they would be completely devoured and their country become a Chinese province (so long as Europe permits it of course!).

They never counted on Yamagata, or his general staff, or his admirable Japanese soldiers, who forced the world to take them seriously. What wondrous pages they added to the glorious history of Japan. A First Army of fifty thousand men was mobilized in days, embarked aboard a fleet of steamships, debarked in Korea where they soon battled the Chinese at Assan,[4] before marching across the country in triumph to seize Pen-Yang and vanquish the thousands of Chinese troops that were defending that fortified city. At sea, Admiral Ito* devastated the Chinese fleet and soon afterwards the Second Army under the command of Marshal Oyama disembarked in Manchuria and went

---

* Itoh Sukeyuki.

on to seize Kinchow, Talien Wan, and Port Arthur. Finally, Weihaiwei succumbed as well and the road to Peking was open to the Japanese army. Li Hung-chang realized this and China capitulated.

Yamagata, Oyama, and Ito had not only won victories through prodigious feats of arms. They had done more. They had, by their troops' exemplary and humane conduct as much as by their courage, achieved a great moral victory. Before these Japanese armies, which responded to the massacres and cruelties of the Chinese by collecting and nursing the enemy wounded and by administering each village, each yard of conquered territory, with sagacity and generosity; before such a display the world bowed in deference. Japan had earned its spurs, and sanctioned as a knight of civilization and progress, she entered at last into the great family of civilized nations.

By dint of one of those ironies so common to life, the man who contributed the most to forming and molding the Japanese forces, to elevating them to the degree of perfection they attained, did not participate in any of the fighting which these soldiers—his children, as he called them—had with the Chinese. Marshal Yamagata was not present at a single battle.

After the defeat of the Chinese at Assan and the occupation of Seoul by the First Army, Marshal Yamagata embarked for Korea to take command of this army, even though he had been ailing for a number of years. The Chinese were entrenched at Pen-Yang and everyone was convinced they would defend it furiously. Li Hung-chang had pronounced the city impregnable.

Marshal Yamagata understood the Chinese character very well, he knew the strange nature of this being capable of defending himself heroically when attacked from the front but who lost all courage when hope for retreat was gone. The basis of all of Yamagata's plans was to surround the Chinese, however long it might take, and to leave them absolutely no avenue of escape. This was the entire Japanese strategy; it succeeded marvelously.

It was at Pen-Yang as it was at Kinchow, at Port Arthur, and at Weihaiwei. The Japanese army, commanded in the absence of Yamagata by Lieutenant General Notzu,[5] was divided into three offensive corps under the commands of Generals Notzu, Oshima, and Tatsumi. These corps attacked the Chinese from the west, south, and east respectively, while a fourth column, disembarking in Korea, was through a forced march able to cut off the Chinese avenue of retreat to the north.

The generals had decided in Seoul on September first that the date of the attack would be the 15th or 16th of the same month. At the time it appeared certain that General Marquis Yamagata would be able to rejoin the army before the battle began. Unfortunately, this was not to be the case: still weak and in pain, the marshal was forced to halt for a time in Seoul and could only make the trip between that city and Pen-Yang in very short stages, not arriving until September 26th.

General Notzu did not wait for Yamagata before striking, fearing any delay might permit the arrival of Chinese reinforcements, and as it was the city was only seized by the Japanese on September 17th after some resistance by the more respectable Chinese elements.

Marshal Yamagata accompanied the First Army out of Pen-Yang, and throughout the long and strenuous campaign north into Manchuria. This army suffered much more than Marshal Oyama's Second Army, the victor of Port Arthur. The Siberian climate and privations of all sorts proved more detrimental to the marshal's health.

Yamagata suffered without complaint and without repose. His doctors wanted to force him to slow down, to take tonics, wine, cognac, all of which the marshal vigorously refused:

"No, no!" he exclaimed. "Never! How can I take such things when my brave soldiers are lacking everything, even water, and when we can hardly even get the needed medicines to our wounded?"

And weak as he was, each day the marshal took only a simple meal of boiled rice—the rice of the common soldier, the only food he would eat—until one day the beloved chief was forced to halt in a small Manchurian village.

Yamagata handed over command to Notzu, who was soon promoted to marshal. The Japanese emperor had sent his best doctor to the marquis' side, who slowly improved and was then taken back to Japan. With the assistance of General Kawakami he continued to guide the army, now under the overall command of Marshal Oyama, through its string of victories leading ultimately to China's suing for peace.

The marshal is the simplest man in the world, and when the emperor dispatched him as special ambassador to the coronation of the Czar, he astonished Europe and America by this extraordinary simplicity. The contrast between this modest victor and the representatives of the vanquished—the Chinese embassy—stunned the world.

Likewise, the voyage of Yamagata through the United States left quite an impression. The simplicity of Franklin, of Grant, of Lincoln is a bygone thing.

If Americans lack titles of nobility and decorations, they make up for it with enough stripes and epaulettes to shame even the most ornamented of European armies. If American ambassadors lack uniforms, their military officers have plenty to spare.* When Yamagata's special New York train arrived at Buffalo, his carriage was overrun by the General Staff of the New York governor, which had come to welcome him and invite him to a special banquet in his honor. It is impossible to say who was more astonished: Yamagata upon seeing such brilliant uniforms, decorated in gold, with superb epaulettes and prodigious plumes; or the American officers when they saw that this famous marshal, the Japanese Moltke, was a small, diminutive figure, simple and without pretension, practically timid, and dressed in a somber outfit that looked to be worth about ten dollars at the most, without a single stripe or decoration of any sort, in short, nothing indicating his rank or declaring to this crowd of gawkers: "I am the man who brought Japan victory and glory!"

---

* The uniform of the regular army is among the most basic; what I am speaking of here are the uniforms of the various "State troops", the militias of each state that together comprise a sort of reserve force of the United States Army [author note].

18 The Red Cross

The prowess of the Japanese army and navy during their 1894 war with China is renowned the world over. One is familiar with how the army vanquished the Chinese in Korea and Manchuria; how it seized Pen-Yang, Port Arthur, and Weihaiwei while the navy destroyed the Chinese fleet at the mouth of the Yalu. However, what is less known are the immense services rendered by the Japanese Red Cross under the presidency of the Her Majesty the Empress. One might say that this organization, like the army itself, was just a newborn and had yet to be put to the test, and one could not have been blamed for fearing it would not be up to the enormity of the task suddenly thrust upon it. Events proved such fears to be unfounded; the various services of the Red Cross covered it with glory and earned it the just admiration of the entire world. It is not the number of victories the Japanese won, but rather the method in which they were won, which definitively place that country among the ranks of the great civilized nations.

It was at Pen-Yang in northern Korea that the ambulances and hospitals of the Red Cross experienced their baptism of fire. This fortified city, occupying a practically impregnable position, had been admirably fortified by the Chinese and was defended by eighteen thousand regular Chinese troops that had arrived from Tientsin and Manchuria.

The Japanese attacked Pen-Yang from four directions simultaneously. However, three of those attacks were but feints, while all the glory—as all the suffering of that terrible day—fell on the Japanese troops attacking the Chinese positions from the front. Under the orders of General Oshima, these soldiers commenced their attack on the Chinese advanced positions at three o'clock in the morning and only overran them after twelve hours of bloody combat. With his troops already exhausted, General Oshima, convinced he could not overwhelm the second line of defense (forts armed with rapid fire cannon) before nightfall, fell back to occupy the previous days' positions.

As the battle raged the ambulances of the Red Cross were tireless in their efforts to lavish care upon the day's wounded—*be they Chinese or Japanese*—who were transported to combat hospitals in the rear. As for the Chinese, they had neither ambulances, nor hospitals, nor surgeons, and they abandoned their wounded to die like dogs. When the firing ceased, the Japanese stretcher-bearers headed for the battlefront with the intention of gathering up the Chinese casualties, but they were prevented from doing so by the enemy, which fired at them from atop the forts. And so they waited for nightfall when they courageously returned to the battlefield, even up to the very walls of the forts, where they gathered up a quantity of Chinese wounded. Meanwhile, can you imagine what sort of labor then occupied the Chinese governor and his officers? The massacre of the Japanese prisoners! The following day their horribly mutilated corpses were discovered by the now victorious Japanese. Upon entering the compound only recently abandoned by the Chinese general, the commander of Japanese forces, General Notzu, discovered the head of a young lieutenant who had been wounded the previous day and been taken prisoner. Do you imagine that faced with such horrors the Japanese gave themselves over to vengeance? Not in the least! The Chinese prisoners were admirably and humanely treated, and a hospital for the Chinese wounded was immediately organized. This is not mere hearsay; I myself visited one of these hospitals and I was given full freedom to question its prisoners.

Daily the moveable wounded were taken by flatboat down the river to the port, where they were placed aboard steam transports that carried them to Hiroshima in southern Japan. There immense hospitals had been set up capable or handling four thousand sick and wounded. One day upon my return to Hiroshima the Japanese Surgeon General, Major General Ishiguro,[1] arranged for me to visit these hospitals. As we were leaving the dispensary he remarked on the first aid kit he held in his hand filled with bandages and antiseptic dressings.

"This here," he told me, "is the work of Her Majesty the Empress. You are no doubt aware that since the outbreak of hostilities Her Majesty and all the court ladies have convened daily in a large hall of the imperial palace to prepare bandages, lint and the like. Despite the victory of our troops, these ladies have completely renounced all indulgences and distractions to dedicate to the Ministry of War the money they'd otherwise have spent on such things as festivals and cosmetics."

The hospital at Hiroshima was located in the countryside just outside the city and surrounded by magnificent gardens. It was comprised of long wards lighted on each side by large windows. The rooms were kept remarkably orderly, and the whole room was of a snow-like whiteness. The beds were white, the patients were dressed in white, and even the sick nurses wore all white uniforms. It was the very image of cleanliness and order. Flowers and other plants brightened every room, and from the open windows came the sound of martial music, which was played daily in the hospital gardens upon orders from the emperor himself. Each patient had newspapers and books at his disposal, and even cigarettes and fruit when it was permitted.

Japanese Nurses Dressing the Wounds of a Japanese Soldier and a Chinese Prisoner.

Figure 24. Japanese and Chinese wounded being nursed at the Red Cross Hospital at Hiroshima (1894). *Munsey's Magazine* (1895).

Among the sick nurses figured many worldly ladies. Countess Néré,[2] the wife of a Japanese admiral, headed these three hundred nurses, who dedicated themselves day and night to the care of the wounded.

All officers had separate quarters, and in one of these I saw a commander being nursed by his daughter, a ravishing child of about fifteen dressed in a superb kimono of embroidered silk. She was so pretty and gracious that I actually envied the commander!

The general gave the bandages prepared by the empress to the officers. It is impossible to describe the respect, gratitude, and love with which they were received. Some poor devil of a lieutenant, who lay on his back wracked with pain, not wishing to receive such a gift from such a disrespectful position, made desperate efforts to sit up.

"Well," I asked a certain young captain, "you must be happy to be so well cared for and to come back to Japan, am I right?"

"Yes," he replied. "But it would be better yet to return to the fight!"

They all thought like this, these wounded. They wished only to throw themselves back into the struggle!

Spotting a freshly cleaned and shaven white-clad Chinese being nursed as if he was a brother, I asked him whether he was comfortable.

"Yes," he replied. "They treat us well enough, but I don't like the Japanese cooking, and I've asked several times for some Chinese dishes without result!"

I was completely dumbfounded. The impudence of this Chinese was so incredible that for several moments I stood speechless.

"You see," remarked General Ishiguro. "These Chinese are never satisfied. They even want us to provide a Chinese cook!"

Meanwhile the Chinese soldiers were killing and mutilating every Japanese soldier that fell into their hands!

The sailors had not been forgotten by the Red Cross Society. The *Kobe Naru,* one of the largest steamships of the Nippon Yusen Kaisha (the Japanese Navigation Society), had been transformed into a well-organized hospital, which was attached to the fleet of Admiral Ito.

Japanese doctors and surgeons are naturally of the modern school and many of them have studied in Paris, Berlin, Vienna, or London. They seem to have a particular knack for surgery, and the few operations at which I assisted were accomplished in a masterly manner.

Before concluding, there is one more example to demonstrate the admirable discipline of the army. When the Japanese army with all its attendant "coolies" entered Pen-Yang a single female was discovered there. She was Chinese, the wife of a telegraph employee. Apparently all the Korean inhabitants had fled, not at the approach of the Japanese but of the Chinese, and they still had yet to return. This woman was young and quite attractive, and no doubt there were among the twenty-thousand Japanese officers and soldiers who seized Pen-Yang not a few strapping fellows who found her to their liking... However, this woman was in no way molested; led before General Notzu, she appealed to his mercy to send her back to China, a request to which the general immediately assented. There was along the river a Chinese fishing junk with three men aboard. It had not taken part in the battle, and it was to these men that the general entrusted the woman. In exchange for a passport allowing them to cross the Japanese naval lines, these men agreed to transport her to Chefoo.

Do these numerous examples not suffice for us to say of the Japanese and the Japanese Red Cross: they merit humanity's praise!

19 The Spy

It happened during the Sino-Japanese War. The First Army under the command of General Notzu had driven the Chinese from Korea and was preparing for the invasion of northern Manchuria. Stealthily and unbeknownst to most, a Second Army had been assembled at Hiroshima, a small and nondescript city in southern Japan where the emperor had been based since the commencement of hostilities. Count Ito, the Prime Minister, Viscount Hijikata, the Minister of the Imperial Household, Count Oyama, the Minister of War, as well as the majority of the other ministers, were there as well. And it was from that place, a quiet and almost unknown corner of Japan, far from parliamentary deputies and reporters, far from Tokyo and Yokohama, far from the foreign legations and the eyes of the curious, that the war was directed. Nobody was allowed to enter Hiroshima unless they possessed a special passport, which was issued only in very exceptional situations.

Upon my return from Korea to Hiroshima, where I had been invited by General Kawakami, Chief of the General Staff, I realized, though it had never been communicated to me, that a second expedition was on the point of departing. Around twenty thousand men were encamped around us while thirty steam transports sat at anchor, already loaded with artillery, munitions, and provisions. Each day two or three of these transports, after having taken aboard troops of all types, lifted anchor and silently slipped away towards a destination unknown. Finally, there was only one steamer remaining, the *Nagato Maru,* which was not allocated as a troop transport but rather to transport certain high ranking persons. But who? No one seemed to know. In the evening I decided to pay a visit to Marshal Oyama, the Minister of War, whom I had known a long time and who had promised me at the end of a banquet a few weeks previous that he would make sure I went "wherever the army went." Though I had just returned from

Korea, where I had seen the First Army in action, I was not satisfied and wished to see the second act upon which I felt the curtain was about to rise.

The Minister of War occupied modest quarters rented from a local merchant in the town center. I was led into a small room where I was surprised to find Count Ito, General Kawakami,[1] Ito Miyouji,[2] the Government General Secretary, and Count Oyama, all seated on floor cushions around a small brazier (for the weather was cold). The presence of documents, maps, writing brushes, and ink indicated to me that serious matters were then under consideration.

Figure 25. Count Oyama Iwao, Minister of War and Commander of the Japanese Second Army. *Leslie's Illustrated Weekly* (1894).

As I felt I had interrupted them I made to excuse myself and depart.

"No, no, please stay," the Minister of War said. "We're happy to see you."

He offered me a cushion and ordered an aide-de-camp to bring tea, liquor, and cigars.

"Well," said the soft voice of Count Ito, who was smiling through his black beard. "When one calls upon a minister at such a late hour, and in wartime no less, it must be for a serious reason."

"The most serious, your Excellency," I replied. "There is only one transport ship remaining and I would be very sorry to see it depart without me. I wish to take part in the expedition."

"Expedition? What expedition?" asked the Chief of Staff incredulously.

"Who told you there was an expedition?" exclaimed Oyama.

"My goodness, messieurs, no one told me a thing, but during my excursions on the excellent horse the general was kind enough to provide me I witnessed encampments of at least twenty thousand soldiers. These have all now vanished, carried off on the transports which at the time of my arrival here danced in the bay. Certainly they are not heading for Korea, for the only Chinese to be found there are the buried ones. It's really quite simple; I wish to go where the army is going."

"Well done," laughed Count Ito loudly, and turning to Oyama, "And your response, marshal?"

"Oh, my response will be brief," said the marshal addressing me. "I have not forgotten my pledge and from the moment you arrived I made arrangements that there be a cabin at your disposal aboard the *Nagato Maru*. We depart first thing tomorrow."

"Us?" I said astonished.

"I will be commanding the Second Army myself," Marshal Count Oyama stated simply.

The following morning an immense crowd had gathered along the length of the quay, anxious to salute the departure of the Commander-in-chief and his Chief of Staff with cries and hoorahs. Aboard the *Nagato Maru* the marshal, in full uniform and surrounded by his officers, bade his farewells to Count Ito, the ministers, and various members of court. Champagne was passed around and everyone was quite exuberant. There was no one, including the Prime Minister who was usually so calm and reserved, who was not carried away by enthusiasm. Striking his glass against mine, he said to me laughing,

"So you're going to eat some Chinese? It'll do you good! Mind the bullets, they can be unwelcome visitors. I hope you arrive over there safe and sound."

"Over there! Over there! But where is *there* your Excellency?"

"Honestly, I have no idea. But tell me, where would you like to go?"

"Why to Peking!"

"That's the spirit! Bravo! Bravo!" cried all the officers. "To Peking!"

The cry of "To Peking! To Peking!" was taken up a thousand times as the *Nagato Maru* set off.

But we would not be going that far.

The rendezvous took place at the mouth of the Tatung[3] River along the Korean coast not far from the Chinese border. Just before emptying into the sea this river makes two bends, forming between them a vast natural port where about thirty vessels had gathered. Aboard them was the Japanese Second Army along with the siege artillery to be used at Port Arthur.

The Second Division of the fleet of Admiral Ito, the victor of the Battle of the Yalu, was at anchor.[4] The First Division, composed of more rapid vessels, cruised the coast while further out the torpedo boats formed our first line of defense. As one can see, the Second Army on board the transports was well protected.

Apparently not all of the preparations necessary for landing and making the march towards Kinchow, Talien Wan, and Port Arthur had been completed, for we remained at anchor for over a week. Aboard the *Nagato Maru* the marshal and the officers of the General Staff were in high spirits and we amused ourselves all day with the deck games so popular aboard transatlantic steamers. On several occasions we undertook small walking excursions ashore and engaged in some pistol practice. In this the marshal and I easily shared the laurels, probably because we had the best arms—those of "Smith and Wessen."

The October nights were long. No light was allowed aboard the transports and this meant pitch darkness before six in the morning. Such a precaution was necessary not only because the location of this enormous fleet had to remain a secret, but because there were concerns over a possible night attack by Chinese torpedo boats.

One afternoon our torpedo boats signaled the approach of a foreign man-of-war. Naturally the air was tense as everyone raced to the bridge. To the general surprise of everyone, this ship, just a simple gunboat, proceeded to cruise through the line of torpedo boats and then through the entire fleet, and then slowly and calmly, in the most impudent manner imaginable, steamed right into the middle of the transport ships, passing just in front us.

It was only then that we noticed it was flying a Russian flag at its stern.

On the bridge of the *Nagato Maru* Marshal Count Oyama, General Yamaji, and the other generals, the entire General Staff and the ordnance officers stood as erect and motionless as statues, their ice-cold glares following the foreign vessel, whose unwelcome presence induced in all these martial souls a fierce and indescribable sentiment.

Arriving at the second bend in the river, the Russian gunship veered about and passed by us once more before regaining the high seas from whence it steered for the Chinese coast at full steam.

While the marshal and the older officers maintained their staid, pensive poses, the younger officers, no longer able to suppress their anger, shook their fists in the direction of the Russian flag, screaming in a hundred furious voices:

"Coward! Cossack! Traitor! Your turn will come, you miserable spy!"

20 The Eggs

There's nothing to impress with traditional Japanese food. Your Japanese is a very light eater; in fact, I have often wondered how he can sustain himself and work the way he does while taking so little sustenance. I doubt there is a more frugal race on earth, and yet thin people are the large minority in Japan. Save for their wrestlers, who are veritable monsters, mountains of flesh, fat Japanese are a rarity as well. In general the Japanese are admirably built, well-proportioned, squat and vigorous. Both men and women do an enormous amount of work each day. They have extraordinary resistance.

The *kuruma*, the man who pulls your jinrikisha across flat ground, up hills and down, seems indefatigable. Dripping with sweat, covered in mud and dust, in wind, rain, snow, or under a grilling sun, he runs on and on, devouring kilometers with admirable vigor and agility. He is an extraordinary being, a superb animal, and I don't know what is to be more admired, his physical qualities or his courage, perseverance, and tenacity when, exhausted, panting, every muscle in his body crying out for mercy and ready to give out, he smiles at his own suffering and urges himself forward to the end, repeating softly to himself, "*Shikata ga nai*," which may be translated as, "since fate dealt me this lot, there's nothing to be done," or put more simply, "what's the use of complaining?"

And when, having arrived, we hand him the few pennies that are to recompense him for this labor as a carriage animal, whether we be generous or not he smiles while toweling off his poor body, doubled over by its exertion, and then even lavishes you with thanks and blessings. Ah! How far we are from Paris and its whip-wielding carriage drivers, from their coarseness and brutality!

Personally, I have always suffered from a certain ineffable sentiment, a mélange of pity and admiration, realizing that I was being

The Eggs

pulled along the road by his human effort alone; it was hard convincing myself I was not guilty of cruelty.

Now then! This human horse that is the *kuruma* subsists on practically nothing. His nourishment would hardly suffice to sustain a twelve year-old schoolboy in the west. A bit of rice, a little dried fish, some fish soup, a little rice wine and sugarless green tea, such comprises about his entire diet.

And he is not the only one in Japan who works hard and eats little.

To say nothing of the peasants, men and women, who toil like beasts of burden, in commerce and industry, in boutiques and textiles, employees and laborers also work fifteen or sixteen-hour days and, what is more extraordinary, in most cases they receive absolutely no remuneration. They are fed—and very poorly fed—and that is all.

After fifteen years laboring for the same company, a worker will often receive from his patrons, in the form of a loan, a certain sum allowing him to set up an enterprise in his turn.

In the foreign trading companies in Japan the Japanese clerks who speak English, French, or German receive contracts of 150, 200, 300 francs or more. But don't imagine they're happy or envied by those who work for a pittance—no, on the contrary. They're pitied, *because Japanese are not treated with the same consideration in these foreign firms as they are in native ones!*

For the Japanese this is the crux: without courtesy life itself loses its attraction. Among them there is but one desire: to be polite; and one anxiety: the fear of being uncivil.

After the greeting "*Ohayo,*" which means, "it is a very honorable early hour," the Japanese never fail to add, "*O! Shikai itashimashita,*" which is to say, "I beg you to forgive my rudeness from our last encounter," a simply delightful request when one recalls the extraordinary politeness they in fact displayed at that last meeting.

To return to the subject of Japanese food and their meager needs, I need only add that ten or twelve francs a month are more than sufficient to feed a Japanese for you to understand the degree of simplicity of life over there.

This sobriety on the part of the Japanese is one of the great strengths of their army, whose commissariat is child's play compared to those of European armies. During the last war with China the Japanese army could never have made the progress it did if it had had to drag across

Korea and Manchuria the provisions, canned foods, and kitchen utensils that generally follow a European army. In a country where roads properly speaking do not exist, where communications are nil, where artillery, munitions, and medicine have to be lugged on the backs of men across vast distances, you need as many porters as soldiers if you want to feed the army on bread, meat, vegetables, canned preserves, biscuits, liquor, coffee, sugar, and so on.

I went to Pen-Yang, Korea, where the First Army was assembled and deprived of provisions. It was only by the grace of General Notzu that I managed not to starve to death. I learned my lesson, and when I departed with the Second Army I brought three months of provisions, a donkey to carry it all and a cook to prepare it. Alas! The Army Chief of Staff, whom I was accompanying, went three times faster than my donkey and cook, the result being they weren't always there when I needed them.

I can never forget the intelligent efforts of Arai (the cook), who did what he could to move things forward as rapidly as possible, and when he did finally catch up with me, no matter how late the hour or how tired he was, he got a fire going and prepared me an excellent meal. That done, he would then set to work on my clothes, giving me a fresh change of linen, before loading my pockets, holsters, and saddle-bags with "Huntley and Palmer" biscuits, chocolate, and canned goods. After a very short rest he would be up again at four, prepare my breakfast and then be off with the donkey, hopefully to meet me again at the end of the day's stage. Arai was devotion personified and I am greatly indebted to him.

Just as I was the first foreigner to arrive at Pen-Yang in Korea, I was the only foreigner to take part in the disembarkation of the Second Army. Catching passage with General Oyama aboard the transport *Nagato Maru,* I accompanied him all the way to the Manchurian coast. There, learning that a brigade under the command of General Yamaji[1] had taken up the vanguard, I left the marshal and with a young interpreter named Okabe, Arai, the donkey, and a single soldier as escort, set off across unknown territory, determined to catch up with the advance brigade. I believe I reached it on the third day, and was almost immediately joined by the French military attaché, Count de Labry, and his Japanese friend Captain Arada. These two officers, whom I had known in Japan, were perfect gentlemen both and filled with vim and vigor. They became my companions and I wish to extend to them here my infinite gratitude for the help they provided me, for the thousand little services they rendered on my behalf, and not least of all for the friendship and concern they displayed towards me.

The Count de Labry and I were the sole foreigners to depart with General Yamaji's advance and to take part in the fighting at Kinchow and Talien Wan and in the ultimate Japanese seizure of those two forts. Anyhow, the combat itself held little interest. The Chinese offered absolutely no resistance. But several of the marches were truly grueling; water was rare, as much for bathing as drinking; we went without food on several occasions, and most unpleasant of all, we had to spend many a night in the notoriously filthy and putrid hovels of China.

Figure 26. The one-eyed General Yamaji Motoharu, Commander of the First Division. *Leslie's Illustrated Weekly* (1894).

On the eve of the fall of Kinchow we marched until eleven or twelve at night, arriving at the end of the leg, just below the Chinese positions, worn out and exhausted.

There were three or four old farmhouses there, one of which was placed at our disposal. Arai had not yet arrived—we had not seen him for forty-eight hours—and we had absolutely nothing to eat. We were about to go to sleep on empty stomachs on makeshift beds of straw when suddenly—oh joy!—we caught the sound of "cock-a-doodle-doos" coming from the rear of the courtyard. Heading over there, we discovered two old chickens.

In a gracious gesture we sent one to the general, keeping one for ourselves.

"Arai's not here. Who's going to prepare the chicken?"

"Oh, certainly not me," said the French officer. "I prefer to sleep. He who sleeps dines, as they say."

"It's the simplest thing in the world," said Captain Arada. "It'll only take five minutes." Suddenly he grabbed the chicken and stuffed it—feet, feathers, innards and all—into a truss of straw which he then stuck in the fire!

You can imagine what ensued. The straw having burned, we recovered something black, shapeless, and disgusting, which only five minutes before had been a chicken. Starving as we were, none of us dared touch it.

I awoke at two in the morning with horrible cramps; my stomach was groaning with hunger. From the glare of the pilot light I could see the Count de Labry was awake as well, and following his gaze I could see it led to the "chicken à la Arada," which the Japanese captain had placed next to us.

"I'm dying of hunger."

"Me too!"

"Should we try it after all?"

"Let's!"

Alas! We had only to taste it before bitterly regretting our decision. It was dreadful!

Before daylight we had once more set off. During the night the Japanese troops had taken up positions on an elevated spot below the city of Kinchow, which was now at the mercy of the Japanese artillery that had been able to advance without the least trouble.

The Eggs

Following General Yamaji, who was surrounded by his General Staff, we galloped as far as as the field artillery positions, which immediately began to open fire on the ramparts of Kinchow, atop of which we spied a large number of brightly-clad Chinese and hundreds of huge standards.

It was truly striking. As soon as the first shells exploded among them the beautiful uniforms scattered as fast as could be, flags and standards shamelessly dropped, and then the Japanese buglers signaled the charge. We watched as the Japanese infantry emerged suddenly from furrows in the terrain to throw themselves headlong against the enemy positions.

An engineering company, which during the night had approached as close as prudently possible, soon reached the city's main gate. One cartridge of dynamite and . . . Boom! Kinchow was ours!

"Forward!" cried General Yamaji, and galloping at full speed we followed him as he charged towards the ramparts, atop of which we could now see, here and there, a Chinese more stubborn and less afraid than the rest still firing his gun.

Several stray bullets whizzed by our ears and we received quite a scare to see the Surgeon General suddenly fall along with his mount. We thought he had been killed, but fortunately this was not the case. His horse had simply made a false step and stumbled but without hurting this brilliant officer in the least.

We were stopped outside the city gate where it was decided we should wait until all areas of the city had been occupied by the army. We no longer cared, for in the meantime we had become more and more hungry.

I remembered that in galloping towards the city we had passed a turnip field, and without informing my companions I set off again and soon returned with some of these vegetables, which though superb with duck, leave much to be desired when eaten plain.

Once finally settled in the conquered city, though it was nearly abandoned by the Chinese I learned of one old resident who had bravely refused to depart. What's more, he was said to own some chickens. I headed off to his house only to learn—alas!—that he had only one chicken left, and it had been requisitioned for the general.

I was about to leave dejected when the old man added, "But I have eggs."

I jumped. "Eggs," I cried. "I'll take them! Hurry, where are they?"

The old man disappeared for a few minutes to reappear carrying an egg in each hand.

"I only have two," he said.

"Very good. How much do you want?"

He shook his head. "I can't sell them just like that," he told me.

I was confused.

"No, I want to sell this one first," he added, showing me the egg in his right hand. What a crazy old fool, I thought.

"Well, then how much do you want for that one?"

"You can have it for two centimes."

"Very good, I'll take it. And the other?"

"Ah, the other," he said, caressing it lovingly. "This other one will cost you a franc."

I was perplexed.

"Listen old man," I exclaimed. "Would you mind explaining how this one is worth a franc while this other is only worth two centimes?"

"Well the other one, the two centimes one, is fresh. It was just laid yesterday."

The more I heard the less I understood.

"So you're telling me you want two centimes for a fresh egg and one franc for the other?"

"But the other one is really much older. I've been preserving it for over two years."

"Well my good fellow, you can keep it two more years if it makes you happy."

But the interpreter accompanying me, his eyes glowing with lust, asked if I might advance him a franc on his salary since he really wanted to treat himself to this extraordinary egg.

I consented, on condition he eat it at least five hundred meters from our quarters and not come within my presence until tomorrow. I simply could not trust the odor of a two year old egg.*

---

* The Chinese preserve eggs by placing them in a bed of lime to prevent air from penetrating their interior. Preserved eggs are considered extreme delicacies [author note].

21 Chiu-Ji

Animals played prominent roles in my Sino-Japanese War experience. Before embarking with Marshal Oyama and the Second Army I had asked the authorities if it would be permissible for me to bring a horse along with my baggage. I was told the marshal would arrange a mount for me upon arrival in China. And in fact, just before I left to catch up with General Yamaji's advance guard a small Japanese horse was put at my disposal.

It had a weak back and weak knees, and only with difficulty could it lift itself up on its pitiful trembling legs. Nevertheless, it carried me all the way to Yamaji's camp. I arrived late at night with a terrible head cold after a very chilly day's journey. Throughout the ride I had had watery eyes, a runny nose, and a high fever. I went to bed very anxious that I might be unable to depart with the army advance guard the following day.

To my surprise, I awoke the next morning feeling perfectly refreshed and with all traces of the virulent cold gone. But my astonishment did not stop there. A few minutes before departing Arai arrived to announce that my horse was very ill. The army veterinarian I requested examine it pronounced the animal had caught a chill and was suffering from a "serious cold." Everyone was convinced that this intelligent and devoted creature had relieved me of my cold by generously taking it on himself. Whatever the case, the poor beast was incapable of advancing further, and my predicament would have been serious indeed had Captain Arada not felt obliged to put an ordnance horse at my disposal (to the great chagrin of the poor cavalry soldier who was then forced to make the march on foot, and in a uniform not exactly designed for marching).

Japan possesses very few horses and so the cavalry plays but a negligible role in its army. Of the hundred and five-thousand men that comprise Japan's peacetime army, the cavalry makes up only three thousand. The seventeen-thousand man Second Army (not counting the nearly ten-thousand coolies hired to transport provisions), had only three squadrons of a hundred twenty sabers apiece, or a total of three-hundred sixty cavalry soldiers to clear and protect the army's flanks against any surprise. In other words, horses were so rare that I had held out little hope of replacing mine. I kept the ordnance horse until the siege of Kinchow, when numerous excellent mules fell into Japanese hands.

Figure 27. Japanese soldiers during the Sino-Japanese War. *L'Illustration* (18 August 1894).

Thanks again to Captain Arada, a superb white mule was then put at my disposal. The Japanese soldiers, who had never seen a mule (they do not exist in Japan), gazed at it with the curiosity an Eskimo would have for an elephant. They called it a "Chinese horse," and one day I attempted in vain to explain the origins of this animal to a group of foot-soldiers. They laughed so hard they looked like they'd been seized by fits of apoplexy.

If the soldiers regarded my white mule with untold astonishment, Japanese horses on the other hand displayed a violent antipathy towards the beast. The first time I called upon Marshal Oyama's Chief-of-staff, proudly seated on my new mount, the chief's steed along with those of the other officers were seized with a sudden terror and began to kick and jump before flying off in all directions, prey to some comical fright. This happened so suddenly that half the General Staff was actually thrown from their horses. Had a Chinese shell landed amidst this gathering, though it might have created more havoc, it certainly would not have caused as violent a commotion as did my white mule, which, furious with its rude reception, let off with violent kicks on all sides.

This devilish beast exhibited all the characteristics of its race, and its stubbornness was not the least of it. Several times it took it into its head to follow a different route from that of the General Staff. It would suddenly take off in a gallop towards some unknown destination, giving me a very disagreeable half hour during which I naturally became obsessed by the idea that I had become completely separated from the army and would soon fall into the hands of the Chinese. It took a dreadful struggle to get the beast back on the correct path.

When on November 19th we arrived at Doshioji, within artillery range of the advanced defenses of Port Arthur, and believing that the attack would come the following day, I concluded that I would never have the courage to ride into battle on the back of this dreadful mule. What if he became eager to rejoin his former Chinese masters and galloped off at full speed in their direction? That'd be a fine pickle. So I decided to pay a visit to the Deputy Chief-of-staff, to whom I communicated my fears.

"My good man," he said to me. "Though we don't possess a tenth of the horses we need, if you are a good rider maybe I can solve your predicament. One of my private mounts has just arrived. It's a young and solid stallion that hasn't been ridden in three or four weeks and I'm certain won't be very cooperative. If you like I could certainly lend it to you."

In place of the white mule! Why I happily accepted on the spot, but my joy was short-lived.

This stallion had the devil in him. No sooner had I mounted him the following day than I realized I was astride a veritable volcano. I passed such a frightful day at the front struggling with the maddening beast that as soon as I'd returned to the encampment I went to see the Deputy Chief-of-staff to reclaim my infamous white mule, which had the honor of carrying me before the battle of Port Arthur after all. You can be sure that it was with a feeling of triumph that I finally entered that city.

Arai and the provisions donkey followed soon behind me, brave Arai proudly carrying in his arms a little Chinese dog that I had acquired under some very touching circumstances.

Soon after the first forts defending the approach to Port Arthur fell to the Japanese, General Oyama and his general staff occupied a certain hill dominating the city. There was a small Chinese temple there that had previously served as an enemy observation post, just below which several Japanese shells had exploded.

Scattered in the temple's vicinity were several Chinese corpses. Just in front of the temple was the body of an officer whose head had been half blown off by a shell fragment. As the Chief-of-staff had ordered a telescope be set up at the spot where the dead officer lay, two or three coolies were charged to carry him off. Just as they did so a delightful little puppy, no larger than a man's fist and trembling with fear, jumped from the hand of his dead master where it had been hiding. With its hair bristling, growling and baring its teeth, the puppy stood its ground, prepared to defend the pitiful corpse.

As soon as the initial surprise had passed the coolies again proceeded to take the body, but the little dog leapt forward and seized the hand of one of these coolies between its fangs and gave him a frightful bight. The coolie let out a painful scream and seizing a large stick would surely have beaten the dog to death had I not stepped in front of him and grabbed the little thing, declaring that I wished to take it under my protection. The creature struggled furiously, growled, and bit, and it took everything I had to subdue it.

Two days after the fall of the city, a general staff officer came to see me and informed me that the marshal was going to have an eccentric assortment of animals found at Port Arthur sent to the emperor. Among these were donkeys, some of those infamous mules, and a camel. He asked me if I might not want to add my puppy to the collection but I refused, having grown quite attached to it.

"What do you call it?" the officer asked me.

My word, I'd been so busy that I still hadn't had time to give it a name.

"Call it 'Port Arthur,' it'll have a historical name."

"Yes, but a little too long a name for such a small creature, don't you think?"

"Well, why not name it 'Faithful'? Its attachment to its poor dead master was certainly touching."

"Actually," I said. "I was thinking I'd give it a Chinese or Japanese name."

"Why, then it's settled! Just call it 'Chiu-ji,' Chinese for faithful."

Needless to say, Chiu-ji never left me. I took it back to Japan and from there we set off together for the United States.

At the time I wasn't aware that a photographer from a large illustrated English paper, *The Graphic* I believe, had taken a picture of the dead Chinaman with Chiu-ji curled up in his arms.

One day while casually perusing the papers in the library of my New York club, a friend reading the latest illustrated newspapers from London cried out,

"Hey, what do you know, it's Chiu-ji!"

As it turned out, on its front page this prominent London paper had reproduced the photograph taken by its Japan correspondent. And by curious coincidence, the English editor had chosen as a caption for the illustration: "Faithful unto death"—*Fidèle jusqu'à la mort.*

Brave little Chiu-ji!

OUR CORRESPONDENT, A. B. DE GUERVILLE AND HIS LITTLE WAR-DOG.

Figure 28. A. B. de Guerville and Chiu-ji (1894). *Leslie's Illustrated Weekly* (1895).

22 Port Arthur

One recalls the uproar that surrounded the seizure of Port Arthur and the strong emotions stirred up in the civilized world by the accounts of certain foreign correspondents concerning the "massacres" or "butchery" of Port Arthur. According to some telegrams dispatched to American and British newspapers "the entire population, men, women, and children" were mercilessly slaughtered. With a peacetime population of several thousand souls, and at the outbreak of hostilities a garrison force of twelve to fifteen thousand men, which was reduced by half at the time of the attack, it was widely assumed that upwards of 20,000 people had been massacred, and a cry of horror was heard from one end of the universe to the other.

I have absolutely no desire to reopen this polemic or to delve into the personalities concerned. Each of us sees things in our own way. I am nevertheless convinced that even those who were harshest on Japan must recognize today, if they are indeed men of good faith, that they went too far with such propositions, and that in fact the Japanese army was never guilty of the great and horrific crime of which it has been accused.

I was present at the siege of Port Arthur. I entered it at the same time as the other foreign correspondents. I stayed there for exactly the same length of time. I was neither drunk, nor mad, nor blind, yet I did not witness this "bloody massacre of an entire population, a massacre that went on for days."

I believe it possible to prove that there was much exaggeration in these accounts. For this it is necessary to briefly recall the train of events.

The Second Army, under the command of Marshal Oyama, arrived before Port Arthur on the night of 18–19 November 1894, after having seized from the enemy the city of Kinchow and the forts of Talien Wan without firing a shot. As it advanced, the Second Army (following the example set by the First Army in Korea) treated the indigenous inhabitants with the greatest consideration. Anyhow, the villages were almost completely abandoned, the population having fled, not from the approach of the Japanese but from the Chinese soldiers come to defend them, and to sack and pillage everything in the process. Of its usual population of eight thousand, Kinchow had barely one thousand by the time General Yamaji arrived.

It was the same case with Port Arthur. A large majority of the populace had fled well before the Japanese seizure of the city, which is proved by the reports of foreign battleship commanders, who were crossing between Chefoo, Port Arthur, and Weihaiwei conducting surveillance. Hundreds of junks and boats of all sorts had carried the majority of the population, women and children, to Chefoo and other Chinese ports. Thus I establish my first point:

Nine-tenths of the population of Port Arthur had left the city well before the arrival of the Japanese.

The city was enclosed behind a line of forts and redoubts defending it from land on one side and from the sea on the other. These forts were armed with eighty pieces of artillery, the majority Krupp cannons.

The Japanese had forty-eight pieces of artillery, which at dawn on the twenty-first of November opened fire on the Chinese positions. At first the Chinese responded vigorously but then they ceased completely. The assault on the forts was opened on the right by General Yamaji, in the center by the 12th Brigade, on the left by a mixed brigade under the command of Colonel Hasegawa. The Chinese abandoned their positions, a certain number taking refuge in the city while others fled in groups either in the direction of Talien Wan or in junks.

By three-thirty that afternoon all resistance seemed to have ceased but the large forts defending the city's seafront still held. The Japanese fleet under the command of Admiral Ito created a diversion but it was insufficient to take the forts in a frontal assault. The forts had to be attacked from the rear, and accomplishing this required Japanese troops pass through the city. Naturally this meant the Japanese had to neutralize the Chinese fugitives who had sought refuge in the city for the risk they posed in harassing their rear and cutting them off from the bulk of the Japanese army.

It appears clear then that *after having abandoned the forts the Chinese soldiers had taken refuge in the city, and it is not surprising that a certain number of them were killed by the Japanese troops that launched an assault on the last holding forts.*

Some foreign correspondents asserted that the men killed in the city were not soldiers as they were not wearing uniforms. I would point out that this was the first battlefield of the war on which these gentlemen were present, and they were apparently ignorant of the fact that at Assan, Pen-Yang, and Kinchow the Chinese soldiers were actually ordered to dispose of their uniforms and thousands of these non-uniformed and ignominious types fell into the hands of the Japanese. One should remember that the Chinese uniform was composed of simple blouse (sometimes, though not always, accompanied by a large pair of pants), and *it was worn over one's everyday clothing.* With his blouse removed a soldier looked like any other civilian.

In Korea the Chinese had taken things even further. In an effort to pass themselves off as Koreans many Chinese even cut off their queues. The streets of Pen-Yang were strewn with enough ponytails to make the fortune of any barber.

Walking the main thoroughfare of Port Arthur, I observed about a dozen or so corpses, a natural enough sight after such a battle. But what struck me—as it did others—was that the bodies were not uniformed.

"Yet these are soldiers," my companion Captain Arada told me. "They all wear military shoes. Look."

It was also reported that the dead were unarmed. But this proves nothing for the simple reason that the Japanese confiscated all weapons belonging to the enemy for fear they might fall into the hands of other Chinese, or even Japanese coolies. By the time the foreign correspondents entered the city the Japanese had already been there several hours. It is natural to assume that by then they had already gathered up the weapons.

From all this it follows that no evidence presented can prove the dead at Port Arthur were peaceful civilians.

It is noteworthy that the correspondents who spoke of a "massacre" and "butchery" did so in very general terms. They spoke of a "population" (which in fact did not exist as it had fled) but they abstained from giving any numbers. But such a figure for the massacred would certainly have been instructive, even if only approximate. One English correspondent assures us that the bodies of "women and children" littered the streets. Yet a French correspondent, who humbly submits his eyes were wide open, provides us with some figures (he was the only one to do so): *one hundred twenty corpses, of which three were women and three children.*[1]

With those numbers I think we approach the truth, and we can now assert—*the fact that only 120 bodies were found in a city that had been bombarded for several hours by forty-eight canons lobbing hundreds of shells and thousands of pieces of shrapnel, and which was then taken by armed assault by troops thrown against the sea forts, proves that here was neither butchery nor a massacre.* Now let us examine the general attitude and behavior of the Japanese troops at the time of these events.

As I have already noted, in Korea, as in Manchuria, the Japanese had treated the Chinese population with the utmost humanity. At Kinchow, which fell into Japanese hands a few days before Port Arthur, the prisoners were treated admirably and the Japanese soldiers even fraternized with the inhabitants that had not fled.

It is true, however, that a tragic event which occurred during the march on Port Arthur had the potential of changing these humanitarian sentiments once and for all. On November 18, three Japanese cavalry squads serving as an advance for the army were surprised and surrounded by three thousand Chinese with artillery. The Japanese put up a heroic defense and an infantry company, which had advanced well ahead of its brigade, soon came to its aid. Surrounded in turn by far superior Chinese forces, it was thanks only to several heroic charges by the cavalry that they were able to break through and retreat. This engagement cost the Japanese about forty injured and fourteen dead, the latter falling into the hands of the Chinese.

The following day the Japanese army passed through the previous day's battle zone, and there all the soldiers witnessed—as I did myself—the horribly mutilated corpses of those fourteen Japanese. Heads, legs, and arms had been hacked off, ears, tongues, eyes torn off or gouged out, and the torsos subjected to even worse mutilations impossible to describe here. It was horrendous. One can imagine the effect such a frightening spectacle had on the army.

The gate of Port Arthur through which the Japanese entered the city was *decorated* with the eyes, ears, and hands of these corpses, and the walls of the city were lampooned with placards signed by the governor himself offering fat rewards for any Japanese soldier living or dead, or even for *pieces of a Japanese*—prices varying by body part! To speak frankly, could one call the Japanese savages even if they did put a hundred twenty Chinese to the sword? What would Europeans have done—what do the most civilized armies of Europe do—in like situations?

At nightfall two days after the fall of Port Arthur I went on a tour of inspection accompanied by Arai, my domestic servant. It was bitterly cold and we were both frozen. Passing through a large household gate we observed towards the back of a courtyard a large open fire around which were gathered twenty or so soldiers. We approached them with the idea of warming ourselves. Imagine my horror when I perceived the forms of two half-charred Chinese among the flames. Disgusted, I was carefully slipping away when I bumped up against a Japanese officer coming from the opposite direction. With the deference characteristic of his race he proceeded to apologize excessively, saying in French, *"Mille pardons, monsieur!"*

I stopped and cautioned him that he was about to enter upon a horrifying scene: they were burning Chinese! In reply he smiled softy and said,

"You have it wrong, monsieur. It is nothing so horrible as that. The bodies you saw in the fire were of two Chinese who took refuge in an obscure cubby hole after being seriously wounded. They soon died there and it was only the revolting smell of their putrefying bodies that led to their discovery. When they were found they were so decomposed that the order was given to cremate them immediately. Due to the freezing temperatures over the last few weeks the earth is quite frozen through and it would take forever to dig a grave."

Consider this very simple explanation as well as the extent of my misunderstanding had I not chanced upon this officer.

I confess that the appearance of dead bodies in the streets of Port Arthur struck me as so natural that I did not think to examine the nature of their mortal wounds. One of the foreign correspondents did do this, however, and he informs us that "all of them without exception—and I verified this myself when I was unsure—had either on their skull, neck, or face one or more gashes from a Japanese saber; *but neither bayonet nor bullet wounds.*"

Now here is a valuable testament. Up until the moment I read these lines I had considered the hundred twenty Chinese "massacred" at Port Arthur to be the victims of Japanese soldiers excited by the heat of battle and perhaps eager to wreak vengeance for their horribly mutilated comrades. But then I realized I had been mistaken. For if these Chinese were in fact killed by sabers then the perpetrators clearly could not have been Japanese soldiers, for they are armed only with rifles and bayonets—*but no swords!* This is clear, logical, and irrefutable.

It is not difficult now to imagine what actually occurred. The evening Port Arthur had fallen neither the general staff, nor the journalists, nor the bulk of the army had yet entered the city. Only two battalions belonging to General Yamaji's division were inside. Several hundred coolies followed in their wake, carrying provisions, munitions, etc. These coolies—the dregs of the Japanese populace—wanted to make the most of their situation by pillaging those houses they thought abandoned. But as we now know, Chinese fugitives were hiding out there. They were discovered by the coolies in search of booty; struggles ensued and the Chinese died of saber wounds—from the well-known blades of Japanese coolies. It is true that Marshall Oyama had ordered all coolies be disarmed, and so they should not have been carrying swords. But the order was poorly executed, and in many cases the coolies—imitating "samurai"—carried two swords and only handed over one. Most, if not all, of them had a spare blade handy and ready to use.

To be sure, I have no way of knowing if events actually transpired as I just described, but whether or not my suppositions are just, what remains evident is that *the hundred twenty Chinese "massacred" at Port Arthur were not killed by Japanese soldiers, because their deaths were caused by gashes from swords which Japanese soldiers do not carry.*

Considering how small this "massacre" of Port Arthur becomes once reduced to its true proportions, it is with great satisfaction that I conclude this incident in no way sullies the reputation of the Japanese army, whose conduct from a military as well as a humanitarian perspective was always commendable and worthy of the highest praise and admiration of the civilized world.

Appendix A

Prominent Personalities of *Au Japon*

ARNOLD, Sir Edwin (1832–1904). After serving as principal of the government college in Pune, India, in 1861 Arnold joined the staff of the London *Daily Telegraph*. He gained real prominence for his blank-verse epic *The Light of Asia* (1879), dealing with the life of Buddha, though the work was attacked both for its alleged distortion of Buddhist doctrine and its tolerant attitude toward a non-Christian religion. Arnold spent his later years in Japan, even taking a Japanese wife. Along with composing numerous volumes of poetry, Arnold translated Asian literature and wrote a number of picturesque travel books, among which *Seas and Lands* (1891) and *Japonica* (1891) dealt with his life in and impressions of Japan.

BEAUGRAND, Honoré (1848–1906). A soldier, journalist, politician and author. Born in Quebec, as a young military officer Beaugrand served with French forces in the Mexican campaigns. After the aborted attempt to install the French Maximilian as emperor of Mexico, Beaugrand accompanied the French troops in their return to France. A few years later found him again in North America, where he became a journalist in New Orleans, and subsequently in St. Louis, Boston, and Chicago. In 1878 he returned to his native Canada where he founded *La Patrie,* a liberal daily in Montreal, which remained in his hands until 1897. He also served two terms as mayor of that city in 1885–1887. From the 1890s, financially secure through his publishing enterprises, Beaugrand dedicated the remainder of his life to travel and writing. It was during Beaugrand's extended trip through the Far East during 1891–1892 that de Guerville met him in Japan.

BRINKLEY, Frank (Francis) (1841–1912). The Irishman Frank Brinkley originally arrived in Japan in 1867 to lecture at the newly established Marine Artillery College. In Tokyo he came to serve as correspondent for *The Times* of London and from 1881 became proprietor and chief editor of the English language *Japan Daily Mail* (as well as its weekly version). He stayed on in Japan nearly four decades, as a teacher, imperial advisor, journalist, businessman, scholar, and renowned collector of, and expert on, Japanese fine arts. Evidence also indicates that he was "in the pocket" of the Japanese—to the extent that his newspaper could not survive without heavy government subsidies—and helped feed positive news reports to the western press before, during, and after the Sino-Japanese War.

CHEN Jitong (1851–1907). Also known as Tcheng Ki Tong or Tchen Ki Tong. A Chinese military figure, diplomat, and writer, Chen served during the 1880s as military attaché to the Chinese legation in France. In Paris he presented a colorful figure, well-known for his receptions as well as his numerous public lectures and writings, such as what remains his best known work today, *Les chinois peints par eux-mêmes* [The Chinese painted by themselves]. Chen's last year in Paris was marred by personal and political scandals—that received their share of attention in the papers—leading to his expulsion from France (alluded to by de Guerville) in 1889. It was soon revealed that almost all of Chen's books—including, ironically, the one mentioned above—were penned by Adalbert-Henri Foucault de Mondion, who in a deal with Chen had placed the name of the well-known Chinese attaché to the book in exchange for a share of the profits. But the scandal did not spell the end to Chen's public career. He went on to serve briefly as the Minister of Foreign Affairs in the short-lived Chinese republic.

COLLIN DE PLANCY, Victor Émile Marie Joseph (1853–1924). A career French diplomat, most of Collin de Plancy's career was spent in the Far East. He was serving briefly as French minister to Japan during the period of de Guerville's sojourn there in 1892 before moving on to serve as French minister to Korea—a post and country he strongly preferred—from 1893. He would remain at Seoul almost continuously until his retirement due to health reasons in 1906.

COOMBS, Frank Leslie (1853–1934). A native of Napa, California, Coombs practiced law before going on to serve for several years in the California State Assembly. Upon the unexpected death of the American

Appendix A

minister to Japan, John F. Swift, in 1892 Coombs was named to replace him. He held the position only briefly from summer 1892 to summer 1893. He later served one term in the United States Congress. It is Minister Coombs to whom Guerville refers in his chapter on the Yoshiwara in *Au Japon*.

HIJIKATA Motohisa (1833–1918). Active in efforts to restore the Meiji Emperor in the years preceding 1868, after that *fait accompli* Hijikata was named Assistant Military Supervisor of Edo (Tokyo). He went on to hold the offices of Chief Cabinet Secretary, and in 1887 Minister of Agriculture and Commerce. At the time de Guerville met him upon his 1892 visit to the imperial court, Hijikata had reached the height of his career as Imperial Household Minister and member of the Privy Council.

HUMANN, Edgar-Eugène (1838–1914). Career French naval officer. At the time of de Guerville's visit to Japan in 1892 he held the rank of vice-admiral as Commander of the French Far Eastern Squadron.

INOUE Katsunosuke (1860–1929). A lifelong diplomat, Inoue was educated primarily in Europe, where he was sent to study at the age of eleven. Nephew and adopted son of the Marquis Inoue Kaoru, one time Minister of Foreign Affairs and one of the most powerful officials in Meiji Japan, Inoue Katsunosuke was named in turn ambassador to Great Britain, Germany, and Belgium. At the time *Au Japon* was being written Inoue was serving as ambassador to Germany. Inoue's wife, Suyeko (b. 1864), was also very westernized and fluent in French.

ISHIGURO Tadanori (1845–1941). An early student of western-style medicine, Ishiguro worked as a medical professor in the years following the 1868 Meiji Restoration before being named surgeon to the army and director of the Medical Affairs Bureau in 1872. At the time de Guerville met him during the Sino-Japanese War, Ishiguro was serving as chief of the ambulance corps. He would later head the Japanese Red Cross.

ITŌ Hirobumi (1841–1909). Itō Hirobumi came from humble farmer origins to become one of the most prominent figures of Meiji Japan. When still a boy his father was adopted into the Samurai Itō clan, thus making the young Hirobumi heir to the educational benefits accorded the sons of samurai. Following Japan's forced opening by the American Commodore Perry in 1858 the young Itō Hirobumi became one of the most conspicuous of the young samurai that stood against the foreign incursion. The story goes that in 1862 Itō stowed away aboard an English cargo ship in order to go gain more insights into European ways. His brief European interlude transformed him from an advocate of "expelling the barbarians" to one of embracing western technologies for the sake of self-strengthening and national advancement. As a "prophet of the new age" Itō then became a staunch supporter of the overthrow of the old samurai system and of imperial restoration, and following the 1868 Meiji Restoration became one of the most prominent statesmen in the Meiji government. He was the first to hold the office of Prime Minister (1881) in Japan's new cabinet system and was also instrumental in the drafting of the Meiji Constitution of 1890. During Itō's second term as Prime Minister the Sino-Japanese War broke out. Itō would go on to serve two more terms as Prime Minister and in 1905 was named the first Resident-General of Korea, following that country's acquisition by Japan as a protectorship. Soon upon finishing his term as Resident-General, Itō Hirobumi was assassinated by a young Korean nationalist at Harbin Station in China.

ITŌ Miyoji (1857–1934). Born in Nagasaki, Itō Miyoji began his work as an official interpreter and went on to accompany Itō Hirobumi on his tour to study the legal and social systems of Europe in 1882. During the Sino-Japanese War Itō served as Government General Secretary but following hostilities was appointed ambassador plenipotentiary to negotiate peace with China.

KAWAKAMI Sōroku (1828–1899). As a retainer of the Satsuma Clan, Kawakami was a strong supporter of the Meiji Restoration. He accompanied the Minister of War Ōyama Iwao on his tour of Europe and during the Sino-Japanese War distinguished himself as a member of the Japanese General Staff. In 1898 he was named Chief of the General Staff.

KESSLER, Count Harry von (1868–1937). De Guerville's contemporary, Kessler came from a quintessentially cosmopolitan background: Aristocratic German father, Irish mother, Paris-born and English-bred.

He was also a homosexual. Kessler began his career as a diplomat, and at the time of his meeting with de Guerville crossing the Pacific he was en route to take up diplomatic duties in his native Germany. The career of a bureaucrat soon grew stale, and Kessler is best known today for his work in publishing and literary criticism and for his expansive diaries.

KIPLING, Rudyard (1865–1936). Little introduction is needed for this preeminent British writer and "poet of empire." Kipling's brief 1892 sojourn in Japan (his second visit), en route around the world, coincided with de Guerville's visit as Honorary Commissioner for the World's Columbian Exposition. Though Kipling's stay was brief it left a lasting impression. Though he is mentioned in *Au Japon*, Kipling and de Guerville never met.

LABRY, Viscount de, (dates unknown). French military attaché to Japan in the mid-1890s. In late 1894 de Labry accompanied de Guerville to the Liaodong Peninsula during the latter's coverage of the Sino-Japanese War, and like de Guerville would witness the events surrounding the fall of Port Arthur. De Labry's own eyewitness report on that city's fall to the Japanese, while not denying completely that excesses of killing occurred on the part of the Japanese, approaches more that of de Guerville than the extremely critical accounts of James Creelman of the *New York World* and Thomas Cowen of *The Times* of London.

LEGENDRE, Charles William (1830–1899). Like de Guerville, as a young man Legendre (or Le Gendre) emigrated from his native France to the United States. Settling in New York City, Legendre saw action as a Union officer in the American Civil War. In May 1864 he lost an eye in the Battle of the Wilderness resulting in his honorable discharge as a brevet brigadier general. Appointed American consul to Amoy, China in 1866, Legendre spent the remainder of his life in the Far East, first as an American diplomat and then as a private military and political advisor to the Japanese and Korean courts, playing a key role in the Japanese military campaign in Taiwan in 1874. When de Guerville met him in Japan in 1892, Legendre was serving as a Vice Minister of the Home Department in the Korean government and visiting Japan as commissioner plenipotentiary attempting to renegotiate Korean-Japan fishing and trade treaties.

LI Hongzhang (1823–1901). Without doubt Li Hongzhang is one of the most preeminent figures of late imperial China. Raised in the traditions of Chinese scholar-officialdom, Li passed the Chinese civil service examination in 1847. During the Taiping Rebellion that rocked late imperial China in the 1850s and 1860s, Li gained fame for his organization of local militia forces and his leadership of military campaigns that helped extinguish the rebellion. In these engagements Li came into contact and worked with westerners, many of whom were mercenaries offering their services to China. From this time Li also developed an interest in creating western-style arsenals and fleets to strengthen the weakening Chinese state. In 1870 Li was named governor of the capital province of Zhili, a post he occupied for twenty-five years, and which he held concomitant with that of Superintendent of Trade in the north, which necessitated his residency at the treaty port of Tianjin. Li became the most familiar Chinese figure to foreigners and a strong advocate of China's self-strengthening. In this latter aspiration, however, Li often found himself frustrated by the more conservative forces at court.

LUO Fenglu (1850-?). A brilliant diplomat and scholar, Luo was sympathetic to the idea of China's modernization, and for this met with frequent and hostile opposition. As a young man he had been a naval cadet at the new Chinese Naval School established through French help. In 1878 Luo began his long familiarity with Europe when he was sent to study at King's College, Cambridge from whence he was later transferred to the Chinese mission at Berlin. From 1881 Luo served as personal secretary and translator to Li Hongzhang, a position he held when de Guerville encountered him in Tianjin. Luo went on to be named Chinese Minister to the Court of St. James in 1897, and then Chinese Minister to St. Petersburg in 1901, a position he was unable to assume due to Russian protestations that he was an inveterate anglophile.

MATSUKATA Masayoshi (1835–1924). A member of the Satsuma Clan and early supporter of the Meiji Restoration, Matsukata was named chief of the agricultural bureau in the early Meiji government and participated in this capacity at the Paris International Exposition of 1878. He went on to serve as Minister of Finance and two terms as Prime Minister.

MILNE, John (1850–1913). A geologist and engineer educated at King's College, as a young man Milne was appointed Chair of Geology and Mining at the Imperial Engineering College in Tokyo. In Japan Milne's interests soon turned to the study of earthquakes, where from 1880–1892 he chaired a society he founded for the study of earthquakes in Japan. He also took a Japanese wife. After a devastating fire in 1894 that destroyed most of his personal papers and instruments, Milne returned with his wife to England, eventually settling on the Isle of Wight, where he established an earthquake observation station. He is today recognized as a founding father of seismology.

MUTSU Munemitsu (1844–1897). With a checkered past that included conspiring to overthrow the government in the mid-1870s, Mutsu went on to serve as Minister to the United States and Minister of Agriculture and Commerce. However, he served most prominently as the Minister of Foreign Affairs during the Sino-Japanese War and for a brief while afterward. As Minister of Foreign Affairs, Count Mutsu played a prominent role in "orchestrating" the Sino-Japanese War for its western audience. De Guerville claimed to be on friendly terms with him, an acquaintanceship that dated back to de Guerville's first visit to Japan in 1892, and which served him well in securing a prime spot traveling with the Japanese First and then Second Armies during their respective campaigns in Korea and on the Liaodong peninsula in China. Shortly before his death Count Mutsu wrote an important diplomatic account of the Sino-Japanese War titled *Kenkenroku*.

NOZU Michitsura (1841–1908). Born into a Samurai clan of Kagoshima, Nozu fought with the imperial loyalists in 1868, participating in many battles in northern Japan. During the Sino-Japanese War then Lieutenant General Nozu was given command of the First Army following the resignation of General Yamagata. It was Nozu who oversaw the conquest of P'yŏngyang before leading the First Army into Manchuria. In 1895 Nozu was promoted to General and went on to lead an army during the Russo-Japanese War (1904–1905).

ŌKUMA Shigenobu (1838–1922). A native of Saga prefecture, from his youth Ōkuma had close contact with foreigners when he studied English from a Dutch missionary. After the Meiji Restoration of 1868 he was named a judge to handle affairs with foreigners in Nagasaki. He went on to serve as Minister of Finance and Home Minister. After being named Prime Minister in 1888, Ōkuma worked tirelessly to revoke the unequal treaties Japan held with the industrialized western nations. After a foiled assassination attempt that cost him his left leg, Ōkuma resigned in 1889 but remained involved in government affairs as a member of the Privy Council. Ōkuma went on to serve again as Prime Minister in 1898 and from 1914 to 1916 and was one of the most distinguished of Japan's elder statesmen, or *genro*. Besides government work, Ōkuma was involved in political organization, journalism, and higher education, establishing the Tokyo Semmon Gakko, the predecessor of Waseda University.

ŌYAMA Iwao (1842–1916). An early supporter of Japan's imperial restoration of 1868, as a young officer Ōyama led an artillery unit in support of the imperial forces. Ōyama spent several years in Europe and America, including a year observing the Franco-Prussian war of 1870 and another three years studying in France, experiences that afforded him firsthand observation of the emergence of German military dominance in Europe. Upon his return to Japan Ōyama rose steadily through the military and civilian ranks, serving as vice-chief of the Army General Staff, director of the Army Staff College, Minister of Education, and, in 1891, Minister of War. Through the 1890s Ōyama, along with Yamagata Aritomo and others, worked to establish a modern style army in Japan. During the Sino-Japanese War General Ōyama served concurrently as Minister of War and commander of the Second Army tasked with seizing Port Arthur. He again commanded Japanese armies in Manchuria during the Russo-Japanese War (1904–1905). Despite his wide worldly experience, to the end Ōyama remained more of a military than political figure. He was noted for his reticence of character and for his large-featured, pock-marked face.

SMITH, Charles Stewart (1832–1909). New York businessman, banker, and public figure. Beginning his career as small dry goods merchant in New York City, Smith rose to remarkable commercial and financial success. Smith retired in 1887 but went on to serve as head of the New

York City Chamber of Commerce and Chairman of the "Committee of Seventy," a citizens' political group organized to break the hold of Tammany Hall on New York politics. Smith declined the Committee of Seventy's nomination to be mayor of New York. In 1892 Smith made a working trip to Japan as head of the New York City Chamber of Commerce. As a prominent resident himself of New York City, de Guerville would no doubt have been familiar with the Smith name.

TESHIMA Seiichi (1849–1918). Educated in the United States, Teshima's life was one dedicated to the education of his fellow Japanese. First appointed director of Tokyo Kaisei School and then director of the Tokyo Educational Museum, in 1890 he was named principal of Tokyo Workers School (the school de Guerville tours, and now Tokyo Industrial University). Teshima was also named Commissioner General of the Imperial Japanese Government to the World's Columbian Exposition, and it was while returning to Japan from a working trip to Chicago that de Guerville met him aboard the *City of Peking*.

WATANABE Kōki (1848–1901). As a young man Watanabe studied medicine and English and in 1871 accompanied the Japanese envoy Iwakura Tomomi on a diplomatic mission to Europe and America. Later he served as Governor of Tokyo (1885) and President of Tokyo University (1890) before being named Japanese ambassador to Vienna (Austro-Hungary). In 1892 Watanabe was elected to the lower house of the Diet and resigned his ambassadorship to take up his new political duties in Tokyo. It was in the course of returning to Japan via the United States that Watanabe met de Guerville, then on his way to Japan as Honorary Commissioner for the Chicago World's Fair.

WINSTON, Frederick Hampden (1830–1904). A prominent Chicago Democrat and delegate from Illinois to the Democratic National Convention of 1876. Winston went on to serve from 1885–86 as United States Minister to Persia, during the Grover Cleveland administration. During the early 1890s he served as Corporation Council for the City of Chicago under Mayor Harris. In 1892 he traveled to Japan as an official representative of the Chicago World's Fair Planning Committee. He was never, as period Japanese newspapers and even de Guerville, claim, the Director of the World's Columbian Exposition.

YAMAGATA Aritomo (1838–1922). Born into lower Samurai status, Yamagata went on to become one of the leading *genro* (elder statesman) of the Meiji period and after. Yamagata served as a staff officer in the imperial forces during the struggle for imperial restoration in 1868. After a tour of Europe and America in 1869 he returned to Japan to be named vice-minister of military affairs, and soon took on the enormous task of modernizing the nation's military forces. Yamagata was named Minister of War in 1873 and after a series of high-level posts, eventually became Prime Minister in 1889. The outbreak of the Sino-Japanese War signaled Yamagata's return to military affairs when he was named commander of the Japanese First Army, but was soon recalled to Japan due to illness (though rumors purported he had been recalled over strategic differences regarding his support of a Japanese advance on Peking). After the war he would continue to serve in both civilian and military roles, including another stint as Prime Minister and Commander-in-chief of the General Staff during the Russo-Japanese War of 1904–1905. Yamagata was also a skilled poet.

YAMAJI Motoharu (1841–1897). Like Ōyama, Yamaji was a member of the loyalists surrounding the Meiji Emperor during the restoration of 1868. With the restoration's success Yamaji was appointed chief of staff of the army's Third Brigade and in this role helped suppress the Satsuma Revolt of 1871. He achieved the rank of general in 1886 and was made a baron two years later. During the Sino-Japanese War General Yamaji commanded the First Division, under the Second Army commanded by Ōyama, which besieged and then seized Port Arthur. Due to a childhood accident that left him blinded in one eye, after Port Arthur he gained the sobriquet "Dokugan-ryu"—the one-eyed hero. James Creelman, in his memoir *On the Great Highway*, relates, perhaps apocryphally, that as a schoolboy Yamaji had plucked out his own eye to prove his courage.

Sources

Giles, Herbert A. *A Chinese Biographical Dictionary.* Taipei: Literature House, 1898.

Hoare, J.E., "Captain Francis Brinkley (1841–1912): Yatoi, Scholar, and Apologist." In J.E. Hoare, ed. *Britain & Japan: Biographical Portraits,* Vol. 3. Richmond, United Kingdom: Curzon Press, 1999:99–107.

Hummel, Arthur W., ed. *Eminent Chinese of the Ch'ing Period (1644–1912)*. Washington, D.C.: United States Government Printing Office, 1943.

Iwao, Seiichi, ed. *Biographical Dictionary of Japanese History* (translated by Burton Watson). Tokyo: Kodansha International, Ltd., 1978.

Taillemite, Etienne. *Dictionnaire des marins français*. Paris: Tallandier, 2002.

The Japan Biographical Encyclopedia and Who's Who. Tokyo: The Rengo Press, Ltd., 1961.

Who Was Who, 1897–1916. London: A & C Black, Ltd., 1935.

The Dictionary of Canadian Biography. Toronto: University of Toronto Press, 1966.

The National Cyclopaedia of American Biography. Clifton, NJ: J.T. White, 1926.

Appendix B

The Writings of A. B. de Guerville
(not including newspaper articles)

1892

"Japan and the World's Fair, a Commissioner's Lecture before the Emperor." *Leslie's Weekly* (22 September 1892): 214.

"Japanese Humor in Politics." *Leslie's Weekly* (13 October 1892): 266–67.

1893

"Mme. Chrysanthème at Home." *Leslie's Popular Monthly* 35 (January 1893): 26–31.

"Li Hung Chang, the Viceroy and Master of China." *Leslie's Weekly* (15 June 1893): 386.

"Children in Japan." *Leslie's Weekly* (9 November 1893): 303.

1894

"A Holiday Visit to Colombo." *Leslie's Popular Monthly* 37 (February 1894): 148–60.

"Russia in Asia. Has She Designs upon Corea?" *Leslie's Weekly* (26 April 1894): 275.

"Experiences in China, A Journey on the Pehio—Life in Tien-Tsin." *Leslie's Weekly* (10 May 1894): 314.

Appendix B

"Socialism and Anarchism in Europe I: In Spain—Interview with the Minister of the Interior." *Leslie's Weekly* (5 July 1894): 4.

"Socialism and Anarchism in Europe II: In Spain—Interviews with Señor Salmeron and Señor Pi i Margal, Ex-Presidents of the Republic." *Leslie's Weekly* (12 July 1894): 26.

"Socialism and Anarchism in Europe III: the Anarchists of France and Italy." *Leslie's Weekly* (19 July 1894): 42.

"An Interview with Senor Castelar." *Leslie's Weekly* (26 July 1894): 60.

"The War in the East: The Situation in Japan—Confidence of the Government and People." *Leslie's Weekly* (18 October 1894): 259.

"The War in the East: The Embarkation of Japanese Troops for Corea—Efficiency of the Japanese Military Administration." *Leslie's Weekly* (8 November 1894): 301.

"The War in the East: Our Correspondent with the Japanese Army tells the Story of the Capture of Ping Yang." *Leslie's Weekly* (15 November 1894): 313.

"Our Correspondent in the East. Affairs in Corea—Interview with the King's Father." *Leslie's Weekly* (22 November 1894): 332.

"Our Correspondent in the East: The Japanese Hospital System Described." *Leslie's Weekly* (29 November 1894): 345.

"Our Correspondent in the East: The Second Japanese Army in China." *Leslie's Weekly* (6 December 1894): 364.

"The War in the East. The Movements of the Second Japanese Army Detailed by our Special Correspondent." *Leslie's Weekly* (20 December 1894): 414.

1895

"In Defense of Japan, the Alleged Atrocities at Port Arthur Denied." *Leslie's Weekly* (3 January 1895): 10–11.

"The War in the East: Japanese vs. Chinese Inhumanity." *Leslie's Weekly* (24 January 1895): 55.

"The Murdered Queen of Corea." *Leslie's Weekly* (7 November 1895): 295.

"The Royal Household of Spain." *Leslie's Weekly* (21 November 1895): 331.

"Turkey and its Capital, the Fighting Resources of the Empire." *Leslie's Weekly* (28 November 1895): 350.

"Li Hung Chang's Gratitude." *Leslie's Weekly* (26 December 1895): 435.

"The Red Cross in the Far East." *Munsey's Magazine* 14 (1895–1896): 47–51.

"Japan's Fair Daughters." *Munsey's Magazine* 14 (1895–1896): 341–51.

Civilization and Barbarism. Tokyo: Tsukiji Type Foundry, 1895.

1896

"January Days in Morocco." *Leslie's Popular Monthly* 41 (January 1896): 74–82.

"Pope Leo XIII and the Vatican." *Leslie's Weekly* (9 January 1896): 23.

"Madame Sarah Bernhardt." *Leslie's Weekly* (6 February 1896): 94.

"The King and Queen of Italy." *Leslie's Weekly* (16 April 1896): 257.

"The Situation in Cuba, pt. I." *Leslie's Weekly* (23 April 1896): 275.

"The Situation in Cuba, pt. II." *Leslie's Weekly* (30 April 1896): 298.

"Li Hung Chang." *Leslie's Weekly* (10 September 1896): 171.

"Is the Sultan the 'Great Assassin'?" *The Illustrated American* (26 September 1896): 429–32.

"Japan of Today." *The Illustrated American* (17 October 1896): 521–25.

1897

"Castelar on the Cuban Question." *Leslie's Weekly* (18 March 1897): 182–83.

"Reawakened Greece." *Leslie's Weekly* (8 April 1897): 229.

"The United States, Spain, and Cuba." *The Illustrated American* (10 April 1897): 489.

"The Situation in Crete." *Leslie's Weekly* (15 April 1897):245; (29 April 1897): 261.

"Army and Navy of Turkey." *The Illustrated American* (1 May 1897): 591–93.

"Music in the Far East." *Pearson's Magazine* 3 (June 1897): 690–93.

"War or Peace with Spain?" *The Illustrated American* (27 November 1897): 679–80.

"The Plain People of Spain." *The Illustrated American* (4 December 1897): 710–12.

"Beauties and Horrors of a Spanish Bullfight." *The Illustrated American* (11 December 1897): 741–44.

"Santa Claus around the World." *The Illustrated American* (18 December 1897): 767–70.

"Another War Scare." *The Illustrated American* (25 December 1897): 801–02.

1898

"Alphonse Daudet." *The Illustrated American* (1 January 1898):6–7.

"The Chinese Empire." *The Illustrated American* (8 January 1898): 41–43.

"Li Hung Chang in Peking." *The Illustrated American* (15 January 1898): 69–71.

"France and the Jews." *The Illustrated American* (29 January 1898): 128–29.

"The Women of Japan." *The Illustrated American* (5 February 1898): 162–63.

"The Situation in Spain and in Cuba." *The Illustrated American* (12 February 1898): 192.

"Woman's Love in China" [by General Tcheng-Ki-Tong, reviewed and translated by A. B. de Guerville]. *The Illustrated American* (26 February 1898): 256–58.

1904

Au Japon. Paris: Alphonse Lemerre, 1904.

La Lutte contre la tuberculose. Paris: Alphonse Lemerre, 1904.

The Crusade against Phthisis [English translation of *La Lutte contre la tuberculose*]. London: Hugh Rees, 1904.

1905

La Nouvelle Egypte, ce qu'on dit, ce qu'on voit du Caire à Fashoda. Paris: Librairie Universelle, 1905.

1906

Das Moderne Aegypten [German translation of *La Nouvelle Egypte*]. Leipzig: Spamer, 1906.

Egypten i våra dagar [Swedish translation of *La Nouvelle Egypte*]. Stockholm: Norstedt, 1906.

New Egypt [English translation of *La Nouvelle Egypte*]. London: William Heinemann, 1906.

1907

Der Kampf gegen die Tuberkolose [German translation of *La Lutte contre la tuberculose*]. Leipzig: Spamer, 1907.

"The Situation in Egypt." *Eclectic Magazine of Foreign Literature* 148.4 (April 1907): 312-317.

Au Japon Notes

Preface

1. Admiral Evgeny Ivanovich Alekseyev, illegitimate son of the late Czar Alexander II, uncle of Czar Nicholas II, and at this time Viceroy of the Russian Far East.

2. The Sino-Japanese War (1894–1895) resulted in the Japanese seizure of the Liaodong Peninsula. Initially allotted to Japan as part of its victory settlement, the European powers, notably Russia, found such a Japanese presence in Manchuria intolerable. In 1895 the "Triple Intervention"—diplomatic pressure brought to bear by Russia, France, and Germany—convinced Japan to reluctantly recede the Liaodong, a source of lingering bitterness in Japan for the next decade.

3. Dalian

4. The Trans-Siberian Railway, begun in 1891, was still incomplete in 1904 when *Au Japon* was published. However, enough rail had been laid, and the most challenging portion around Lake Baikal completed, to cast into doubt de Guerville's assertion that Russian troops could only advance through Siberian in winter "with greatest difficulty." The difficulty rather, lay in how to get Russian troops from Vladivostok (the terminus to the Trans-Siberian) to Port Arthur (near Dalian on the tip of the Liaodong peninsula) via Manchuria.

Chapter 1: To Japan

1. De Guerville is curiously and uncharacteristically remiss about the date. It was 1892.

2. P'yŏngyang

3. Jinzhou

4. Dalian

5. This refers to the multinational force sent to relieve a Peking besieged by the Boxer armies in 1900. Composed of French, German, Russian, British, American, and Japanese troops it was led by the British General

150

Gordon. The participation of Japanese troops alongside those of the western powers signified to many—most particularly the Japanese—the emergence of Japan as an industrial and military power on par with the industrial, and imperial, nations of the west.

Chapter 2: The Ambassador's Wife

1. *The City of Peking* was actually the vessel de Guerville took in 1894 en route to cover the Sino-Japanese War. On this 1892 voyage as representative of the Chicago World's Fair, the vessel was the *Oceanic*. Writing over a decade after the events in question, de Guerville might be forgiven for his confusion in ship names. In fact, on most details de Guerville is surprisingly accurate, suggesting he kept a detailed journal or could boast a prodigious memory.

2. Watanabe Kōki and wife (see Appendix A). This is the only case in *Au Japon* where the author attempts to completely disguise a name.

Chapter 3: Teikoku

1. Teshima Seiichi (see Appendix A)

2. Literally, "you're a cuckold," i.e. a man married to an adulterous wife.

3. *Teikoku* comes off the Francophone tongue sounding much like "tu es cocu" - *you're a cuckhold*. Teikoku in Japanese can mean "imperial," or by association, "excellent", "capital.".

4. Honoré Beaugrand (see Appendix A)

Chapter 4: A Tokyo "Five O'Clock"

1. Count Harry von Kessler (see Appendix A)

2. A popular nineteenth century French song. King Dagobert's tutor and advisor Eloi notes the hole in Dagobert's stocking to which the king replies, "You are right, let me have yours." Eloi goes on to make seventeen complaints concluding with, "My king, death is at hand, and it is time to confess," and Dagobert replies, "Why can't you confess, and die instead of me?"

Chapter 5: The Yoshiwara

1. In fact, it already had been. See J.E. De Becker, *The Nightless City* (1899).

2. Frank L. Coombs (see Appendix A). De Guerville is likely confusing Edwin Dun, American minister to Japan during de Guerville's sojourn

there as war correspondent in 1894, with Coombs, the American minister to Japan during de Guerville's first visit in 1892 and the clearly subject of this anecdote.

3. A four-wheeled carriage with front and rear passenger seats that face each other and usually boasting a detachable roof.

4. Charles William Legendre (see Appendix A)

Chapter 6: A Socialite

1. Inoue Katsunosuke (see Appendix A), who served as Japanese ambassador to Berlin from 1898–1908.

2. Besides the chapter in this volume dedicated to Japanese women, de Guerville wrote fairly widely on the topic. See A. B. de Guerville, "Mme. Chrysanthème at Home" (1893); "Japan's Fair Daughters" (1895); and "The Women of Japan" (1898).

3. Edgar-Eugène Humann (see Appendix A).

4. Viscount de Labry (see Appendix A).

5. The Mexican minister to Japan at this time was Mauricio Wollheim, so it is not clear to whom de Guerville refers.

Chapter 7: Tokyo

1. John Milne (see Appendix A)

2. "Amongst the latest arrivals in Japan is a Mr. A. B. de Guerville . . . already materials for an interesting letter have been obtained by Mr. de Guerville, for, the very night after his arrival, Tokyo was kind enough to furnish a conflagration for his behoof, and he succeeded in taking a number of photographic views of street scenes by the light of the blaze, a feat never before performed in this country, we believe." (*Japan Weekly Mail*, 23 April 1892). Ironically, these photographs likely perished in the fire that consumed de Guerville's offices at *The Illustrated American* in 1898.

3. *badaud* may be defined generally as a nosy bystander, or one who likes to gawk and be idly curious.

4. *sergot* was period French slang for policeman.

Chapter 8: A Few Silhouettes

1. Frank (Francis) Brinkley (see Appendix A), who was actually an Irishman by birth.

2. The Meiji Restoration of 1868.

3. A kiss is a sweet thing indeed/you realize it from their rosy lips.

4. Itō Hirobumi, Ōyama Iwao, Mutsu Munemitsu, Hijikata Motohisa, Inoue Katsunosuke, Matsukata Masayoshi, Ōkuma Shigenobu (see Appendix A)

5. Li Hongzhang (see Appendix A)

6. The treaty ending the Sino-Japanese War (1894–1895).

Chapter 9: Their Women

1. He who goes softly goes safely, or "slowly but surely."

2. "Shame on the one who thinks ill of it." De Guerville makes his point while also taking a jibe at the English, as this is the motto on the British coat of arms.

3. A general Japanese term for young lady.

Chapter 11: At the Imperial Court

1. De Guerville refers to the Anglo-Japanese Alliance of 1902 (renewed in 1905), contracted primarily to counter the Russian threat perceived by both those powers.

2. De Guerville gave this presentation on May 5, 1892. See A. B. de Guerville, "Japan and the World's Fair" (1892).

3. A small pointed beard grown below the lower lip, and named after the beard worn by Napoleon III.

4. Frederick Hampden Winston (see Appendix A)

Chapter 12: The Real Madame Chrysanthemum

1. That is, Pierre Loti himself, who by 1904 was a celebrated professor of literature.

Chapter 13: A Visit with His Excellency, the Governor of O . . .

1. Nellie Melba (1861–1931), Australian born soprano and one of the most celebrated opera singers of her day. The nature of De Guerville's relation to her is unclear.

2. The Sino-Japanese War (1894–1895)

Chapter 14: The Missionary

1. Based on this description, this would be the author's August 1894 voyage to Japan, aboard the *City of Peking*, as a war correspondent for the

New York Herald and *Leslie's Weekly*. By "Gascon ancestors," de Guerville seems to be alluding to James Creelman, correspondent for the *New York World* who shared the author's journey across the Pacific. *Gascon* is French slang for boaster or braggart, perhaps a reference to Creelman's sensational and controversial account of a massacre at Port Arthur, the accuracy of which de Guerville openly questioned.

2. Pusan

3. De Guerville was writing four years after China's bloody Boxer Uprising (1900), which had strong anti-foreign elements and during which scores of westerners were killed, many of them missionaries.

Chapter 15: From Tokyo to Tientsin

1. Pusan

2. Modern Inch'ŏn

3. Li-Hong, or Yi Hong. Yi was the family name of Korea's King Kojong (1850–1919), the penultimate monarch of Korea. His predecessor, King Ch'ŏlchong, had died childless in 1864. In situations such as this it was the senior dowager queen who chose the royal successor, in this case the child Kojong, a nephew of the deceased king. Tai-Wan-Kun, or Taewŏngun, interprets literally as "prince of the great court" and was an honorific title given to a monarch's father when that father had never reigned himself. In this case it referred to Kojong's father, Yi Ha-ŭng. As regent Yi Ha-ŭng became a potent political force during the king's minority and after, and was the effective Korean monarch from 1864–1873. So central a figure did he become in Korean politics in the late nineteenth century—usually representing conservative resistance to outside influence—that in historical terms the title Taewŏngun has come to refer specifically to him. De Guerville interviewed the Taewŏngun in Seoul in 1894 while covering the Sino-Japanese War. See de Guerville, "Our Correspondent in the East. Affairs in Corea—Interview with the King's Father" (1894).

4. This is Queen Min, consort of King Kojong. In 1895 she was murdered by Japanese soldiers within the compounds of this same palace. That she was indeed a woman of "exceptional intelligence and will" proved her undoing as Japan began to insist upon ever more control over Korean affairs following its defeat of China in the Sino-Japanese War. See de Guerville, "The Murdered Queen of Korea" (1895).

5. January 20, 1897. The talk stirred up some more controversy for de Guerville as the New York papers claimed he had spoken at his presentation of an imminent United States-Japan Alliance, something de Guerville later publicly denied.

Notes

6. De Guerville refers to the Second Opium War, or Second Anglo-Chinese War, (1857–1860) and specifically to the British attack on the Taku Forts in 1860, which ultimately led to the occupation of the Chinese capital.

7. Tianjin

8. The Geary Act passed in 1892 put a stop to Chinese immigration and even called for the deportation of many. China never did participate officially in the World's Columbian Exposition of 1893 at Chicago, though a coalition of Chinese-American merchants did put together a modest Chinese exhibit.

9. For a fuller account of de Guerville's encounter with Li Hongzhang in Tianjin see de Guerville, "Li Hung Chang, the Viceroy and Master of China" (1893).

10. Luo Fenglu (see Appendix A)

11. Chen Jitong (see Appendix A). He had actually only served as military attaché to the Chinese legation in France.

Chapter 16: Ayama

1. De Guerville was writing—and recollecting—after the passage of a decade, and he naturally demonstrated a few lapses in memory regarding names (or rather initials). These are almost certainly Frederick Hampden Winston and Charles Smith, both of whom arrived in Japan on the same steamer as de Guerville in October 1892 and who like him were connected with the Chicago World's Fair. De Guerville would host a dinner in their honor at the Imperial Hotel in mid-October 1892, at which were present the American Minister, the French attaché in Japan (and future minister to Korea) Victor Collin de Plancy, and General Charles Legendre. They were also both relatively elderly and accompanied by their wives.

2. Specifically the "Tianjin Massacre" of French missionaries in 1870. De Guerville is also alluding to the killing of foreigners in Tianjin during the Boxer Uprisings of 1900.

3. Victor Émile Marie Joseph Collin de Plancy (see Appendix A)

Chapter 17: Marshal Yamagata

1. Yamagata Aritomo (see Appendix A)

2. Sino-Japanese War (1894–1895)

3. P'yŏngyang

4. Asan

5. Nozu Michitsura (see Appendix A)

Chapter 18: The Red Cross

1. Ishiguro Tadanori (see Appendix A)
2. Apparently the wife of Admiral Nire Kagenori (1831–1900).

Chapter 19: The Spy

1. Kawakami Sōroku (see Appendix A)
2. Itō Miyoji (see Appendix A)
3. Datong
4. The Battle of the Yalu between the Japanese fleet, commanded by Admiral Itō Sukeyuki, and the Chinese Beiyang fleet took place on September 17, 1894. Though it resulted in the decimation of the Chinese fleet it was not a total victory as the Chinese had succeeded in landing their troops before the battle commenced.

Chapter 20: The Eggs

1. Yamaji Motoharu (see Appendix A)

Chapter 21: Port Arthur

1. De Guerville here is referring to a certain Laguerre, who covered the war for *Le Temps* of Paris.

Index

Allen, Horace Newton (1858-1932), xviii, lvii
Arnold, Edwin (1832-1904), xlviii, li, liv, lv, 36, 37, 133

Beaugrand, Honoré (1848-1906), 14, 133
Bennett, James Gordon Jr. (1841-1918), xxiii, xxxvii
Brinkley, Frank (Francis) (1841-1912), xx, xxxix, xl, xli, li, lix, 12, 133, 152

Chen Jitong (1851-1907), ix, xxvii, lii, lvi, 89, 134, 155
Collin de Plancy, Victor Émile Marie Joseph (1853-1924), 96, 134
Coombs, Frank Leslie (1853-1934), 20, 134, 151
Cowen, Thomas (dates unknown), xxxii, xliii, 137
Creelman, James (1859-1915), xxiii, xxv–xxvi, xxxii, xxxvi–xxxix, xli–xlviii, liv–lv, lvii, lix, lxi, 137, 142, 154

Geary Act (1892), xx, 155
Grossmith, George, xxi
Guerville, Amédée Baillot de (1869-?): and Port Arthur Massacre, xxxii *et passim*; and *The Illustrated American*, xxvi; and tuberculosis, xii, xxvii *et passim*; as public lecturer, xxi; at *New York Herald*, xxiii; birth, x; establishes *Courrier Français* (Milwaukee), xiv, 151; divorce, xxviii; family, x; immigration to the United States, xii; *La lutte contre la tuberculose* (The struggle against tuberculosis) (1904), xxx, 148; *La Nouvelle Egypt* (*New Egypt*) (1906), xxxi, lvi, 149; marriage, xxvi; return to Europe, xxix
Guerville, Paul Louis Amédée Baillot de (dates unknown), xi

Hijikata, Motohisa (1833-1918), 39, 52, 109, 135
Humann, Edgar-Eugène (1838-1914), 26, 135

Inoue Katsunosuke (1860-1929), 23, 39, 56, 135, 152

Ishiguro Tadanori (1845-1941), 105, 107, 135
Itō Hirobumi (1841-1909), 39–41, 109–111, 135
Itō Miyoji (1857-1934), 110, 136
Itō Sukeyuki (1843-1914), 100, 107, 112, 127

Japan Gazette, xx, xl, xlvi
Japan Weekly Mail, xvi, xix–xxi, xxxv, xxxvi, xxxix, xl, xli, xlvi, xlix, li, lvi, lvii, lix, lx, lxi, 152

Kawakami Sōroku (1828-1899), 102, 109–110, 136
Kessler, Harry von (1868-1937), xviii, lvii, 15–16, 18, 136
Kipling, Rudyard (1865-1936), xvii, lv, lvi, 36, 137
Kojong (Korean king) (1850-1919), xix, xlviii, 154

Labry, Viscount de (dates unknown), 26, 116–118, 137
Legendre, Charles William (1830-1899), 22, 25, 37, 137, 155
Li Hongzhang (1823-1901), xix, xxii, xxiii, xxvii, liii, lvii, lix, 40, 86–88, 96, 99, 101, 138, 144, 146, 148, 155
Luo Fenglu (1850-?), 88, 138, 147

Matsukata Masayoshi (1835-1924), 39, 138
Milne, John (1850-1913), 28–30, 139
Milwaukee Women's College, xiii, xiv, xvii
Min (Korean queen) (1851-1895), xix, xlii, lii, 81, 154
Mondion, Adalbert-Henri Foucault de (1849-1894), ix, 134
Mutsu Munemitsu (1844-1897), xxxviii, xli, lix, lx, 39, 139

New York Herald, xxiii, xxv, xxxi, xxxv, xxxvii, xxxix, xli, xlviii, lvii, lix, lx, lxi, 86, 154
New York World, xii, xxiii, xxv, xxxii, xxxvi, xlii, xliii, xlvi, lv, lx, 137, 154
Nire Kagenori (1831-1900), 156
Nordach Clinic (Germany), x, xxx, xxxi
Nozu Michitsura (1841-1908), 101, 102, 105, 108, 109, 116, 139

Ōkuma Shigenobu (1838-1922), 39, 140
Ōyama Iwao (1842-1916), xxxviii, xlii, 3, 39–40, 56, 100, 102, 109–111, 113, 116, 121–122, 124, 126, 131, 140

Port Arthur Massacre (1894), liii, lv, 126 *et passim*
Pulitzer, Joseph (1847-1911), xii, xxiii

Sannomiya Yoshitane (1843-1905), 24, 39, 40, 52, 56
Sino-Japanese War (1894-95), x, xx, xxii–xxvi, xxxi–xxxii, xxxiv–xxxvii, xli, xliii, xlviii, li, liii, liv–lvi, lx, 3, 98 *et passim*
Smith, Charles Stewart (1832–1909), 91, 140
Spraker, Laura Belle (dates unknown), xxvi, xxviii

Taewŏngun Yi Ha-ŭng (1821-1898), xli, 81–82, 154
Teshima Seiichi (1849-1918), xix, 10, 141

Villiers, Frederic (1851-1922), xxxii, xlii–xliii, xlv, xlviii, lxi
Watanabe Kōki (1848-1901), 7, 9, 141

Winston, Frederick Hampden (1830-1904), 57, 91, 141

Yamagata Aritomo (1838-1922), xlviii, 97 *et passim*, 139, 140, 142
Yamaji Motoharu (1841-1897), 113, 117, 119, 121, 127, 131, 142
Yoshiwara (district of Tokyo), lv, 19 *et passim*, 73, 75, 135, 151

About the Translator

Daniel Kane received his BA in French and History from Southern Illinois University, Carbondale in 1992. After a time in Korea in the military he went on to study Korean History at the University of Hawaii, where he received his MA in 1999. He is currently completing a doctorate in Korean history from the University of Hawaii while working there as the Korea Specialist Librarian.

www.ingramcontent.com/pod-product-compliance
Lightning Source LLC
Chambersburg PA
CBHW030137240426
43672CB00005B/158